Created and Directed by Hans Höfer

INSIGHT GUIDES
Venezuela

Edited by Tony Perrottet
Principal photography by Eduardo Gil

Managing Editor: Andrew Eames

HOUGHTON MIFFLIN COMPANY

APA PUBLICATIONS

VeneZueLa

First Edition (3rd Reprint)
© **1994 APA PUBLICATIONS (HK) LTD**
All Rights Reserved
Printed in Singapore by Höfer Press Pte. Ltd

Distributed in the United States by:	Distributed in Canada by:	Distributed in the UK & Ireland by:	Worldwide distribution enquiries:
Houghton Mifflin Company	**Thomas Allen & Son**	**GeoCenter International UK Ltd**	**Höfer Communications Pte Ltd**
222 Berkeley Street	390 Steelcase Road East	The Viables Center, Harrow Way	38 Joo Koon Road
Boston, Massachusetts 02116-3764	Markham, Ontario L3R 1G2	Basingstoke, Hampshire RG22 4BJ	Singapore 2262
ISBN: 0-395-65779-2	ISBN: 0-395-65779-2	ISBN: 9-62421-175-2	ISBN: 9-62421-175-2

ABOUT THIS BOOK

Venezuela is one of Latin America's great unknowns. The country has been traditionally bypassed by the "gringo trail" that winds from Mexico City to Tierra del Fuego, and travelers who have visited almost everywhere else in the region confess to never being lured to its shores. Even foreign journalists who regularly cover South America have been known to shrug and ask: "What's in Venezuela – besides oil?"

This is largely a holdover from the 1970s, when petrol-rich Venezuela was one of the most expensive countries on the planet and Venezuelans were the tourists, not the hosts. It is an unfortunate truism that travelers often benefit from a country's economic woes, and with the local currency's decline, Venezuela has become a bargain destination. First gaining attention for its 2,500 km (1,750 miles) of pristine Caribbean coastline, Venezuela is now one of South America's hot spots.

The boom happened so quickly that little has been published on the country – a fact that baffles the tourists now flocking there. *Insight Guide: Venezuela* was conceived to fill that glaring gap, adding one more title to Apa Publications' portfolio of South American titles that includes *Argentina*, *Buenos Aires*, *Brazil*, *Rio*, *Chile*, *Peru* and *Ecuador*.

Apa's editor-in-chief for South America, **Tony Perrottet**, used his years of experience as a foreign correspondent in the region to put together an expert team for the project. Australian-born Perrottet graduated in history at Sydney University before embarking on a highly mobile career as a freelance journalist and photographer. Drawn by tales of relatives who worked on the sheep farms of southern Patagonia, he ended up in South America in the mid-1980s and was based in Buenos Aires for many years working for international publications. Perrottet, who now lives in New York, has lost count of the number of times he has visited Venezuela.

Apart from editing the volume and providing several photographs, Perrottet wrote the chapters on history, the Llanos (where he ended up in a beer-drinking competition with cowboys on a remote cattle ranch) and the Gran Sabana or "Lost World" region (where he became lost for several days but enjoyed every minute of it). This is the fifth book that he has edited for Apa Publications.

The Writers

Perrottet divided much of the writing between US journalists Mary Dempsey and Anne Kalosh, two friends who first worked together on Venezuela's English-language newspaper, the *Daily Journal*.

Mary Dempsey worked on the Insight Guides to South America, Peru and Ecuador, but admits that Venezuela was her first love. She was brought up in America's Midwest where she contracted the "incurable case of wonderlust" that inspired her move to Caracas in the early 1980s. As an editor for the *Daily Journal*, Dempsey traveled every corner of the country and eventually the rest of South America. Although now a resident of the US, Dempsey makes at least one trip to Venezuela every year, and for this volume contributed the chapters including Caracas, the east coast, fiestas and popular culture – as a result of which, she confesses, her knowledge of Venezuelan *telenovelas* (soap operas) is now encyclopedic.

Anne Kalosh made her first visits to Vene-

Perrottet

Dempsey

Kalsoh

Gil

zuela were by sea, when she was working as a shipboard newspaper editor on a cruise vessel that sailed the world. She returned to Caracas for two years as features editor for the *Journal* and stringer for several US magazines and is now a freelance writer based in Miami Beach, where she has written for publications including *Travel and Leisure* and *Newsweek*. For *Insight Guide: Venezuela*, Kalosh has written on the Andes, the Amazon, western beaches and provided a feminist take on Venezuelans' obsession with appearance and beauty pageants.

Explaining the intricacies of Venezuelan society and politics is **Ed Holland**. Having lived for a decade as a correspondent for the *Miami Herald* in Caracas with his Argentine-born wife, Holland has had ample time to study Venezuelans at work and play. He warmed to the challenge of writing about his adapted compatriots: "Venezuelans are not an introspective people," he notes, "and almost nothing has been written in the way of social analysis." Tackling the chapters on sports and diving is the *Daily Journal*'s sports editor, **Eric Jennings**, who himself plays a mean outfield in baseball, Venezuela's *yanqui*-imported national sport.

Chief amongst the many photographers involved in producing the spectacular visual side to *Insight Guide: Venezuela* is the Argentine **Eduardo Gil**, already well known to readers of Apa's other South American guides. Gil studied sociology and worked as a commercial pilot before dedicating himself to photography. Having spent several years as director of the Buenos Aires Cultural Center (and resigning in a row over censorship), Gil is now represented in New York by the Black Star photo agency.

Also represented is the work of US photographer **Keith Mays**, who spent two years in Venezuela; the Liechtenstein-based nature photographer **Andre Bartschi**; and the Venezuelans **Ray Escobar**, **Cheo Pacheco** and **Eduardo Vigliano**.

The Final Touches

Special thanks go to **Juan Wendehake** of Viasa airlines in New York and **Scott Swanson** of Lost World Adventures for their assistance in putting the book together. The final proof-reading and indexing were completed by **John Goulding**.

History

Features

Places

Maps

TRAVEL TIPS

Compiled by Mary Dempsey

*For detailed information
see page 281*

WELCOME

Venezuela is a country that defies easy classification. Should you have any preconceived ideas about Latin America, the 40-minute drive from Maiquetía airport to the center of Caracas might give them a jolt. Your taxi – probably a shiny, US-made gas-guzzler of the sort largely abandoned outside of Texas – will pull out of the terminal, nudge past decrepit trucks carrying fruit, then head onto a new, six-lane highway.

The long tunnels that cut through the surrounding mountains are feats of modern engineering – one is, in fact, the most expensive tunnel, inch for inch, ever built – yet the hillsides are covered in dismal shanty towns. Look closely and you see that from almost every tin roof protrudes a TV antenna. Finally, driving through central Caracas, you will find an almost intimidating array of glass skyscrapers and modern kinetic sculptures, while the side streets are filled with impoverished vendors selling cheap American music tapes and T-shirts with messages in English.

Welcome to Venezuela, or at least a couple of its many faces. The wealthy Caracas of glass and concrete was shaped in the 1970s at the peak of the petroleum boom, when the price of crude oil quadrupled overnight and the country was dubbed "Saudi Venezuela" by its envious neighbours. Its alter ego, the impoverished Caracas that exists alongside, is a legacy of the oil crash of the 1980s. Yet rich or poor, Caracas in the 1990s has become the most *yanqui*-fied part of South America – a Caribbean city where the bulk of the population is under 20 years of age and addicted to baseball, fast food, soap operas and MTV.

Even so, you only have to drive a few kilometers away to enter a totally different world. Life in much of the Andes of Mérida, in the tiny fishing villages along the Caribbean coast or the "Wild West" style outposts of the Amazon jungle could not be more traditional. In fact, these far-flung provinces can seem to be stuck in the 19th century – local cowboys still chase across the remote *hatos* or cattle ranches of the Llanos, for example, much as they have for centuries – until you realize that, even here, satellite dishes are now picking up cable TV from the US.

The mix of high technology and tradition affects every part of Venezuelan life, and visitors should be aware that things are not as efficient as they often look: in the true *mañana* spirit, time is an elastic concept for Venezuelans even in Caracas; transport runs late, connections fail to materialize and people make appointments that they have no intention of keeping. Even so, take Venezuela in the right spirit and it is one of the most spectacular, sensual and easy-going countries in the whole of Latin America – and one that never ceases to be surprising.

Preceding pages: view from a light plane over the Gran Sabana; the Canaima lagoon, Gran Sabana; the San Antonio fortress at Cumaná; flamingoes over the Llanos. **Left,** sun-worshippers at work.

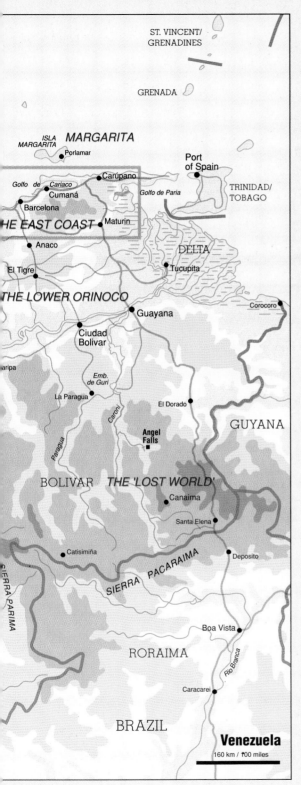

Venezuelans like to travel but, unlike other South Americans, tend not to leave their country permanently. When you ask why, the answer inevitably has something to do with the nation's natural beauty, be it love for the rolling plains of the Llanos, the crystalline coastal waters, or the Andes mountains of Mérida.

This explanation needs no elaboration – when it comes to geographical variety, Venezuela is privileged. It is a Caribbean beach paradise. It is also an Andean country, with snow-capped peaks. And it is a rainforest nation, with steamy jungles inhabited by primitive Indians like the Yanomamis and exotic wildlife. It is a territory of superlatives, with the Caribbean's longest coastline, the world's highest waterfall and Maracaibo, the continent's largest lake, atop one of the planet's largest crude oil deposits.

Silky white sand: Although the geography of Venezuela is more hospitable in many ways than Peru, where the Andes are mightier, Brazil where the jungle is far more immense, or even Argentina where the temperature extremes range from tropical to sub-polar, the gentleness of the landscape does not diminish its astounding beauty. Venezuela's best known attributes may be its coast and islands. This Caribbean coastline is a paradise of silky white sand lapped by aquamarine waters and shaded by palm and coconut trees. Its waves are bathwater-warm year round and most visitors make a beeline for the best known beaches near Puerto La Cruz. Offshore, the swimming, surfing and sunning capital is Margarita, the largest of Venezuela's 72 islands – many of which have good beaches, fishing and diving.

South of Margarita is Cubagua, once the center for the pearl fishing industry. When the pearls were fully harvested four centuries ago, the island was abandoned by all except for a few fishermen. Today developers are in the middle of a multi-billion dollar project to turn Cubagua into the nation's biggest resort. Farther west, off the mainland coast, is

the archipelago of Los Roques, shadeless sandy islands. Their calm waters are filled with exotic fish and their beaches are dusted with powdery sand. The inaccessibility of these islands is appealing for many visitors – they are reachable only by propeller plane or private yacht.

Primeval wilderness: While beaches are its most visited attribute, the so-called "Lost World" immortalized by Sir Arthur Conan Doyle in his book of the same name is Venezuela's most haunting and astonishing terrain. This is the Gran Sabana, a valley of more than 100 flat-topped mountains called *tepuis* (the Pemón Indian word for mountain), their sheer walls the ultimate test for climbers, their tops covered with prehistoric sandstone labyrinths and thick vegetation.

The lopped-off *tepui* peaks are often hidden by thick cloud cover for days without a break, but the isolation is an integral part of this region. Most of the *tepuis* have never been explored and some of their flora and fauna are unique to this area. Scientists who have reached this eerie locale say the sandstone is more than 1.8 billion years old – predating even the most primitive marine life by more than a billion years.

The Gran Sabana, Venezuela's largest plateau some 1,000 meters (3,300 ft) above sea level, is home to the Roraima *tepui* reaching up 2,810 meters (9,220 ft) above sea level. In his classic novel, Conan Doyle imagined that dinosaurs might still be roaming on its isolated roof. Today it is home to Canaima National Park. Located at the confluence of the Carrao and Hacha rivers, it is one of the world's largest natural reserves – a steamy jungle where 500 kinds of orchids have been identified and the home of Angel Falls, the world's longest cascade of water, careening in a graceful plume off the top of a *tepui*.

Cloud buildup over the *tepuis* unleashes up to 380 cm (150 inches) of rain annually, waters that rush to feed the headwaters of the Orinoco River system concentrated in what is known as Guayana Territory, a vast region that covers nearly 45 percent of the nation. This is Venezuela's Wild West, where Indians struggle to maintain their customs and territory against incursions by gold and diamond prospectors. The remoteness of the region has not been a block to progress:

Closing in on a bighorn in the Llanos.

asphalt highways lead to Puerto Ordaz and Ciudad Guayana, two jungle cities that are the focal point for construction and engineering work on the mammoth Guri Dam. The damming of the Caroní River to provide hydroelectric power for Venezuela represents one of the world's largest such projects. Scores of other rivers, including the Orinoco, flow into Delta Amacuro, which became Venezuela's 21st state in 1991.

Farther south along the Orinoco is Venezuela's jungle, a lightly-populated virgin zone abutting Columbia and Brazil. Most of the residents here are indigenous people and military men assigned to the outpost of Puerto Ayacucho. Attempts to colonize this region for farming have been thwarted by Mother Nature and part of the territory has been declared off limits to all but anthropologists studying the Indians there, scientists interested in the unique plant and animal life, and missionaries.

Mountains and cattle plains: In contrast to the low, steamy jungle are the Andes Mountains, cold, crisp peaks cut by green valleys and icy lakes. Venezuela's Andes are novel because they are the only spot in this Caribbean country where residents can see snow. Half the snow-capped area belongs to Pico Bolívar and another bit pertains to Pico Espejo, the latter being accessible in a cable car from Mérida that reaches an altitude of 4,763 meters (15,626 ft). On the mountain slopes, and in the valleys at their feet, potatoes, grains and flowers are cultivated. The rivers rushing down from the snowy peaks are brisk and crystal, filling the region's 172 trout-laden lakes.

The highlands run down into the Llanos, expansive cattle breeding plains dotted with *morichales* (oases with moriche palm trees). These flat prairies roll over more than 300,000 sq. km (115,840 sq. miles) of Venezuelan territory, with changes in elevation so slight as to be undetectable. Because of this lack of relief, these grasslands are flooded from rainfall much of the year and the cowboys or *llaneros* who herd cattle here ride bootless to avoid foot diseases associated with the wetness. The Llanos have one of the country's most varied and unusual collections of plants and animals, luring naturalists, birdwatchers and photographers.

Diamond miners await an air taxi, Gran Sabana.

BEGINNINGS

Most histories of Venezuela commence in the year 1498, when the navigator Christopher Columbus first laid eyes on the Orinoco River and declared that it must flow directly from Eden, the biblical paradise. Of course, Columbus was the first European to visit South America, but it was hardly a "discovery" – native Americans had been living here for some 10,000 years, ever since the great migrations following the last Ice Age.

Dozens of unique cultures inhabited the vast region of mountains, desert, plains and jungle that the invading Spaniards would eventually bring together under the name of "Venezuela". Convinced to his dying day that he had found the Orient, Columbus called these inhabitants "Indians", and the misnomer has stuck (although, in Spanish, native Venezuelans now prefer to be referred to as *indígenas*, or "indigenous people").

These Indian groups did not build the sort of magnificent civilizations or glittering cities later found in Mexico or Peru. Instead, they lived in semi-nomadic, hunting and gathering societies, or small agricultural villages. Although Europeans would dismiss their societies as primitive, the pre-Columbian world was in fact highly complex: each society had its own language, mythology and cultural traditions, its long history of warfare and survival. Some, like the Caribe Indians, were fierce and warlike, descending on their enemies in canoes and turning their bones into flutes; others, like the Aruaks, were sedentary, spending more time cultivating small fields than fighting.

With no knowledge of writing, these pre-Columbian societies kept no records, and little is known about dozens of ancient cultures. Remote groups like the Goajiras around modern-day Maracaibo and the Piaroas in the Amazon managed to survive the murderous onslaught of Europeans, but the majority were simply wiped out. Their exotic-sounding names, like Mixtecas, Goyones and Taironas, would soon only crop up in the disjointed chronicles of the conquerors.

Preceding pages: a monument to the encounter between Europeans and Amerindians, Cumaná. **Left** and **right**, European visions of Indian life.

First contact: Yet when Columbus's tiny caravelles weighed anchor in the gulf of Paria on his third voyage, there was little indication of the wholesale devastation that European contact would bring. The navigator decided that this new fruit-laden land was "the loveliest in all the world" and its people surprisingly open and friendly. Canoes full of Paria Indians came out to great the newcomers, and Columbus eagerly noted that they wore jewellery made of gold and pearls.

The virtual flood of explorers that fol-

lowed soon abandoned Columbus's idea that the New World was Asia. After sailing up and down Venezuela's beach-lined coast, they were also decidedly unimpressed with what it had to offer in the way of riches. Apart from a few small baubles, the Caribbean yielded no quantities of precious metal, silk or spices. One of these first explorers, the Italian Amerigo Vespucci, gave Venezuela its name – literally, "Little Venice" – when his sailors commented, no doubt ironically, that the native villages on stilts in Lake Maracaibo reminded them of the canals of Venice. But this growing suspicion that the Americas were hardly worth bothering about drastically changed when Cortes conquered Mexico in 1519. News of the great city of Tenochtitlan accompanied boatloads of gold to the royal court in Spain. Suddenly it seemed that kingdoms of unimagined wealth might lie deep in the heart of any new territory – and Venezuela, as the most accessible part of the new continent of South America, became top candidate for conquest.

The Spaniards had half-heartedly set up a pearl fishery on the desolate island of Cubagua, but now they decided to found a town on Tierra Firme – "the mainland," or, to foreign tongues, the Spanish Main. In 1521, a few mud huts were established around a square plaza by the Caribbean and called

wilder shores of Venezuela proved most difficult to conquer and settle.

The invasion begins: The tone for colonizing Venezuela was set by the disastrous 1530 expedition led by one of Cortes' most trusted captains, Diego de Ordaz. Convinced that there was a link between the glow of the sun and the color of gold, the aging conquistador set off from Spain with over 600 men towards the hottest place then known in South America: the Equator, between the Orinoco and the Amazon.

After a difficult crossing of the Atlantic, Ordaz and his men spent several wretched months wandering the Orinoco delta. Tropical diseases and hunger quickly took a bitter toll

Cumaná, marking the first Spanish town in South America. But even this outpost had to be fought for: relations with local Indians had soured long before, thanks to regular Spanish slave raids. Slave traders would simply surprise Indian families fishing on beaches and transport them to the miserable sugar plantations being set up on Trinidad.

As a result, when Spaniards began mounting expeditions from Cumaná into the interior of Venezuela, the Indian reaction was often immediately hostile. Paradoxically, while the huge and more "advanced" civilizations of Mexico and later Peru collapsed quickly under the Spanish onslaught, the

amongst the unacclimatized Spaniards. "There were men who, from one day to the next, had their entire feet consumed by cancer from the ankle to the toes," one chronicler recorded, and the daily pile of Spanish dead were simply flung into the river. Finally the desperate Spaniards found a large fishing village of Aruak Indians: the conquistadors went straight for the native women, whom one chronicler breathlessly noted were naked except for "a rag in front of their private parts, which is loose and just long enough to cover them... Thus when they sway, or in a wind, everything is revealed."

Before long, the Spaniards became convinced that the Aruaks plotted to steal their pigs and began a fight in which the whole village was burned. At another village, Ordaz put hundreds of unarmed Indians to the sword because they refused to give food (and then burned the village to make sure none escaped by feigning death).

Only some 200 Spaniards were still alive when the expedition stumbled into the endless flat plains of the Venezuelan Llanos. They wandered this near-deserted country, still following the Orinoco, until Ordaz finally agreed to turn back. The only good news was from an obviously terrified Indian prisoner, who announced under questioning that vast gold could be found in the nearby

out trace in the steaming jungles of the Amazon or succumb to starvation in the Llanos. Strangely, many of these ill-fated groups were led by Germans. Forming a unique chapter in the history of the Spanish conquest, the whole of Venezuela was temporarily granted in the 1500s to the German banking house of Welser, a group of merchant adventurers who had interests from India to Africa, patronized the artist Albrecht Dürer and to whom the Spanish king Charles I owed thousands of ducats in debt.

Historians have been fascinated by the German expeditions mainly because of their cruelty, stunning even by the callous standards of the day, and their almost total futility.

empire of Meta, ruled by a one-eyed prince.

The German conquistadors: Although Ordaz himself died on the way back to Spain, the myth of Meta would inspire dozens more expeditions into Venezuela's inhospitable interior. Before long, Meta would blend with the enduring fantasy of "El Dorado," a fabulously wealthy land where an Indian king was covered daily with gold dust.

Dozens of expeditions set off into the Venezuelan interior, often to disappear with-

Left, the quest for El Dorado inspired the exploration of Venezuela. **Above**, fanciful vision of a Spanish *conquistador*, mounted on a llama.

A wealthy young cloth merchant from Ulm, Ambrosius Dalfinger, led hundreds of finely equipped soldiers to the sandy wastelands near Lake Maracaibo, losing a third of his force without finding even a single gold earring. When he finally did find gold on another trip, the soldiers sent to transport it became lost, turned to cannibalism, then all died of starvation.

Another German captain, a calculating 24-year-old named Nicolaus Federmann, became convinced that the Pacific Ocean lay not far south of Coro. He tricked tribe after Indian tribe into offering his men help before turning on them and either slaughtering or

AGUIRRE THE MAD

The 16th-century Venezuelan frontier was a remote and often desperate place, where Spaniards were as willing to turn on one another as to fight for any common goal. Months by sea away from any instructions from Spain, *conquistadores* made their own self-serving law, and dozens of intrigues and civil wars were played out in the power vacuum.

Entering this chaotic scene in 1562 was perhaps the most notorious conquistador of them all, Lope de Aguirre, whose exploits were immortalized for modern audiences in the 1972 Werner Herzog film *Aguirre, Wrath of God*. The historian John

Hemming has described Aguirre as "a man of unmitigated evil, cruel, psychopathic and gripped by an obsessive grievance against the whole of Spanish society." The terms would have seemed charitable to the Spaniards and Indians who had to face him in a voyage of destruction that ended up in Venezuela.

Expelled from Peru after joining the wrong side of a civil war, Aguirre signed up for a large expedition leaving Cuzco for the Amazon basin. The object, as ever, was to search for the chimerical El Dorado. But as the inexperienced group of 370 soldiers stumbled through the

Above, Spanish *conquistadores*.

steaming jungle, Aguirre soon found a wellspring of discontent. He incited a mutiny and had the expedition's leader, Pedro de Ursua, skewered in his hammock. Another Spanish noble was elevated to the leadership, but his rule was shortlived: Aguirre had him put to the sword as well, and his beautiful *mestizo* mistress hacked to death.

Described as a thin, scrawny man with one lame leg, Aguirre was nevertheless one of the most experienced and ruthless fighters in the New World. Now, floating down the Amazon river on a barge, he declared his intention of leading the rebels back to conquer Peru – a plan that meant following the Amazon to the Atlantic, travelling via Venezuela around the north of South America then marching back to where they had started.

En route, Aguirre began to indulge his long-standing grudges against Spanish society and some more recently aquired psychoses, turning the expedition into a floating death camp. According to chroniclers, Aguirre "determined not to carry with him any gentleman or person of quality, and therefore slew all such persons; and then departing only with the common soldiers, he left behind all the Spanish women and sick men." The surviving Andean porters were also left by the banks of the Amazon to die. Meanwhile, Aguirre began suspecting soldiers of plotting against him, and ordered so many of his men to be garrotted for treason that the expedition's numbers were reduced from 370 to 230.

Aguirre's rantings and paranoia were at fever pitch when the rebel barges arrived in Venezuela, weighing anchor on the palm-fringed Margarita Island, now the country's premier tourist resort. The Spanish governor welcomed them, but he was quickly seized and executed. Aguirre instituted a reign of terror over the island – putting to death any local citizens or his own soldiers who seemed to be "lukewarm in his service."

Desertions had long been depleting Aguirre's forces, but now, as he fled royalist forces and began an ascent of the mountains near the present-day Venezuelan city of Valencia, the trickle of escapees turned into a flood. Realizing that the end was near, Aguirre decided to go out in typical style. He went to meet his 16-year-old daughter Elvira, whom he had escorted through the whole ghastly expedition unharmed, kissed her on the forehead and placed a crucifix in her hands – then ran her through with his sword. Hearing the screams, Aguirre's own men then decided to put an end to the tyrant, and riddled him with their arquebuses. ∎

enslaving them as porters. These were chained up by the neck so that if one collapsed or died of exhaustion, the body could be quickly discarded by simply chopping off the head.

Typical was his treatment of the Guaicari Indians, who came to meet Federmann's men in an apparently peaceful fashion. "While I distracted them with words," the Teutonic conquistador proudly recorded, "I arranged that they should be surrounded by the horses, which would attack them.

"We took them by surprise and killed five hundred. The horsemen charged into the thick of them, knocking down as many as they could. Our footsoldiers then slaughtered these like pigs... In the end they tried to

hide in the grass, or the living hid beneath the dead, but these were found and many of them beheaded after we finished with those who were fleeing."

In the end, Federmann found a race of dwarfs – only 76 cm (30 inches) tall, he reported, but perfectly proportioned – and even some golden trinkets, but little else. After about 20 years of similarly atrocious depradations, the Spanish Crown ordered an inquiry and revoked the German lease. With poetic justice, many of the Germans came to

Above, English pirates became the scourge of Venezuela's coast.

sticky ends: Federmann wasted the rest of his life searching for El Dorado, Dalfinger fell riddled with Indian arrows in Colombia, and several others were executed by Spanish conspirators.

The frontier secured: Although no cities paved with jewels were ever found, these misdirected quests did attract the manpower needed to secure much of Venezuela for the Spanish Crown. Giving up on El Dorado in the 1540s, colonists turned to securing more towns and routes through the Andes to the rest of the empire. It was an uphill struggle: the scattered groups of Venezuelan Indians were now aware of the Spaniards' cruelty and put up tenacious resistance to their advance, in many areas halting it completely. The town of Caracas, later to become Venezuela's colonial capital, was founded several times, only to be wiped out again and again by hostile tribes.

In fact, Spanish colonists bitterly expected the struggle to go on for decades and ruefully looked at other American provinces like Peru and Bolivia where silver mines were making penniless adventurers into grandees overnight. Then an unexpected European weapon broke the Indian resistance: smallpox. While Spaniards had a strong immune system to the disease, it was unknown in the Americas and wiped out entire Indian communities. In the embattled Caracas valley, for example, a wave of the plague in 1580 killed no less than two-thirds of the native population – a toll considerably worse than the Black Death in medieval Europe.

The forgotten provinces: With this ignoble victory, Venezuela entered its long period of colonial control. These centuries as a dismal and forgotten backwater in the Spanish empire are often skipped over as a forgotten and somewhat irrelevant time, not least by modern Venezuelans. But the structures set up during the colonial era have shaped – and distorted – the fate of Venezuela to this day.

The small outposts at Cumaná, Caracas, Mérida and Maracaibo grew to be muddy villages and then established towns as colonists began arriving in numbers from Spain. Still marking Venezuela's towns and cities is the original monotonous grid-iron street plan, spreading out from the *cabildo* (town council) and cathedral as a symbol of rational empire-building. Houses were mostly of adobe mud, although a few of the richest settlers built in brick; most were set around a whitewashed patio and garden, and were kept one story high to avoid damage in case of earthquakes. Attempts were made to create genteel enclaves of Hispanic style in this tropical setting: children were still married off at age 14, heavy imported wine went down with meals and a long siesta after lunch was *de rigueur*.

Pirates soon replaced Indians as the main threat to Venezuela's new towns. Prowling the Caribbean coastline were packs of English, Dutch and French corsairs waiting for gold-laden galleons but not above pillaging a whole town for its wealth. On one occasion in 1595, Sir Francis Drake even attacked Caracas: taking 500 men on a secret night march through the mountains, he surprised the town and burned it to the ground. According to the chroniclers, most of the inhabitants fled, leaving a single old man to confront the invaders. In true Don Quixote fashion, he took a lance and charged Drake's men on horseback, only to be felled by a volley of arquebus fire.

Cattle and cacao: After building towns as bases, the Spaniards claimed the countryside. In the grand colonial plan, Venezuela become half plantation, half ranch.

Missionaries often turned out to be the shock troops of settlement: fiery-eyed Franciscans, Capuchins and Jesuits filtered through the Venezuelan hinterland to make contact with the remaining Indian groups. Although many ended up martyrs, they succeeded in setting up the missions that would convert the *indígenas* and prepare for their eventual submission to the Crown.

Across the warm valleys of the coast spread *haciendas*, semi-feudal plantations growing mostly the native South American plant cacao. With Indians dying out, the Spaniards brought in boatloads of black African slaves as laborers, adding a new and lasting racial element to Venezuelan society. Slavery lasted here long after it was abolished in Europe: as late as 1840 travelers were appalled to find every Venezuelan town had its covered slave market. Blacks up for sale had coconut oil rubbed into their skin to make it shiny and, as if they were horses, had their teeth checked by prospective buyers to confirm their age and health. Conditions on the plantations were pitiless, and regular slave revolts were repressed quickly and ferociously.

Meanwhile, the fertile grasslands of the Llanos were opened up to cattle. *Hatos*, or ranches, began to dot this remote area and, as in the pampas of Argentina, half-wild herds were soon wandering the empty plains, unrestricted by fencing. Since beef was near-impossible to transport, *llaneros* – the breed of skilled horsemen, usually drawn from the fringes of society, who worked the Llanos – would slaughter steers just to eat the tongue and take the hide, leaving the carcasses to rot in the wilderness. While there were chronic shortages of almost every other domestic item in colonial times, leather was abundant and used for almost anything: it made the backing for tables and chairs, replaced glass for windows, and, when used in thongs, could be substituted for rare iron nails.

The shape of colonial society: The majority of initial settlers were young unmarried men, and coaxing Spanish women to brave the uncertainties of an Atlantic crossing and rough life in the New World would long remain a problem. Those that did come were somewhat horrified to find that they might have to share their new husbands with one or more Indian or black slave mistresses, and even accept a collection of bastard children.

Indeed, the mixture of races was soon to be the main feature of Venezuelan society. By 1700, "free-coloreds" or *pardos* – including everyone from freed slaves to half-castes – would make up some 45 percent of Venezuela's whole population, with black slaves and Indians comprising 15 percent each. *Blancos* or whites only made up about 25 percent of the total (and even then, as one foreign writer observed with studied prejudice, they were "rarely free of any connection to the blood of the colored class").

This white elite – often called "Gran Cacao," in deference to the source of its power – was acutely conscious of its vulnerability, and in a primitive form of apartheid made sure that *pardos* could not wear the same Hispanic clothes as whites, could not enter the Church or study at university. There were even attempts to have *pardos* carry a certificate denoting their racial status "to avoid doubts and confusion," while the motto *Todo blanco es caballero* ("every white man is a gentleman") became the rule. As a result, *pardos* were kept in the more menial trades or worked as laborers on *haciendas* and on the wild, free-ranging cattle ranches.

As the colonial era progressed, the *blancos* became divided between a small group of Spanish-born newcomers and the vast bulk of creoles – as whites who were born in the New World were called. Both groups emulated the styles and manners of far-away Madrid. The visiting German scientist Alexander von Humboldt would record of Venezuela that "in no other part of Spanish America has civilization assumed a more European character," with *blancos* holding elegant soirées, playing cards, dancing and earnestly discussing the latest French farce or Italian opera.

Still, the Venezuelans could hardly avoid some creole eccentricities: von Humboldt

short, Venezuela was an unknown tropical backwater. What changed all that, strangely enough, was chocolate.

When Europe and the United States developed a passion for this by-product of cacao in the mid 1700s, Venezuelan plantations geared up to meet the demand. Most other crops were abandoned in pursuit of this single valuable export – creating a monoculture that some modern writers claim has affected Venezuelan agriculture to this day. The old dreams of El Dorado were resurrected in the boom climate, and Caracas, as the center of the trade, began to dominate the rest of Venezuela economically and politically. By the 1770s Venezuela had been

was astonished to see aristocratic families on hot evenings pick up their chairs and carry them into nearby rivers, chatting with friends and smoking cigars as the water flowed up to their knees, quite unfazed by the many small crocodiles splashing about their feet or the playful dolphins spraying them with water.

The chocolate empire: Despite the Venezuelans' European airs, their six scattered provinces were for almost all the colonial period amongst the least important, successful or wealthy parts of the Spanish empire. In

African slaves at work on an 18th-century cacao plantation.

pushed from obscurity to the most valuable non-mining colony in the Spanish empire, and the Gran Cacao *blancos* could scarcely believe their luck. The fancy-dress balls in Caracas and concert recitals in Cumaná were never so lavish as at the end of the 18th century, their champagne, fine cheeses and olives imported thanks to the sweat of their black slaves.

But this Golden Age was the calm before the storm. The wars of independence would soon hit Venezuela with an unexpected ferocity, turning its *haciendas* into cemeteries and pushing the country's progress back more than 100 years.

The soporific calm of colonial Venezuela was shattered at the beginning of the 19th century by the wars of independence against Spain. Although Venezuela would play a key role in liberating much of South America, most Venezuelans entered the struggle hesitantly and failed to anticipate its enormous cost. Nowhere else on the continent was the fighting more cruel and destructive: after two decades of bloodshed, Venezuela would be lying in ruins and its tenuous colonial prosperity lost.

Inseparable from this dramatic conflict is the figure of Simón Bolívar, *El Libertador*. Every Venezuelan village, no matter how small, boasts a bronze Bolívar statue along with a plaza, main street or municipal building named in honor of the romantic national hero who, despite his many victories, died a bitter and broken man. A heavy shroud of mythology lies over his memory: Bolívar is Latin America's Washington, Napoleon and Hamlet all rolled into one.

El Libertador: Notoriously short in stature, thin and wiry, a fine horseman and swimmer, Bolívar could discourse as easily about military strategy as the works of Rousseau. He inspired the passionate devotion of his soldiers and the praises of everyone from South American patriots to the English poet Lord Byron, who named a boat that he owned *Bolívar* and planned to sail it to Venezuela. Exiled twice, escaping numerous assassination attempts (once when a slave knifed a fellow patriot sleeping in Bolívar's hammock), Bolívar squandered one of the greatest family fortunes in the New World pursuing his dream of a united Latin America. The dream took him in campaigns across the Andes to Colombia, Ecuador, Peru and the nation named after him, Bolivia. Looking back from the 20th century, few historians deny that Bolívar was a genius.

Yet as the 19th century turned, there was no indication that Venezuela would soon push for independence or that the young Bolívar would be involved. The wealthy,

white creole elite, while annoyed at certain aspects of colonial rule, rarely questioned the basis of Spanish control that had served them so well: more worrisome to the *blancos* was that the black and colored population might rise up against them in rebellion. Meanwhile, Simón Bolívar was just another young man about to inherit a fortune from his Gran Cacao family and destined for a life of ease – although on his teenage travels to Europe, Bolívar had met the German scientist Alexander von Humboldt, and been as-

tonished by the suggestion that the Spanish American colonies were ripe for freedom.

The first push towards independence actually came from outside Venezuela in 1808. Sensational news arrived from the Napoleonic wars in Europe: mother Spain had been occupied by the French army, the Spanish king had abdicated and Napoleon's brother been placed on the throne. But rather than declare Venezuela independent, leading *Caraqueños* formed a junta in support of the Spanish king. Only by 1810 did the wealthy elite decide that Spain was in such confusion that they should try self-government.

The rest of Venezuela did not agree. Coro,

<u>Left</u>, paying homage to Simón Bolívar at the Plaza Bolívar in Caracas. <u>Right</u>, the young "Liberator."

Maracaibo and Guayana refused to sign a new constitution, and even the mass of *Caraqueños* failed to be impressed by the *blancos'* rule. An aging radical named Francisco de Miranda was made dictator, but was unable to control the situation. In 1812, 300 royalist troops led an easy counter-revolution, and many patriots fled into exile in the Caribbean, leaving their so-called First Republic in tatters.

The slaughter begins: One of the exiles was Bolívar, who had thrown himself into the lower echelons of the independence movement as if to help forget the tragic death of his young wife. He had gone to London as the new Republic's ambassador (only to be dis-

though Venezuelan-born captives would get a second chance). The violence escalated and drew more of the Venezuelan population into the conflict: armies devastated great swathes of the countryside.

Adding to the carnage was the arrival of the *llaneros*, the wild horsemen of Venezuela's interior plains who became a devastating irregular cavalry force – first on the side of the royalists, then for the patriots. The *llaneros* lived off the land and took as pay what they could pillage. They did not even need to be supplied with weapons, since they could replenish their lance-points from an outcrop of palm trees.

By 1814, Bolívar had recaptured Caracas

appointed in his pleas for support) and risen to the rank of colonel in the patriot forces, but his true leadership potential had remained untapped. Now, during his first exile, Bolívar slowly began to exert his charisma and assume command of the patriots.

First came what the Venezuelans call *La Campaña Admirable* (the Admirable Campaign) when Bolívar and other patriot generals regrouped their forces and began a "War to the Death" against the Spaniards. Responding to the brutality of royalist forces, who regularly executed captured prisoners without trial, Bolívar declared that any Spanish-born prisoner would be shot (al-

and declared the Second Republic, but made the mistake of trying to force all mixed-blooded Venezuelans to carry certificates of race (although, curiously, Bolívar himself had a trace of black heritage, as earlier portraits of the General reveal). The *llaneros* mobilized against him, sweeping into Caracas and forcing the patriots, yet again, into exile. Their commander, José Tomás Boves, became notorious as the Spanish "butcher": he personally supervised the massacre of entire villages, wandering through the ruins

Above, *Llanero* lancers feign a retreat, only to return and attack again.

THE BRITISH LEGION

L a Legión Britannica, or British Legion, is the shorthand term for the more than 5,000 English, Scottish, Irish and Hanoverian soldiers who journeyed across the Atlantic to join Simón Bolívar's revolutionary army in Venezuela. In one of the least-known aspects of the South American wars of independence, battalions drawn from far away London, Glasgow and Dublin fought alongside *criollos* throughout Venezuela, with many following the Liberator even into the harsh Andes of Peru.

Recruiting in Britain began soon after 1815, when the battle of Waterloo finally brought the Napoleonic wars to a close. Multitudes of demobilized veterans were returning to their homes, only to find few jobs and dismal prospects.

In 1817, Bolívar ordered his agent in London to recruit any officers that wanted to serve as mercenaries in South America. The response was overwhelming. An officer named Gustavus Mathius Hippisley – who, like most officers, was chafing under a half-pay army pension – immediately came forward with an officer corps ready to form a regiment of hussars in Venezuela. They were followed by three more regiments of cavalry officers, one of rifles and an artillery unit – some 1,000 soldiers in all.

Alarmed by the potential exodus, the British government decreed that any departure was prohibited. On learning the news, Hippisley ordered that the boats would leave immediately – weighing anchor so quickly, in fact, that many recruits were left behind. Although it departed unmolested, the flotilla hit a storm in the Channel and one of the troop ships was wrecked on the French coast, drowning 200 recruits.

The 800 who made it to the New World found themselves stranded in the British Antilles for months waiting for their arms. Tropical diseases hit, followed by massive desertions, and only 240 made it to Angostura (now Ciudad Bolívar) in Venezuela. They were immediately despatched to join Bolívar's army in the steaming Llanos, where they took part in the battle of Semen. Hippisley only arrived some time later, but argued with Bolívar and returned to England soon afterwards.

Despite this inauspicious start, officers and soldiers arrived from Britain in a steady stream until the British government finally stopped the

flow in August 1819. Historians estimate that some 6,500 set out for South America and 5,300 arrived. The bulk were English, although there was a battalion of Scottish highlanders and a separate "Irish Legion".

Despite being on the winning side, very few of the British Legion would survive the grueling years of war. The major killer was not weaponry but disease: soldiers succumbed to everything from malaria to typhoid.

The so-called "Albion Battalion," composed mostly of English soldiers, fought with distinction in Venezuela, at the battle of Boyacá in Colombia and beneath the volcano of Pichincha in Ecuador before being disbanded in 1822 for lack of numbers. The First Venezuelan Rifles

continued to march with Bolívar through the royalist stronghold of Lima and up into the *altiplano* of Peru, where it took part in the climactic battle of Ayacucho in 1824.

The Irish contingents performed less gloriously, with one group surrendering to the royalists only to be executed en masse. Others mutinied on Margarita island, seized some boats and fled to Jamaica. Yet one Irishman, General Daniel O'Leary, stayed in South America and became one of Simón Bolívar's most trusted confidantes. O'Leary stayed by the Liberator's side until his dying moments – then went on to write a 34-volume memoir, which remains the most important historical source on Bolívar's life. ∎

Contemporary drawing of a patriot in Bolívar's army.

with a sinister smile. On one occasion, when his troops captured the city of Valencia, Boves ordered the wealthiest citizens to bring their finest silver to a feast. But after an elaborate series of toasts, Boves ordered the men to be dragged out for execution, while the horrified wives and daughters were forced to waltz with the cavalry officers. After years of such gruesome jests, Boves finally met a violent end, skewered on a lance in battle.

The last chance: Hiding out in Jamaica, Bolívar prepared to fight yet again. Realizing the importance of the *llaneros*, he offered them land as a reward for joining his cause: the confiscated estates of royalists would be distributed amongst them. The *llanero* leader – a Herculean, illiterate cavalryman named José Antonio Paez, who always appeared with a towering black bodyguard – agreed. And since the *llaneros* followed strong figures rather than any particular cause, Bolívar gained the backbone of a new army.

Hiding out in a guerrilla base in the Orinoco, Bolívar is reported as a wild figure with huge sideburns and shoulder-length hair, wearing a cast-off uniform including the helmet of a Russian dragoon and carrying the skull-and-crossbones flag, with the words "Liberty or Death." In time, a loose form of discipline was imposed upon the *llanero* army, and Bolívar returned to his Europeanized elegance as its general.

In a change of strategy, Bolívar gave up on Venezuela and led his army over the Andes into Colombia. This march is considered one of the most audacious and desperate strokes of Latin America's liberation. Many of the soldiers crossed the icy mountain passes without shoes, and more than a quarter of the army died on the march. But, bolstered by the experienced troops of the British Legion (*see page 41*) the campaign was a success, and Colombia became a base in 1819 for a return attack on Caracas.

This time Bolívar did not mean to fail in his homeland: "The war will not be to the death, nor even a normal war," he wrote. "It will be a holy war, a struggle to disarm the enemy, not destroy him." Luckily, the royalists were losing heart, as political chaos in Madrid was distracting both attention and troops from the New World. Fighting dragged on until the battle of Carabobo in 1821, and Bolívar finally entered Caracas to be declared President.

The Liberator's dream: But Bolívar's career as *El Libertador* was only beginning. Being president of both Colombia and Venezuela was hardly enough: Bolívar not only planned to extirpate the Spanish presence from Latin America, he wanted to see the former colonies united as the world's largest nation. It was a vision that drove him onwards to liberate the Andean nations, and one that held together for a remarkably long time given that Bolívar may have been the only Latin American to believe in it.

Thousands of Venezuelan troops followed the general into battle amongst the volcanoes near Quito, the Inca ruins of Cuzco and the bleak *altiplano* beyond Lake Titicaca. After

the last Spaniards had surrendered at the Andean battle of Ayacucho, Bolívar was feted in Lima and seemed close to achieving his dream. Yet even as he danced all night through the glittering ballrooms of America's wealthiest city and gained an enduring reputation as a Casanova (one cavalry officer reputedly moved out of the Presidential Palace because the shrieks of love-making ruined his sleep), things were going awry.

News soon arrived that the confederation of La Gran Colombia – a country uniting modern Colombia, Venezuela and Ecuador, and a cornerstone of Bolívar's plan – was cracking up. The *llanero* Paez had been left behind in Venezuela, and planned to lead the country to secede. Bolívar rushed back to Caracas and patched up the confederation, but it was doomed: local interests were too strong to keep the Americas together.

Even so, Bolívar spent the last years of his life vainly staving off the inevitable. Wracked by tuberculosis, his disillusion took on a tragic dimension (brilliantly captured by the Colombian writer Gabriel García Márquez in his bestselling novel *The General in his Labyrinth*). One by one, his supporters turned against him, while his only possible successor, Marshal Sucre, was assassinated on a mountain highway. In Colombia, Bolívar escaped another assassination attempt only

decades of Latin American history. "America is ungovernable," he declared. "Those who serve the revolution plough the sea. The only thing to do in America is emigrate."

Repairing the ruin: For most Venezuelans, although they helped finance Bolívar's later campaigns, nominal independence was secured in 1821. But Venezuela had fragmented into regions controlled by *caudillos* (strongmen) and there would be another 10 years of fighting before the country was more or less under stable rule.

Although the country remained a part of La Gran Colombia for several years out of deference to Bolívar, Paez finally did order the formal break in 1829, and by 1830 the

by leaping out his bedroom window; in his home country, Venezuela, he was finally outlawed as a traitor. Jeered at in the streets by the same people who had cheered him a few short years before, the general left Bogotá for exile in Europe, but never made it: he died in 1830, almost penniless, in a small town on the Caribbean coast.

Shortly before his death, Bolívar penned a bitter prophecy that has echoed through the

Left, Bolívar ponders Latin America's fate on the heights of Chimborazo in Ecuador. **Right**, the remains of Bolívar are now kept in the Panteón in Caracas.

new country of Venezuela began the process of reconstruction.

By any reckoning, the independence wars had been devastating: at least 150,000 Venezuelans died in the fighting; working *haciendas* were destroyed; roads and bridges were in disrepair; livestock numbers had fallen from 4½ million head to somewhere around 250,000. The treasury was bankrupt, and the new administration only survived on a high-interest British loan.

Others besides Bolívar were beginning to wonder what it had all been for. Although the independence struggle is often referred to as a revolution, the basic colonial social structure was intact: Venezuela proved the ancient adage that the more things change, the more they stay the same.

Bolívar had honored his promise to divide the lands of royalists amongst the *llaneros* and other veterans, on a sliding scale of size from generals down to foot-soldiers. But in a process that foreshadowed a history of failed land reform in Latin America, the impoverished soldiers sold out their smaller shares to the officers at a fraction of the real cost. The old white landowning elite gained some new members, mostly of white officers, whose descendants own much of Venezuelan agriculture to this day. Otherwise, their power was unbroken.

leged classes." Male *blancos* tied the vote to owning property, kept important military posts and controlled everything from the presidency down to the most obscure local municipal offices.

Years of chaos: The rest of the 19th century is a complicated morass of coups, civil wars and separatist movements. Yet all were to some extent arguments amongst the white elite over who would control and profit most from foreign trade. The chief players were the elegant, educated *Caraqueño* bureaucrats and a series of rougher *caudillos* who commanded armed bands left over from the independence wars. The legacy of two decades of brutality was that might was right in

Meanwhile, slavery still existed. Bolívar had freed his own slaves, but few other landowners followed. It was only in the 1850s that they decided that slavery was actually unprofitable, and that slaves could be kept tied to plantations by making them nominally free but charging exorbitant rents (an arrangement that the US South would repeat after the American Civil War, turning slaves into indebted sharecroppers). The mixed blooded *pardos* were also kept out of positions of power: even Bolívar had dreaded the prospect of *pardocracia*, or rule by the colored masses, which he said "will ultimately lead to the extermination of the privi-

the politics of Venezuela.

The most famous *caudillo* was Bolívar's old ally, the *llanero* Paez. From 1830 to 1848 he established a modicum of order in Venezuela, hunting down bandits, crushing rebellions and, when he was not president himself, choosing who should rule. The illiterate plainsman of old remained a figure in local politics until the 1860s, when he was finally exiled to die far from his native world in New York City. Even so, Paez gave Venezuela a chance to rebuild some prosperity – largely thanks to a coffee boom – and enough stability to survive the upheavals that would regularly occur in the next generations.

As in several other South American countries, the ruling elite split into two factions that called themselves the Liberals and the Conservatives – although, rather like the Republican and Democrat parties in the modern United States, their differences were more about the fine tuning of government than any serious social change. Transfers of power between the two groups occurred in violent fashion, but any suggestion of an uprising by *pardos* or blacks was met with ruthless, united action.

The Liberals and the Conservatives plunged Venezuela into five years of civil war after a period of economic decline in the 1850s. In theory, the argument was about

whether Venezuela should have a federal system or be controlled directly from Caracas, but although the Liberal-Federalists had won by 1863, regional revolts and battles continued for decades.

Despite the turmoil, some changes were occurring. Most noticeably, the city of Caracas was growing further apart from the rest of the country. With its direct links to the outside world, the capital became increasingly affluent and cosmopolitan: its streets,

Left, European-style public buildings sprang up in Caracas during the late 19th century, despite endless civil wars (<u>right</u>).

buildings and the dress of its educated bureaucrats mimicked the styles of Europe. President Guzmán Blanco was particularly keen to create a Caribbean version of Paris, ordering the construction of the Parque El Calvario with a French gothic chapel and French garden designs that needed one hundred full-time gardeners to maintain them.

At the same time, Simón Bolívar was rehabilitated in the eyes of history, and his personality cult begun as a symbol of national unity. The Liberator's remains were brought back to Caracas from Colombia and installed in a national pantheon; statues of Bolívar were erected around the country; and Venezuela's first national currency was set up in 1879, to be called the bolívar.

Birth of a nation: As the 19th century stumbled on to a close, the old regional *caudillo* style of politics looked increasingly outdated. Presidents could no longer be earthy and charismatic men with enough guns to fight to the top, but were expected to have professional credentials.

More importantly, the President was increasingly able to force his will on the rest of the country. The central government in Caracas began to build up its armed forces with modern weapons, against which the smaller *caudillos* could no longer compete. New communications such as the telegraph and railroad ensured that they could no longer plot in secrecy.

Naturally, few *caudillos* accepted the changes lying down, and the 1890s were a particularly chaotic period of regional uprisings. Eccentric presidents like Cipriano Castro – who built the elegant Palacio de Miraflores in Caracas, complete with an iron-plated, earthquake-resistant bedroom – still made it to the presidency, but Venezuelans quickly tired of them: Castro's haphazard style led to such serious economic problems that the government defaulted on its European loans. Then as today, debt default was considered the most heinous of economic crimes: in 1902–03, England, Germany and Italy began a naval blockade of Venezuela and bombarded its coastline to make it pay up.

Despite these hiccups, the era of the regional *caudillos* was coming to an end. With the discovery of oil in the early part of the 20th century, a new technocratic President, Juan Vicente Gómez, would fling the country headlong into the modern age.

THE BOOM YEARS

The first Spanish explorers to land on the sun-scorched shores of Lake Maracaibo noted a thick black oil oozing from the sandy earth. Local Indians used the sticky liquid to caulk their canoes; it could be made into candles, spread to trap animals and even used as a medicine. But for the Spaniards it held no interest, and for the next 400 years – apart from the odd pirate who needed a gum to caulk a leaking ship – nobody but the Indians gave the oil a second thought.

By the turn of the 20th century, the invention of the motor car had given this black fluid new value. Even so, Venezuelans were not at first enthusiastic about the costly task of crude oil extraction. Explorations around Lake Maracaibo were desultory: a few small wells were dug, a pipeline and tiny refinery built, but nobody expected much from the new discoveries.

Then, in December 1922, a Venezuelan subsidiary of Shell restarted drilling at a well named Los Barrosos No. 2, near the sleepy village of La Rosa on the east coast of Lake Maracaibo. Four years earlier, drilling had been suspended in disappointment at a depth of 164 meters. But this time, in a scene straight out of the Hollywood film *Giant*, the well "blew out": on the first day of drilling, 100,000 barrels of oil spurted from the earth, eclipsing the entire previous Venezuelan production of 8,000 barrels a day.

The find was dubbed the Bolívar Coastal Field and made immediate world news. For Venezuela, oil was like manna from heaven. Petrodollars would change the country's face forever, ending generations of stagnation and giving Venezuela the highest per capita income in Latin America. In what one writer has dubbed "a compression of historical time," Venezuela was transformed by the 1960s from an agricultural society characterized by political chaos to a consumerist, relatively stable democracy. Unfortunately, the easy oil money was not always wisely used, and when the boom was over, Venezuelans would look back on the heady years

of wealth with a mixture of wonder, pride and despair at a lost opportunity.

Oil rush: In the two years after oil was discovered, some 73 different foreign companies flocked to Lake Maracaibo to begin exploration, encouraged by the promise of enormous profits with minimal taxes. The skilled workers were mostly from the United States, the hired muscle Venezuelan: hard-bitten engineers from Texas and Oklahoma descended on this primitive tropical backwater and in a remarkably short time had

carved oil empires from the wilderness.

In the initial years of exploration, conditions were appalling: the lakeside was either virgin rainforest or bleak desert. Imported heavy equipment was slowly unloaded on the docks of Maracaibo – with 75,000 inhabitants, by far the largest town in the area – and taken in small sailboats to the shore. From there, machinery could only be dragged by oxen and mules to the oil sites, with workers following on foot.

Soon more sophisticated oil camps were set up with every modern convenience for the foreign engineers. The fields were fenced off with barbed wire, and even had their own

Preceding pages: oil towers on Lake Maracaibo. **Left**, the discovery of oil in the 1920s transformed Venezuela. **Right**, dictator Juan Vicente Gómez.

police. Makeshift towns sprouted from nowhere along the lake's shore, with all the hallmarks of a "black gold" rush: bars and brothels outnumbered food stores 10 to 1, while fortunes were gambled or drunk away overnight. Everything was imported, including fresh water, which fetched a price per litre higher than the crude oil being dug up. Even the prostitutes were given nicknames like "Pipeline," "Four Valves," "Derrick" or "Hoist."

Although it was initially considered impossible, techniques were invented for offshore drilling on Lake Maracaibo. Soon hundreds of towers had sprouted across the waters in a floating steel forest. Although they no

enda, its inhabitants peons who needed to be looked after like children. The Gómez political philosophy was not complex: trusted friends and relatives would be given positions of power and wealth; enemies real or suspected were hunted down, tortured, exiled or simply murdered.

In 1908, having risen through the army to the rank of general, Gómez advised President Cipriano Castro to travel to Europe for a medical operation before declaring him an outlaw and seizing the presidency. Gómez quickly turned the army into his personal Praetorian Guard, with loyal officers from Andean states given positions of favor. For the more subtle tasks of social control a

longer function, these towers with their ghostly flames are still the most powerful image the world has of Venezuela.

The iron fist: The oil boom coincided with the dictatorship of Juan Vicente Gómez, whose brutal 27-year rule marked Venezuela irrevocably and set the scene for the country as it is today.

In many ways, Gómez fits the classic caricature of a Latin American dictator. An ex-cattle rancher and accountant from the Andean state of Táchira, he was a colorless, taciturn and unimaginative figure who ran Venezuela like a latter-day Roman emperor. The country was treated like a private *haci-*

secret police was formed to hunt down anyone who plotted against or even bad-mouthed the dictator. Nothing was left to chance: even the formation of a Rotary Club in Caracas was banned in case it should turn into a political organization.

Having built this vast, corrupt apparatus of control, Gómez moved from Caracas – whose European pretensions he never felt comfortable with – to a cattle ranch in nearby Maracay. From there he could pronounce the major decisions of Venezuela's fate, while allowing the bureaucrats of Caracas to look after the day-to-day details of government. Civilian ministers, foreign diplomats and heads of local businesses all made the journey out to this rural outpost, begging cap in hand for the favors of the surly Patriarch.

The carnival king: With Venezuela firmly under his control, Gómez greeted the news of the 1922 oil boom in typical imperial style. As the Uruguayan writer Eduardo Galleano has described it: "While black geysers spouted on all sides, Gómez took petroleum shares from his bursting pockets to rewards his friends, relations and courtiers, the doctor who looked after his prostate, the generals who served as his bodyguard, the poets who sang his praises and the archbishop who gave him a special dispensation to eat meat on Good Friday."

Lavish tax concessions to US oil companies meant that the Venezuelan government only received some seven percent of the total oil profits from 1919 to Gómez's death in 1935. Even so, the money had fallen from the skies as far as Venezuelans were concerned and – to a government accustomed to surviving on minimal local taxation – it seemed like a fortune. Roads, housing and port facilities were built, often to the petroleum company's specifications, while the city of Cara-

Lifestyles of the oil-rich and famous: left, young Bohemians in Caracas and, right, a chic matron promenading.

cas began the modernization that would wipe out its colonial past forever.

Local entrepreneurs jumped on the development bandwagon and made themselves rich, creating a Venezuelan middle class. The bolívar remained strong throughout the Great Depression, and Venezuelans began to appear in the salons of Paris and jewelry shops of New York. Soon the oil-rich Venezuelan was a semi-mythical figure to stand alongside the robber baron of Texas and cattle king of Argentina.

Not surprisingly, everyone wanted a piece of the action. Rural peasants flocked to the burgeoning oil camps and suburbs of Caracas to pick up some work. Landowners gave up their farms to head for the big smoke, where they could indulge in the more lucrative trade of brokering the sale of drilling rights from the State to US companies. Agriculture declined rapidly and there was no hope of starting up a manufacturing industry: Venezuela was importing everything from beans to refrigerators.

Autumn of the Patriarch: Sealed up in his remote cattle ranch, Gómez succumbed to illness and senility. He began to suspect his closest allies of betrayal: palace intrigues racked the extended Gómez family – which by now controlled everything from the national newspapers to cabinet posts – and a new rank of secret police thugs was brought to power in the struggle. Rumors of Gómez's imminent death circulated around Venezuela every week, without foundation. The military watched the wretched spectacle of the President's last years, biding its time for more control.

When word finally leaked from Maracay in 1935 that the Patriarch was dead, riots erupted around Venezuela. Thousands of *Caraqueños* flocked into the streets to celebrate the autocrat's demise, sacking the houses of the most hated *gomecistas*, and, where possible, lynching them from telegraph poles. The military was too busy getting a new government ready to protect the old figures – having regarded them with some contempt anyway – and Venezuelans were given tacit permission to purge the country.

The Gómez decades had transformed Venezuela, but they also left a curious political void: the dictator's brutal repression had wiped out all previous political traditions and there was hardly anyone left capable of running the country. Thousands of exiles who had been living in Europe and the United States for years began returning to Caracas, to be greeted by avalanches of flowers and emotional reunions in the docks and airports.

The most famous and capable group were known as "the Generation of '28." As students, they had led a great anti-Gómez riot in 1928 which led to their wholesale exile. Now they came back with a vision for Venezuela.

It was now that many Venezuelans wholeheartedly accepted the idea that their country could and should take its place in the First World. Modernity became a national obsession, and the national model would be the United States. Petrodollars would supply the

Venezuela a 30 percent share of the oil company's profits.

The trienio: This slow process of reform came to an abrupt end in 1945, when the Generation of '28 leaders in AD convinced a group of young military officers to stage a coup. Having seen the fall of Fascism in Europe, intellectuals in Venezuela felt that the time had come for drastic action against the autocrats of the South. Some 2,500 people died in bitter fighting during the coup, mostly in the streets of Caracas, but Medina Angarita stepped down. To this day, the AD decision stirs heated debate in Venezuela: the coup eventually ushered in a moment of democratic rule, but was followed by a right-

cash, the Generation of '28 the ideas: Venezuela would become the industrialized democracy of the Caribbean.

Gómez's Minister of War, Eleazar Lopez Contreras, assumed the presidency, proclaimed a new constitution and declared that he would lead the way to the democratic future. New institutions like a central bank were created along with laws giving Venezuela slightly more control of its oil wealth. Some indirect elections were allowed, and the Generation of '28 figures formed a political party called Acción Democrática (AD). Lopez's successor, Medina Angarita, used the need for oil in World War II to guarantee

wing backlash that brought on the harshest dictatorships the country has ever known.

A junta now forced through the reforms needed to change Venezuelan society to an ideal image. Free elections were held, and the famous novelist Romulo Gallegos became president. Unfortunately, the author of *La Rebellion* and *Doña Barbara* proved a better writer than politician. Too many changes were pushed through, without popular support. Reformers misjudged the traditional sectors of Venezuelan society, and

Above, a petrol refinery built in the 1970s, at the height of the boom.

failed to notice that the military officers who had led the coup of 1945 had no intention of being left out of power.

In 1948, a military junta seized power in a bloodless coup, sent the novelist-President into exile and set about undoing most of the reforms of the previous 13 years.

Chief amongst the young bloods now in power was General Marcos Pérez Jiménez. This ruthless manipulator took over as president in 1952 after holding an election and declaring it void when it looked like he might lose. In a throwback to the Gómez days, secret police once again patrolled the streets of Caracas in search of the regime's opponents – only this time they could use modern phone taps, radio surveillance and electric cattle prods in the pursuit of their goals. Any union action or student demonstration was immediately crushed. AD leaders went into exile, although the party survived in hiding despite torture, assassinations and jailings.

Strikes by oil workers were now a thing of the past, and US companies like Standard Oil were pleased in 1954 to receive tax cuts of US$300 million. Despite his brutality, Pérez Jiménez became a staunch ally of the United States: in the same year as the tax cuts, he was the first to recognize a CIA overthrow of the elected government of Guatemala. The regime had already become the most feared and hated in Venezuelan history when US President Eisenhower awarded Pérez Jiménez the Legion of Honor.

Still, the oil money was flowing more freely than ever and Pérez Jiménez began a program with the 1984-style title "New National Ideal" for the "conquest of the physical environment." Huge public works like six-lane highways in Caracas, the giant Humboldt Hotel, high-rise office buildings and sumptuous clubs for military officers began to spread across the Venezuelan landscape. Corruption went hand in hand with the construction, disgusting even some members of the military.

The regime seemed increasingly clumsy and capricious in its activities. When Pérez Jiménez finally held a plebiscite in 1958 – and once again blatantly rigged the result – Venezuelans had had enough. Riots and a general strike led to the general packing his bags full of US dollars and boarding his private jet to Miami.

The new era: Venezuelans now had a second chance of forming a democratic regime, and this time the political leaders – older and more moderate – decided to go in for slow reform. One of the Generation of '28, Romulo Betancourt, became president in 1958 at the head of an AD government, starting a democratic era that has survived to the present.

Through the 1960s, a succession of governments guided the country through threats by right-wing military officers and a left-wing guerrilla operation, but at the end of the decade stability was assured. As a major oil producer, Venezuela began taking its role on the world stage: in 1960, it took the lead in forming the international oil cartel, OPEC, which met regularly in Caracas. Venezuela joined the Andean pact and formed a regional common market with its neighbors – although a long-standing border conflict with Guyana took the country to the brink of war.

Oil money poured in throughout the 1970s in ever greater sums. Taxes were raised so that Venezuela received nearly 70 percent of foreign oil revenues, and the Arab oil embargo of 1973 brought Venezuela a US$50 billion windfall.

Much of the money was used by President Carlos Andrés Pérez to nationalize industries from natural gas to iron, until finally oil production was taken over. The move was made cautiously, compensation was provided and the transition went smoothly. Soon a "Venezuelization" of oil company jobs would make some nine-tenths of the employees locally born.

Yet even at this time of surplus, things were going awry, as Eduardo Galleano observed in the mid-1970s: "Caracas chews gum and loves synthetic products and canned foods; it never walks and poisons the clean air of the valley with the fumes of its motorization; its fever to buy, consume, obtain, spend, use, get hold of everything leaves no time to sleep. From surrounding hillside hovels made of garbage, half a million forgotten people observe the sybaritic scene. The gilded city's avenues glitter with hundreds of thousands of late-model cars, but in the consuming society, not everyone consumes. According to the census, half of Venezuela's children and youngsters do not go to school."

The middle class was drunk on oil money; everyone else intoxicated by the thought of one day getting some. Few pondered what would happen when the hangover hit.

VENEZUELA TODAY

Since the 1970s, Venezuela has gone from being South America's richest nation into a nouveau-poor society in search of an identity. Once known as the Saudis of the West, Venezuelans have seen their economic fortunes decline in exact proportion to the general fall in world oil prices. Even so, Venezuela's many problems were hidden from view until relatively recently, when austerity measures heralded the sort of economic crisis so painfully familiar to other Latin American countries. Runaway inflation, currency devaluations and even food riots have marked this new phase in Venezuelan history, to which the country is still trying to adjust.

"Saudi Venezuela": Venezuelans still live with the memories of the oil boom years, which began in earnest with the nationalization of the petroleum industry in 1976 and ended with a crash in 1983. The government coffers overflowed with revenues. Although a good deal was spirited away by corrupt politicans, some trickled down in the form of scholarships to study abroad, loans for small businesses, or jobs created by an expanding government bureaucracy.

These were the days when middle-class Venezuelans grew accustomed to regular shopping trips to Miami, leaving Caracas with empty suitcases that returned packed with designer clothes, home appliances, gourmet foods and even titles to property in south Florida. In Miami, Venezuelans became know as merry spenders, their slogan the refrain, *Está barato, dáme dos*. ("It's cheap, I'll take two.")

Where consumer goods had been concerned, the word "imported" became synonymous with "quality" and "national" (domestic) with "inferior quality". One of the richest agricultural producers during colonial times, Venezuela by 1983 was importing more than 70 percent of its food.

Black Friday: World oil prices began to slide in 1982, but Venezuelans did not feel the effect until February 18, 1983, a date now recalled as "Black Friday." Alarmed by a capital flight which had reached almost 200

Left, Unionists march to protest against austerity measures in Caracas.

million dollars a week, the government of President Luis Herrera Campins imposed exchange controls and devalued the mighty bolívar, which had remained stable for more than a decade and was widely regarded as the blue-chip Latin currency.

The devaluation more than doubled the price of the US dollar. For most Venezuelans, this meant no more shopping trips to Miami and a general restriction of the opulent lifestyle which many had come to accept as their birthright. Not surprisingly, Venezuelans decided to "kill the messenger" and determinedly threw the government out in the next elections.

The more populist Acción Democrática

(AD) party won the election that followed despite the lackluster presidential campaign of Jaime Lusinchi, a physician by training. The affable, avuncular Lusinchi manoeuvred his way through the deepening crisis with measures designed to maintain social peace and bolster his rating in the polls. Inflation was kept in check by controlled consumer prices.

Industry enjoyed a preferential exchange rate for raw materials and spare parts, keeping industries operating and the unemployment rate down – but at the cost of burning up the country's foreign reserves.

A Venezuelan Evita: Lusinchi's administra-tion was sullied by a scandal which many Venezuelans still consider among the most shameful in the country's history – the president's much-publicized affair with his personal secretary, Blanca Ibáñez. Ibáñez, a petite, attractive redhead who rose from an impoverished family in the Andes to a private office in the presidential palace, sought to create an influential place for herself in Venezuela comparable to that of Eva Perón in Argentina.

With none of Evita's charisma or media appeal, Ibáñez could only emulate her role as official distributor of government largesse to the poor. Unfortunately, Blanca's popularity was practically nil, except among those who admired her audacity.

"Blanquita" often played the role of first lady at presidential functions, ruffling the feathers of diplomats and protocol officials. The *affaire* of state between her and Lusinchi also caused a rift within Acción Democrática when the president unsuccessfully tried to muscle a place for Ibáñez on the party's 1988 election slates.

The president's doting on a much younger woman – and the power she attained – subjected him and the country to ridicule. Even more galling to nationalistic Venezuelans were rumors that the most powerful woman in the country was born in Colombia. As the Peruvian magazine *Careta* put it: "For the president of Venezuela to have a lover who is a Colombian, is somewhat similar to President Reagan having a lover who is a Sandinista."

The return of "El Gocho": Venezuela's current president, Carlos Andrés Pérez, has in many ways been the dominant figure in Venezuela's modern democratic history. Pérez was born on a coffee *hacienda* in Rubio near the Columbian border in the Táchira region which has produced a regular crop of Venezuela's dictators. Known as "El Gocho," the nickname for natives of the Andean region, the charismatic Pérez had been the mastermind behind Venezuela's oil and iron nationalizations during his first presidency in the 1970s. Then, in 1988, he overcame opposition within his own party to win first the nomination and then the presidential sash again – and immediately set about undoing most of the reforms achieved during his first term in office.

Pérez drew up a privatization plan for state

companies, followed by a harsh adjustment program designed to win approval and credits from the International Monetary Fund. Price controls were removed from most consumer goods, causing the inflation rate to soar by 23 percent in one month alone. Subsidies were cut from government-produced goods and services, including gasoline, electricity and water. A free floating exchange rate was introduced for the bolívar, which predictably drove the dollar price and the cost of imported goods to new highs.

It was economic shock treatment. Even so, nobody expected the popular uprising that followed, unlike anything in Venezuela's modern history.

rounding hillside shanty towns to loot commercial areas, carrying off everything from video cassette recorders to sides of beef. Once it was clear that the police had lost control, middle-class Venezuelans joined in the pillage. Live television broadcasts of the looting probably contributed to its spread to the other parts of the nation, with disturbances ultimately recorded in 16 cities across the country.

The decision to use military force to quell a civilian uprising led to many senseless deaths. Some army troops sent into the *barrios* returned sniper shots by spraying entire apartment buildings with automatic weapons fire. Others fired at citizens who appeared in the

On February 27, 1989, three weeks after Pérez took office, an increase in public transport fares provided the spark for three days of nationwide rioting and looting that forced the government to suspend constitutional guarantees and send the army into the streets to restore order. The center of the rioting was Caracas: hundreds were killed and millions of dollars in property damage inflicted as slum-dwellers poured down from the sur-

Left, the Paseo de los Próceres, a monument ot the heroes of Venezuela's past, in Caracas. **Right**, Carlos Andrés Pérez (left) in his second term as president.

windows of their homes after curfew. The number of people who died in the riots remains a topic of conjecture. Official accounts say 297 were killed, but Venezuelan human rights groups say at least 500 died in Caracas alone.

One foreign reporter who covered the riots said he felt the looters were reaching to grab a piece of the Venezuela they now knew was gone forever. More than just a "food riot," or "gasoline price riot," the disturbances were a tragic lesson in how easily the whole fabric of society could unravel. Hard times had struck with a vengeance and Venezuelans, who had lived so well for so long, showed they were capable of reacting in violent and unexpected ways.

The new Venezuela: Long after the dust from the riots had cleared, the collective trauma remained. Even so, the Pérez government reaffirmed its commitment to the economic program, with the expected results: the next year was the worst the Venezuelan economy had seen for decades.

The country fell into a deep recession. Pérez ran into problems within his own party. Already unpopular for filling key economic posts with young, foreign-trained technocrats (the so-called "yuppie cabinet"), he now looked hell-bent on losing the next elections.

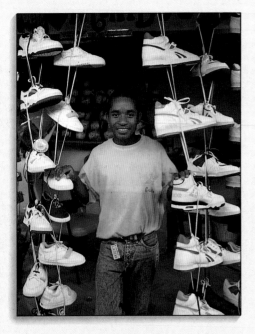

But as the program progressed, signs of economic recovery began to show. Public finances were put in order, and the deficit was reduced. A tremendous (53 percent) growth in non-oil exports took place in 1989, as the government sought to wean the country away from its oil habit.

Then, in 1990, Venezuela got an unexpected boost from the Persian Gulf crisis, when an extra US$4 billion in oil income came in as a result of the increased demand from customers needing to make up for production lost by Iraq and Kuwait.

Instead of easing up, the government kept up the push towards a free-market economy.

Dissatisfaction grew to such a point that in February 1992 there was even an attempted coup led by a small segment of the armed forces. The vast majority of the military proved loyal to the government, however, and the plotters quickly surrendered after some isolated fighting at rebel bases. Venezuelan political, union and Church leaders unanimously joined to condemn the coup attempt, the first the country had seen in 30 years.

Urban crisis: There are signs that Venezuela's economy may be reviving with inflation under control – although at the price of increased urban poverty and expanding slums. A rise in street crime in the capital has completely changed the way *Caraqueños* live. With the government powerless or unwilling to deliver adequate police protection, the country has been turned into a nation of homebodies and the sheen has come off Caracas's vibrant nightlife. Except for the Sabana Grande pedestrian mall, which itself has grown seedy in recent years, walking alone on the streets of the capital at night is considered a reckless adventure.

Crime has also turned Venezuela's moneyed class into a prisoner of its own privilege. The typical middle to upper class *Caraqueño* resides in a *quinta* (private house) surrounded by high walls, or in an apartment building where the windows and doors are covered by metal grates.

Offices are similarly equipped. As a result, wealthy *Caraqueños* spend their work day going from one locked environment to another, usually in an automobile equipped with a crook lock, pedal lock, gas cutoff and the obligatory car siren which is heard night and day in the city, and is as much a part of the scene in Caracas as it is in any mainland US destination.

Despite the country's ongoing problems, Venezuelans have good reason to be optimistic. After 33 years, their democratic institutions have proved their durability. While the oil boom may be long gone, Venezuela holds a wealth of other natural resources – gold, diamonds, coal, bauxite, hydroelectric power – waiting to be exploited. A more rational use of the country's great resources could provide the key to a more enduring, less volatile prosperity.

Left, LA Gear in Caracas.

THE POLITICS OF PATRONAGE

One of Venezuela's greatest achievements has been to maintain a functioning democracy for more than three decades. It has survived a serious leftist guerrilla threat in the 1960s and the nationwide popular uprising of February 1989. Venezuelans are rightfully proud of their democracy and see a direct link to the country's founding father, Simón Bolívar.

But democracy has also made Venezuela a highly politicized society in which the two principal parties (Acción Democrática and the Social Christian COPEI) have an influence on peoples' lives which goes far beyond the experience of most other countries.

A Venezuelan's party loyalty affects everything from the awarding of government contracts, promotions in business, entry into a private club or professorships at the university. A card identifying a citizen as a member of the ruling party can even help him or her to negotiate a traffic violation or jump to the front of the line at a government office.

Party membership is widespread – Acción Democrática claims to have two million members nationwide – but that still leaves a lot of Venezuelans out in the cold.

The asphyxiating influence of the parties is due partly to the tremendous power of the central government in doling out patronage. Until recently, the president appointed all state governors and was empowered to dictate economic policy by decree, without consulting Congress. Meanwhile, congressional figures can act as patrons themselves.

And, since the electoral system still requires the voter to select all the congressional candidates on one party's slate, without being able to pick and choose each one, everyone down to the most minor official ends up being an apparatchik from the ruling party – with little or no sense of responsibility to the voters.

The National Ports Institute (INP), recently privatized, was a perfect example of patronage and the influence of parties on public sector employment. In 1979, at the end of the first administration of President Carlos Andrés Pérez, the INP had 3,000 workers, almost all of them from the governing Acción Democrática party.

Right, even basic public services are dictated by patronage.

After COPEI presidential candidate Luis Herrera Campins took office, the INP's workforce was doubled with the addition of 3,000 workers, all of them *Copeyanos*.

This procedure continued during the next two presidential terms. By the time the government finally got around to privatizing the ports, the INP had 14,000 workers, of whom it admitted 60 percent were unnecessary. The INP was dissolved in mid-1991 and its workers dismissed.

Venezuelans have begun to rebel against this system and the injustices it provokes. The first direct elections for state governors and municipal offices were held in December 1989; a year and a half later, President Pérez relinquished absolute presidential power over economic policy. An

electoral reform movement is now seeking to abolish the system of party slates and replace it with a one person, one vote rule.

Another encouraging feature has been the emergence of neighborhood civic associations (*asociaciones de vecinos*) which try to do for their communities what corrupt and inefficient government entities do not: fix potholes, guard against crime, and prevent new construction in areas where it is not legal.

The neighborhood associations are taken seriously by the government and are seen as a way to circumvent local politics – getting basic services performed no matter what party card the neighborhood might be carrying. ∎

PATILLA
3 Kilos x 30

To the casual visitor, Venezuelans seem to import culture wholesale from the United States. There is little evidence of Venezuelan history in the public buildings of its cities; no sign of the ancient indigenous cultures so prominent elsewhere in Latin America. Instead, Venezuelan radios blare a steady diet of Madonna and New Kids on the Block. Young people sport designer jeans and T-shirts with slogans in English, while drivers race at breakneck speeds down the urban highways in their late-model Fords and Chevrolets. The impression is of a place that is trying desperately to be like South Florida but has so far only managed to approximate the climate.

This attraction to the United States is even reflected in sport, as Venezuela is the only country on the South American continent where baseball is more popular than soccer. Interest in US professional baseball leagues – where a dozen or more Venezuelan players have made their mark – is so great that there are live nightly TV transmissions of the games, with simultaneous translation.

All this may lead one to ask – where is the real Venezuela? The answer is, this is it: an overwhelmingly young, urbanized society, with a large but shrinking middle class, whose eyes are constantly fixed northward (although not much further north than Miami); a country in permanent, frantic motion, eating fast food and drinking its coffee from disposable plastic cups; a country that has lived through a debauch of fabulous wealth which it can't quite believe is over, despite the cold shower of austerity doled out in recent years.

City folks, country ways: Yet this breakneck Americanization of Venezuelan society is a relatively recent occurrence. Indeed, few of the world's countries have changed so much in such a short time as Venezuela, thanks to the discovery of oil. From a poor, isolated, agricultural nation that was the fiefdom of successive dictators, it was transformed within the space of a few decades into the

consumerist, high-tech society that visitors see now, one with a democratic government and all the trappings – if not always the benefits – of development.

It has all happened so quickly that Venezuelan society is still trying to keep up with the changes – leading to an often bewildering mix of traditional and modern traits.

Venezuela today is the most urbanized country in Latin America, with 83 percent of its 19.7 million people living in a handful of big cities. Yet Venezuelans persist with a

surprisingly rural lifestyle. They rise early, often before dawn, and are usually required to be at their jobs by 8am. Workers take two hours off at midday, during which time they are likely to return home for lunch. This routine may be logical for rural workers avoiding the noonday sun, but in a city the size of Caracas or Maracaibo it creates four traffic jams a day instead of two.

And while Venezuelans are surrounded by skyscrapers and high technology, they often display a surprising lack of sophistication. Even the telephone, which has been in use in Venezuela for decades, is an instrument to which many people seem unaccustomed.

Preceding pages: folk musicians in the Andes; *cafecito* break; watermelon for sale. **Left,** a pretty young *Caraqueña*. **Right,** a businessman wearing the *liqui-liqui*, traditional Venezuelan dress.

Telephone callers are regarded with suspicion unless they are known personally. Seeking even the most innocuous information by telephone is often a frustrating enterprise, which ends when the caller is bluntly told, "You'll have to come here personally, we can't give out that information over the telephone."

Keeping up with the changes: Obviously, Venezuela hasn't quite shaken off its long history as a poor farming country largely isolated from the outside world. Only a few generations ago, it was a nation with a small population, few roads and little overall national coherence. As late as 1945, the day trip to the German immigrant colony of Colonia

evident than in the capital city, Caracas. In 1945, Caracas had a quarter of a million inhabitants and only a few buildings higher than two stories tall. Three decades later, the population had increased sevenfold, and the "city of red tile roofs" had all but disappeared. The city's shape reflected the new Venezuelan society: a high-tech heart of glass skyscrapers for the petroleum elite to work in; gardened suburbs for the *nouveau-riche* middle class; and a ring of slums – the so-called "cordon of misery" – for the growing number of Venezuelans unable to get a slice of the country's wealth.

Adolescent nation: Meanwhile, a population boom in the 1970s has led to Venezuela

Tovar, only 38 km (23 miles) from Caracas, had to be made on muleback.

This meant that Venezuela developed as a fragmented rural country with strong regional identities. Everything was upset when oil wealth hit in the 1920s. Agriculture was no longer very important, and there was massive migration from the country to the cities. During the period from 1936 to 1971, the rural-to-urban population ratio turned around completely; while a quarter of Venezuela's people lived in cities during the 1930s, by the 1970s that proportion had changed to three-quarters.

The velocity of change was nowhere more

becoming overwhelmingly young. Today, some 67 percent of the Venezuelans are under 30 years old and 39 percent under 14 years of age. Only 6 percent are over the age of 60. Perhaps as a result, Venezuelan culture is decidedly youth-oriented, as reflected in advertising and in the national passions for sport, beauty contests and other youthful – the country's critics might say "superficial" – pursuits.

At the same time, Venezuela has become a much more cosmopolitan nation. The vast majority of Venezuelans are still *mestizos* – people whose descent mingles the blood of Spanish settlers with the indigenous Indians or African slaves. But after World War II, a wave of immigrants from Europe and Latin America arrived, encouraged by Venezuela's last military dictatorships to come in search of opportunities. From 1948 to 1959, an estimated 412,500 immigrants entered Venezuela, a huge number for a country that had less than five million inhabitants when the 1950s began.

The large number of first-generation Venezuelans today has given rise to ethnic stereotypes: the Spanish taxicab driver, usually a Galician (*Gallego*); the Portuguese grocery store or bakery owner; and the Italian car mechanic.

Besides the Europeans, there are also re-

Today the racial mix is 65 percent *mestizo*, 20 percent white, 8 percent black and 7 percent Indian.

Yankees stay here!: As for North Americans, their numbers are few (European immigrants actually outnumber them by 50 to one) but their influence great. A small group of North American families have put down roots in Venezuela and founded successful businesses or industrial conglomerates which have made them part of the country's moneyed elite. One case in point is the Phelps family, who own the daily newspaper *El Diario de Caracas*, Radio Caracas television station and Aerotuy airlines.

The Americans who have come to Ven-

cent immigrants from nearby Latin American countries – particularly from Colombia, Ecuador and Peru They came during the oil boom of the 1970s and the early 1980s to work as laborers and domestics. Blacks from Trinidad, Guyana and other Caribbean countries also arrived during that time. Many of the poorer immigrants have returned to their respective countries since the crisis hit, but a large number have stayed to raise families and take on Venezuelan citizenship.

Left, farmer in the Andean region of Mérida; Goajira Indian woman in Maracaibo. **Above**, a big grin in Margarita island; Caracas vice.

ezuela have, on the whole, been technocrats – oil industry engineers or executives with the multinationals. All have come to further their own interests but have nonetheless made contributions in terms of technology, science and culture. (For instance, the late patriarch of the Phelps family, Mr William Phelps, was an ornithologist who wrote the definitive guide to Venezuelan birds. His widow, Kathy Deery Phelps, is an author, philanthropist and ardent environmentalist.)

Perhaps as a result, there is little in the way of resentment towards North Americans or foreigners in general. The word *musiu*, a corruption of the French *monsieur*, which refers to a light-skinned foreigner, is not an insult. Similarly, Venezuela is racially very tolerant, with marriage between *mestizos*, blacks and whites commonplace.

The only exception to this open-mindedness is the attitude towards the Colombians, Venezuela's poorer neighbors to the west, who have entered the country in large numbers, often illegally, since the oil boom days. In Venezuela, Colombians typically work as domestic helps, factory workers, or car body repairmen, often filling positions that most Venezuelans would instantly turn down. They are viewed with suspicion by poor Venezuelans, who regard them as both astute and untrustworthy.

Defining "Venezuelan": So, after all this, what are Venezuelans like? The contemporary *criollo* might still be anyone from a barefoot cowboy in the Llanos or a shopowner in Caracas recently immigrated from Portugal; a high-powered oil industry executive in Maracaibo or a Yanomami Indian in the Amazon basin whose lifestyle has not changed much from that of his forebears, thousands of years ago.

In general, Venezuelan society is unusually open, friendly and informal. Spanish speakers are sometimes surprised to note how quickly – often immediately – Venezuelans discard the polite *Usted* form of address and use the more familiar *tú*. To some, this is an excess of familiarity, bordering on disrespect. But in Venezuela, it is merely an indication that your interlocutor considers himself an equal.

Depending on your mood, Venezuelans may seem exceedingly polite and unfailingly generous or hopelessly frivolous and maddeningly inconsistent. Friendships are struck up quickly but rarely last; people seem unwilling to take any relationship beyond the superficial level. On the other hand, someone with whom you have only a fleeting acquaintance will often greet you effusively, as if you were a long-lost friend.

Ironically, while Venezuela is on the surface a very open society, it is also remains impenetrable to foreigners beyond a certain level. Although they display little overt xenophobia, Venezuelans also show little interest in meeting or forming friendships with people from abroad. This attitude persists even among the young Venezuelans who have been educated overseas. The only foreigners who get an inside view of Venezuelan society are those who marry into local families.

Superficial lifestyles: Unlike their southern neighbors the Argentines, who tend to psychoanalyze every conceivable issue, Venezuelans are little given to self-examination – a fact that may explain the surprising lack of literature about the country itself. Conversations often remain on the anecdotal level and people seem more comfortable with humor than serious topics.

Some Latin Americans regard Venezuela as a *nouveau-riche* society where the prevailing norm is money without good taste. Others admire it for having maintained a democratic government during a period when almost the entire South American continent was ruled by dictators. (The conventional wisdom is that Venezuela's military has no need to stage a coup d'état because the government has already bought them everything they've asked for and more.)

Perhaps the dominant aspect of the Venezuelan mindset is its transitory view of life. Marriage, business, career, family, are all regarded as short-term concerns which could be here today, gone tomorrow. Venezuelans who invest in a business, for example, usually do so with the intention of making a quick profit within a short time and then selling out – something akin to buying a lottery ticket.

Women's role: Although Venezuela shares the cult of machismo with other Latin American countries, Venezuelan women have managed to achieve a place in society that would be the envy of their sisters in many developed nations. The first woman was named a cabinet minister in 1968 and the first female presidential candidate, Ismenia Villalba of the Unión Republicana Democrática, stood for election in 1988 (the same year Geraldine Ferraro was the Democratic party's vice-presidential candidate in the United States).

Women business executives, medical

apparent success sits alongside such traits as a national obsession with traditional beauty contests and cosmetics (*see The Business of Beauty, pages 85–89*). Venezuela's professional women maintain a high sense of glamor, playing up their femininity much more than their North American or European counterparts.

At least part of the progress of Venezuelan women has been due to necessity. In Venezuelan society, infidelity is widepread and men often support, not only lovers, but entire second families. Many women have learned not to count on their husbands as a steady source of income.

Another factor is divorce, which was le-

doctors, judges, engineers and architects abound; in some professions, such as law, women actually outnumber men in the current graduating classes. The push for sexual equality has been accomplished without the help of any nationwide women's organization or any cohesive feminist movement. Some writers believe their success in a male-dominated society has been due to their non-confrontational – and therefore non-threatening – approach.

Foreign feminists find it bizarre that this

galized in Venezuela in 1909 and since then has become a fixture of family life – often seeming to be the rule rather than the exception. Most people approaching their forties are on their second marriage; men often refer to "my first marriage" as if that were a normal phase in life. When you ask a Venezuelan couple how many children they have, the response is usually to list the ones they have had together and then the ones from their previous marriages.

All this has given rise to a disjointed family structure in which half-brothers, step-parents and in-laws co-exist – at times even under the same roof – in a manner that is

Left, Piaroa elders in Amazonas. **Above,** *Llaneros* (cowboys) strut their stuff in the Llanos.

often baffling to outsiders. Even so, family life is considered sacrosanct and Venezuelans view the home as a refuge not open to outsiders. Unlike other Latin Americans, they do not often invite friends to their homes, which are generally reserved for the immediate family and in-laws.

Problem case for the Pope: Venezuelans are not on the whole a religious people, with the exception of the western Andean region, where the the Catholic faith has very strong roots. In general, the Church is regarded as a traditional but somewhat irrelevant institution, its role largely ceremonial. Church attendance is so low that, prior to the visit of Pope John Paul II to Venezuela in 1985, the

Remnants of traditional culture: The US cultural invasion of recent years doesn't mean that the centuries-old Venezuelan culture has been completely wiped out. You just have to look a little harder for it.

Music is a good place to start. Venezuela is an eminently musical country, in which singing comes as natural as breathing, and everyone seems to be able to carry a tune. On trips to the beach or at parties, someone will inevitably produce a *cuatro* (the traditional four-stringed intrument, similar to a ukelele) and the singing will begin. Aided by a few good rums, even the shyest Venezuelan will begin to improvise lyrics in the *contrapunto* style which has its origins in the Llanos.

Venezuelan Catholic Bishop's conference began a public relations campaign whose slogan was: "The Pope wants to be your friend." Statistics released by the bishops' conference said that while 80 percent of Venezuelans were baptized, only 20 percent attend church regularly.

Nonetheless, there is a certain amount of devotion to some unusual Catholic icons – like Don José Gregorio Hernandez, a turn-of-the-century physician whose life ended tragically when he was hit by a trolleycar. The bizarre cult of María Lionza, meanwhile, combines elements of Catholicism and witchcraft (*see Fiestas, pages 93–97*).

Among the best traditional artists are the singing group Un Solo Pueblo (One Single People), who have become something of an institution over the past two decades and have even incorporated their children into the group. More than "folk singers," they are serious students of the different trends in Venezuelan traditional music and go to some length to explain it at concerts, detailing the names of the villages where the songs were collected and their particular significance.

Un Solo Pueblo present the wide variety of Venezuela's traditional music: the plaintive country music of the Llanos, with its nasal vocals and whimsical lyrics; the complex rhythms and exuberant dances of the *tambores* or drums of the Afro-Venezuelans in Barlovento and along the rest of the Caribbean coast; the gentle, nostalgic waltzes of the Andes; and the English-lyric calypsos of Guayana, the legacy of the Caribbean blacks who worked in Venezuela's gold rush during the 19th century.

Venezuelans also excel in classical music. One of the country's most accomplished instrumentalists is guitarist Alirio Diaz, who has also served as Venezuela's ambassador to Italy. Caracas alone has four symphony orchestras and many cities in the interior also have municipal orchestras of their own.

In the graphic arts, Venezuela has produced a few outstanding contemporary painters and sculptors. Jesús Soto, of Ciudad Bolívar, is responsible for much of the modern monumental art that graces the new buildings in Caracas, including the entrance to the Teresa Carreno Theatre and the Chacaito Metro Station. Other noted painters include Jacobo Borges and Hector Poleo, both of whose works can both be viewed in the Museum of Contemporary Art.

Venezuela's greatest living man of letters is Arturo Uslar Pietri, a towering figure who has been both a chronicler of contemporary Venezuelan events and a participant in them. The winner of many international literary awards, Uslar has been a novelist, historian, cabinet minister and television commentator, among other things. Now in his 80s, Uslar is remembered for urging Venezuelan governments, back in the 1930s, to "sow the petroleum" – to invest the tremendous income from the country's principal export in productive enterprises. Uslar is held in great esteem for his literary production, which includes the recent *The Visit in Time* (*La Visita en El Tiempo*) which won Spain's Prince of Asturias literary prize in 1991.

Looking to the future: The idea of Venezuela as a country bursting with natural wealth but lacking in human resources is popular, particularly in other Latin American nations. Luckily, the reality is slowly changing, as a generation of Venezuelans educated abroad take the helm of government, the private sector and the professions. They have re-

turned with professional skills and a new style of management which is helping Venezuelan business and industry to modernize.

Many were beneficiaries of a government scholarship program called the Gran Mariscal de Ayacucho which, during the 1970s and early 1980s, sent some 40,000 Venezuelans abroad to study. Others who did not benefit from such scholarships also had the opportunity to travel and study abroad during the "boom years."

Yet while many Venezuelans have lived or studied abroad, very few have emigrated; and, unlike other Latin Americans, very few express the desire to do so. Shortly after the February 1989 riots, there was a move among

first generation Venezuelans – sons and daughters of Spaniards, Portuguese and Italians – to obtain the passports of their parents' fatherlands. However, only a small number actually went through with it.

On the other hand, many foreigners who come for a short stay end up spending years, or even a lifetime in Venezuela.

Despite their frustrations with corrupt politicians and inefficient public services, Venezuelans as a whole love their country and recognize its tremendous potential. While their gaze may be distracted by the latest North American cultural totems, their feet remain firmly fixed at home.

<u>Left</u>, dominoes on Sinamaica Lagoon, near Maracaibo. <u>Right</u>, rooster and shades on the Caribbean coast.

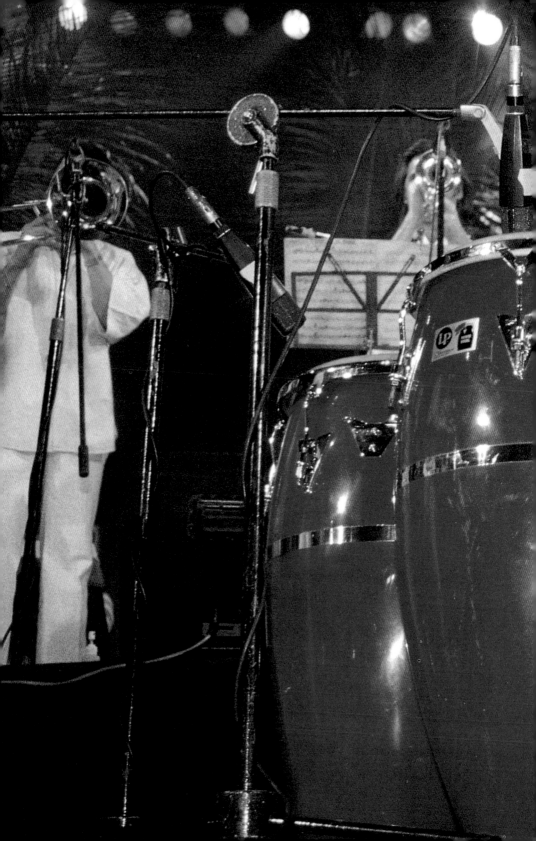

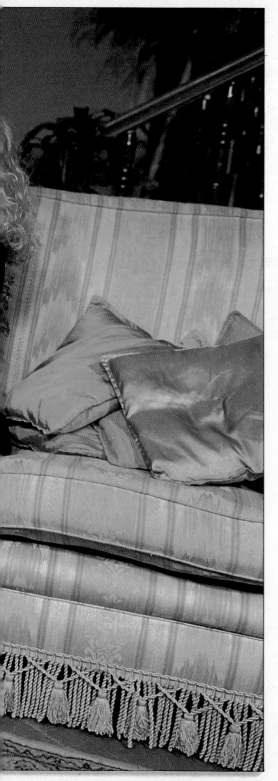

POP CULTURE PARADISE

Put together a disproportionately young audience, plenty of disposable income, a music hotline to Miami and what do you have? Venezuela, the continent's pop culture paradise, a country where it's show time all the time.

As a result, Venezuela has produced a remarkable number of well-known pop singers, and its television soap operas *(telenovelas)* are breaking records in Europe and the United States. Actress María Conchita Alonso appeared in a number of US movies, including *Moscow on the Hudson*, but she got her start as a beauty singer in Venezuela. The Caribbean's unchallenged "Devil of Salsa" is Venezuelan Oscar d'León, who has been shaking it up on stage for several decades. South America's single most successful *telenovela* so far has been *Cristal*, a Venezuelan production that interrupted work and social schedules in half a dozen neighboring countries before taking Spain and Italy by storm. *Farándula*, as pop entertainment is called here, is serious business.

Geographically, Venezuela has everything needed to be a *farándula* heaven. Its proximity to Caribbean islands and countries long known as music spots – including Cuba, the Dominican Republic, Puerto Rico and Panama – has transformed it into the gathering place for performers from the whole region. Not only can they find larger audiences in Caracas, but it costs far less for a Dominican singer to travel to Venezuela in search of fame and fortune than it does to head straight for Miami, the world's undeclared capital of Spanish-language pop music. The wild salsa, merengue, rumba, mambo and calypso beats that find their way into Venezuela's infectious melodies and rhythms are pure Caribbean; much of this hip-shaking music betrays African roots – intrinsic in Venezuelan music.

Afro-Caribbean roots: Pop singer Yordano and the band Adrenalina Caribe claim they were influenced by Cuban *Nueva Trova* performers like Silvio Rodríguez and Pablo Milanés, whose dark jazzy ballads with po-

Preceding pages: belting out the rhythms in a Caracas night spot. **Left**, hamming it up in a *telenovela* (soap opera).

litical themes talk of social inequality, the Latin American identity and regional integration. Even Venezuelan composer/singer Ilan Chester, whose style was most affected by years of music study in England, broke from the European mold by incorporating Afro-Caribbean drum rhythms into his most popular songs.

But Venezuela's success may have less to do with its location on the globe than with its economic power. When it comes to television, at least 83 percent of all Venezuelans own a set, and those who don't generally live in the jungle or outback areas where transmissions won't reach. Even the most modest shantytown developments have television anten-

music, movie and TV stars. Keeping abreast of entertainment developments is not a pastime, it is an addiction.

Key to *farándula*'s success is the country's huge captive audience: 70 percent of the population is under 18 years old and they are chomping at the bit to run out to concerts, buy new tapes or head to the cinema. This audience has money to spend, unlike its counterparts in other Caribbean, Central and South American nations, and industrialists are willing to invest big bolívars to keep the music and film industries competitive.

The interest in *farándula* as a money-making industry began in the 1980s when the bolívar was strong and Caracas was the

nas popping up from their roofs; upscale neighborhoods are easily identified by their plethora of satellite dishes. Some 98 percent of families in Caracas have access to at least one TV set, making that city a wonderland for television advertisers and a dream come true for performers in need of exposure.

Publications are also able to cash in on the craze. Any newsstand in Caracas has a variety of magazines dedicated to pop entertainment. The most popular – and controversial – newspaper column in Caracas is "Chepa Candela," an unsigned gossip strip revealing the alleged loves, sexual preferences, idiosyncracies and marital woes of Venezuelan

world's second most expensive city (after Nairobi). Entrepreneurs and marketing specialists watching Venezuelans fly to Miami for weekend shopping trips recognized an untapped gold mine.

But those who claim Venezuela leads the continent in pop culture shortchange this country, for the sphere of influence extends far beyond South America. When the soap opera *Cristal* aired in Spain, it was one of the most popular TV series ever shown there; another 7 million Spaniards saw Venezuela's second most successful *telenovela, La Dama de Rosa*. Both soap operas broke ratings records in Italy.

Several Venezuelan singers, including José Luis Rodríguez, sell records in the United States where they tape in both English and Spanish and are wildly popular, especially with North America's burgeoning Hispanic population. Although their movie industry is fledgling, Venezuelan directors already boast a number of feature films that have garnered critical acclaim outside the country.

Farándula financial empire: If a performer makes it in Venezuela, his or her success is almost guaranteed and a ticket to Miami isn't far off. Music purists and television critics will argue that Venezuelans are not necessarily more talented than their counterparts in nearby nations but they receive an invalu-

teed hits – are performed by Sonorodven musicians. (The *telenovela* arrangement is so extreme that only local artists' songs can be used as the themes for Venezuelan television programs; the government backs the practice on grounds it boosts local performers.) Rudy Escala's recording of *Cristal's* theme song was hummed in households on three continents. Jorge Rigó's *telenovela* songs have overshadowed his other music to such an extent that he has become irreversibly identified as a soap singer.

Overwhelming media exposure does not necessarily mean only good exposure, particularly in the newspapers. The entertainers frequently protest when newspaper gossip

able amount of promotion thanks to bountiful coffers in Caracas and the local record label's cooperative agreement with CBS records in the United States. Part of this promotion stems from the incestuous relationship which the recording monopoly, Sonorodven, has with new music video firm Video Rodven and TV station Venevision. The trio are owned by the Cisneros Group (which also owns the TropiBurger fast food chain and Pepsi Cola in Venezuela).

Sonorodven artists are advertised extensively on TV and *telenovela* songs – guaran-

obsessed with their private lives begins describing them as "nymphomaniacs", as having "presumed homosexual tendencies" or as "notorious drunks." Still, some entertainers believe bad publicity is better than none. And with a recording and television conglomerate that operates as a dynasty, it's no wonder that foreigners like Peruvian singer Melissa and Peruvian actor Roberto Moll have made Venezuela their home, that Argentine José Alberto Mugravi works from here and that Chilean singer Rigó immigrated to this pop culture capital years ago.

When it comes to music, as with TV, Venezuelans pride themselves on being on

Left, glued to the box. **Above,** high drama.

top of it all, and that means not only the latest songs and dances but the gory details of every performer's life and the ins-and-outs at Sonorodven. It is rare that a musician makes it big unless signed to the Sonorodven label. Conversely, artists may sign with the label then be pushed into the wings, blocked from performing or recording by iron-clad contracts like those offered to movie stars during the Golden Age of Hollywood in the 1930s and 1940s. Some performers not given the promotion they want, like Ilan Chester, are able to wait out the contract time and sign with a US recording label. Others disappear into obscurity.

Singing and soaps: In the crazy world of

world of *farándula*: winning a beauty contest. Annually, Miss Venezuela is virtually guaranteed an acting and/or singing career if she shows even the remotest amount of talent (*see The Business of Beauty, pages 85–89*). And those who don't make it into feature films often have the satisfaction of making it into the advertisements that precede the movie. Every film screened in Caracas follows a Belmont cigarette ad. Advertising like this, common now in many countries, would have little importance except that the Belmont specials are a national institution – usually better known than the movies themselves. It is an enviable thrill to be chosen as one of Belmont's bronzed, bathing-suit clad

Venezuelan pop culture, music and acting are interchangeable. Although actors can make it without singing, singers are obliged to take a role or two in local soap operas; *telenovela* work is detailed in recording contracts. Sometimes the TV fame supersedes the music and aspiring singers like Carlos Matta and Guillermo Dávila become better known as leading men than musicians. "El Puma," Jose Luis Rodríguez, began his now stellar singing career as a soap opera leading man; it was his role in the historical soap opera *Estefanía* – not his tropical music – that pushed him to fame.

Women have an additional path into the

men and women destined to scamper across the screen to promote the cigarettes.

Success despite obstacles: Venezuela's successful foray into region-wide *farándula* comes despite formidable obstacles. For one, Venezuelans speak with a Caribbean accent that is difficult for more southern countries to understand. Colorful Caracas expressions like *Epa Chamo* (Hey, guy) and *cónchale vale* (an exclamation) puzzle viewers in Chile and Peru. And the provocative clothing so characteristic of Venezuelan TV is eyebrow-raising in other parts of the continent.

Despite this, *telenovelas* from Caracas shoot to the top of the ratings in Peru, Argentina, Ecuador, Italy, Spain and among the Spanish-speaking audience in the United States. They are more polished than their Mexican counterparts, more scandalous than the Argentine soaps and they are notorious for their astoundingly dramatic endings. In the finale of *Rosa Salvaje*, a train smashed into the villainess's car, a gunfight and arson eliminated the rest of the bad guys and the good characters came together for a wedding. Each episode of a Venezuelan soap is jam-packed with scandal and seduction and sets trends for hairstyles and fashion.

Details in the *telenovelas* may be ridiculous and illogical, but that doesn't matter. In the wildly successful Venezuelan-Argentina

soap opera *Amándote*, half the cast spoke with Venezuelan accents and the other half had clearly identifiable Argentine accents. Families were a mishmash of both – an inconsistency that no one seemed to mind. Often, the soap stars' ticket to success owes more to fate than art. Hopelessly myopic Lupita Ferrer, the grande dame of Venezuelan *telenovelas*, refuses to wear eyeglasses, claiming that her vision problems give her the lost, melancholy look for which she is

Left, TV celebrities mingle with high society at fashionable Caracas restaurants. **Above**, "The Puma" with friend.

famous. Chubby-cheeked Jeanette Rodríguez, Venezuela's highest-paid soap actress thanks to her mythical success as the blonde protagonist in *Cristal*, is generally credited with being photogenic rather than talented. Gigi Zancheta earns more newspaper inches for her fights than for her dramatic roles.

But the spotlights aren't just on the TV personalities. Film stars like attention, too, and rather than hiding behind dark glasses, moaning over the loss of their privacy, they make themselves as visible as possible. Miguel Angel Landa, one of Venezuela's top movie stars, *telenovela* leading man and the host of a television talk show, rides around Caracas in a car plastered with his name and the name of his program. As with the *telenovelas* and music recordings, film artists know that success lies in their ability to promote themselves.

In another sense, Venezuela's fledgling movie industry is a lot like its soap operas – high on drama, light on critical acclaim – but not all is fluff. The nation has produced a number of award-winning feature length films, including *Oriana*, which was lauded at the Cannes Film Festival some years ago.

Art imitates life: Occasionally, Venezuelans use film to turn a critical eye on their own obsession with flash and cash. In *Adios, Miami*, an unfaithful Venezuelan executive played by Gustavo Rodríguez was found out by his wife, who cut off his cash while he vacationed in Miami with his voluptuous girlfriend. In tandem, the government named him in a corporate fraud scandal. Desperate, he tossed himself into the ocean, washed up on Miami Beach and tried to pass himself off as a Cuban refugee.

The more serious *Cangrejo* movies reenacted notorious but unsolved true-life crimes. Based on ex-policeman Fermín Mármol León's investigative *Cuatro Crimenes, Cuatro Poderes* (Four Crimes, Four Powers), this dramatically acclaimed series of films looked at a priest accused of sexual assault, a bomb expert/politician whose wife was killed by an exploding statue, a military man who killed his wife's lover (claiming he was a thief) and a group of rich youths who kidnapped and inadvertently killed a child. In one of his best roles, actor Miguel Angel Lando played the real life Mármol León – a police chief who left the force in disgust with his corrupt bosses.

Venezuela's top two exports? Anyone will tell you – oil and beauty queens.

Let's face it: in Venezuela, looks count. Dressing for success means the tighter the better. You see a woman slinking down the street in a skin-tight mini and spike heels, and you can be sure she's on her way to work – as a bank teller or perhaps a legal secretary. It's cause for concern if a man *doesn't* hiss like an overheated radiator and hoot *Epa, mamita!* (Hey, little mama!) or some other "compliment" as the woman passes. There's so much rubber-necking going on, it's amazing the poor guys don't get whiplash.

That's why enterprising Venezuelans have made a business out of beauty. A Caracas "Miss" Academy (the English word is preferred to Señorita) has groomed three Miss Universes, four Miss Worlds and lots of runners-up. It's a fact that *Venezolanos* are among the highest per capita consumers of cosmetics and personal-care products. And fashion is a matter of national pride – not simply because world famous *haute couture* designer Carolina Herrera was born here.

In this society, beauty opens doors. Every aspiring model knows that entering the Miss Venezuela pageant – which chooses a winner from the "Misses" of the various provinces – can do more to boost her career than a facelift. A 1991 contestant, Moravia Cárdenas, makes no bones about the fact that she did it because she dreams of launching her own clothing line. She termed the Miss Venezuela contest a promotional "bargain."

María Conchita Alonso can vouch for that. The pop singer and actress – now with several Hollywood films to her credit – started her career as a Miss. So did more than one *telenovela* (soap opera) star. Tatiana Capote got even more exposure than she may have bargained for when her strap broke as she paraded down the runway. Fans of the actress say it gave her a chance to show off one of the silicone-inflated breasts of which she often boasted. Of course, malicious tongues claim the slip was no accident.

Preceding pages: moment of truth at the Miss Venezuela pageant. **Left**, standing up to scrutiny: looks count in Venezuelan society.

A feminist's nightmare: In many countries, beauty contests are being downplayed as women's rights advance. Not Venezuela. The Miss pageant has weathered feminism with barely a scratch. In fact, political correctness is the least concern of organizer Osmel Souza, who for years has been packaging beauties like some people turn out products on an assembly line.

Souza's efforts have yielded Miss Universes Maritza Sayalero, Irene Sáez and Bárbara Palacios, and Miss Worlds Susana Duijm, Pilín León, Astrid Carolina Herrera and, in 1991, Ninibeth Leal Jiménez. Not bad for a country of only 20 million people.

As a gesture towards feminism, most pageants elsewhere in the world are de-emphasizing the swimsuit contest and stressing the personality and intellect of the contestants. But this trend hasn't exactly caught on in Venezuela, where physicality and showmanship are cherished. One contestant, Pilín León, even rode an elephant on stage.

In Venezuelan beauty contests, as well as on the street, comfort takes a back seat to style. Women favor spike heels, along with skin-tight skirts and trousers (actress Catherine Fullop is the undisputed "queen of the tight blue jeans"). Ever popular are eye-catching fashion details like cut-outs, feathers, bows, studs, rhinestones and appliques. Jewelry is a must – particularly *fantasía* like gigantic hoops, extra-long dangles and gems in a rainbow of hues. If it glitters, it goes.

Each Miss Venezuela gown is a stunner, for designers also have a chance to make a name for themselves in connection with the pageant. Usually if they're designing for a Miss, however, they already have a name or even their own house. Some of the country's top *couturiers* whip up creations for the pageant, which has the air of a style show.

Surgery for success: As the song goes, you're never fully dressed without a smile. Teeth a little crooked? Nose not exactly like a button? Osmel Souza himself reportedly complained that 1991 was the year of flabby derrières and flat chests, resulting in higher "operational costs." It's no secret that cosmetic orthodontia and plastic surgery are all part of the beauty game. One Venezuelan magazine noted that "before smelling the sweet aroma of success, the majority of the participants have breathed the ether of anaesthesia."

As for makeup, the average Venezuelan woman worships eyeliner, and the Misses are no exception. Cosmetics industry sources say that lipsticks with shades that are "deep," "brilliant" or "bright" sell best. One of the rumors swirling in the rarified air of a recent pageant had Ninibeth Leal, then Miss Zulia, shelling out 60,000 bolívares (about $12,000) for the services of a top makeup artist. The styling must have worked, since she went on to become Miss World in 1991.

When it comes to hair, the simple rule is: lowing morning. To meet the press, the queen traditionally goes to a fabulous mansion. Miss Venezuela 1986, Bárbara Palacios, broke from convention and set tongues flapping by staging her interview at her own family's modest apartment on Avenida Baralt in El Silencio, an old – but most definitely not stylish – neighborhood. Since winning the pageant automatically launches a woman into high society, Palacios' move was seen as a shocking breach of class distinctions.

Production line of beauty: How do women become Miss Venezuela contestants? It's not something they simply sign up for. Far from it. First they must be discovered – as was 1991 Miss Carabobo, Beatriz Lesser.

think big. As for color, despite the fact that most Venezuelans are natural brunettes, a disproportionate amount of Misses sport golden locks. Apparently many women buy the advertising gimmick that blondes have more fun. It is not unheard-of for a peroxide blonde to dye her children's hair as well. Body hair is definitely out. It is even fairly common for women to bleach the hair on their arms or wax it off.

In Venezuela, the Misses are taken very seriously indeed. The pageant is stretched out over three programs: the contest itself, a recap of highlights transmitted some hours afterwards and a press conference the fol-

She happened to be queueing at a bus stop. Chances improve dramatically if a woman's in modeling school or comes from socially or politically prominent stock.

Then she must survive Osmel Souza's Miss Academy. Souza's goal is turning out not just another pretty face, but a woman with that certain something that guarantees her a winner. He plays the roles of talent scout, agent, trainer, stylist, image-maker, fundraiser, producer and, when occasion warrants, whip-cracker. And he knows the best beauty secrets. Need to shrink your waistline? Slather it in baby oil and cinch it in elastic bandages from the minute you wake until you go to bed, Souza advises his *chicas*. And don't even *think* of taking the elevator, he warns them. Climbing stairs firms your muscles and lifts your *pompi* (behind).

If it sounds like a lark making a career out of advising gorgeous women how to keep their buttocks firm, to be fair, Souza has his share of headaches. In 1991, faced with a budget cutback, the state-run television station Venevisión, sponsor of the Miss Venezuela contest, hiked its advertising rates. The Miss Venezuela shows already commanded top advertising dollars – twice that charged for programs featuring famous celebrities. Sponsers baulked.

the Caracas headquarters – a studio in El Rosal covered with mirrors where the Misses can strut in leotards and heels.

Scandal in the Academy: With the cramped budget, the contest – for years an Easter tradition – had to be postponed until May. But that was too late to come up with a winner for the Miss Universe pageant, being staged the same month. Traditionally, Miss Venezuela goes on to compete at Miss Universe and the runner-up goes to Miss World. Pressed for time, Souza was forced to choose – from 40 hopefuls – a Miss to represent Venezuela in the Universe contest.

Before his decision, the rumor mills were working overtime. When Souza finally fin-

Finally, after months of delays and with time running short, the advertisers were lined up and Souza was forced to accept a compromise budget of only about 20 million bolívares ($400,000) from the station. That was barely a drop in the bucket up against costs: his and the other organizers' salaries, the costume designers, the plastic surgeons, the orthodontists, the psychologists, the maintenance of two gymnasiums where the Misses receive complimentary work-outs, and the 50,000 bolívares ($1,000) a month rent for

<u>Left</u> and <u>right</u>, backstage at the Miss Venezuela pageant.

gered the sultry brunette Jacqueline Rodríguez, Miss Miranda and an ex-*Chica 2001* (*2001* is a sensationalist tabloid), the other Misses complained bitterly of being cheated. The incident unleashed a fury in democracy-minded Venezuela. It was unthinkable that a woman should get a stab at Miss Universe without being put through the rigors of the Miss Venezuela contest and selected by a fair vote of the judges. But the decision stuck.

It was not the first time Osmel Souza found himself, as Venezuelan slang would put it, in the *mierda*. Several years back, Souza had rewarded two of his favorite contestants,

Maritza Sayalero and Irene Saéz, with expensive ear-rings. They wore them to the Miss Venezuela pageant and they won the title and runner-up. Coincidence? There was an uproar. Venezuelans fumed that, at the least, it was wrong for Souza to play favorites among the women he prepares for the contest. At worst, people claimed the competitions were rigged, with the judges instructed to look for the women with the special ear-rings. Souza responded that he had the right to give gifts to whomever he pleased.

Prima donnas: Other Miss issues have bordered on the scandalous. Traditionally, each state, territory and the federal district have been represented by a contestant. But in

There's a rule that the Miss contestants must be Venezuelan-born, but Venezuela is a country of immigrants and sometimes rules are bent. In the early 1990s, Colombian-born Beatriz Lesser, who has lived in Venezuela since she was four, emerged as a favorite. But some years back, a major controversy erupted when there was a contestant so newly arrived that she barely spoke Spanish. Paola Ruggieri had just come from Italy yet managed to overcome the objections of the masses to become a winner.

What really counts for a Miss is if she cuts the mustard with Souza, and also if she charms the financial backers. Conni Hernández, 1991's Miss Distrito Federal, was

reality, she is seldom actually from that place. And quite often, the Miss and her "constituents" don't exactly hit it off.

The 1991 competition proved to be a revolving door for would-be representatives of Apure state. The fourth in a line of candidates, a *Caraqueña*, toured "her" state in a *liqui-liqui* (traditional dress) but failed to win the hearts of the locals by criticizing the poor condition of the roads. No. 5, Sonia Briceño, didn't even last a week. She fought over a musical number with the choreographer of the Venevisión program, and quit a few days before the pageant proclaiming, "Nobody messes with me!"

no fool. She made quite a show of eating only health-food products such as lecithin that happened to be marketed by one of the contest's sponsors.

Obsession with appearance: Quite apart from the Miss pageant, looks – feminine and masculine – are both prized and rewarded in Venezuelan society. As one writer noted, Caracas high society is a dazzling society that likes to be dazzled. Being dazzling takes more than raw beauty. It requires style and financial commitment. *Caraqueños* dress up to go out. Women don cocktail dresses for restaurants, clubs and discos; men wear suits and ties. Nails are manicured, moustaches are trimmed, accessories are coordinated.

Venezuelans are characteristically pernickety about personal appearance. They're trained from an early age. While a child can run wild in a restaurant without his parents batting an eye, he's in for a spanking if he soils his clothes.

A cosmetics industry study reveals that Venezuelans are among the world's largest per capita consumers of personal care products, spending a disproportionate amount of family income on those purchases. A president of the cosmetics chamber surmises: "Because we're in the tropics, Venezuelan men and women are very fastidious about their personal hygiene."

During the oil boom era, especially the 1970s, Venezuelans of all income levels developed a taste for fashionable cosmetics. The Miami shopping trip to stock up on cosmetics was one of the hardest things for many Venezuelans to part with when the country's currency was sharply devalued in 1983. Now that consumers have less disposable income for cosmetics, the market has shrunk, according to Tomás Fortson, Avon's general manager. "Nevertheless," he says, "people somehow find a way to keep buying cosmetics – even if it means sacrificing other things."

In Venezuela, 98 percent of urban dwellers claim to use deodorant and women are among the world's most lavish buyers of make-up. A hundred kinds of deodorant, 90 brands of shampoo and 20 lines of make-up are offered through the nation's 20,000 distributors. The cosmetics and personal care industry accounts for retail sales of billions of bolívars annually.

In recent years, with the shift away from the ability to buy abroad and the status-conscious notion that foreign is better, cosmetics manufacturers have started to appeal to nationalistic sentiment. There are more dark-skinned models, photographed in distinctly Venezuelan settings like Margarita and Angel Falls.

Male vanity appeal: And manufacturers have started to target men. After all, the market is there. The father of the country, Simón Bolívar, set a good example by buffing his

own nails up until days before his death, and he had a well-known penchant for soaking a handkerchief in enough cologne to fill an entire room with its scent.

Today, every Venezuelan taxi driver carries a comb and if he stops at a light, chances are it will be to groom in the rear-view mirror. Even the most macho guys are heavy-handed when it comes to scent, and many put clear polish on their nails.

To convey a manly image, Ponds markets its men's line along a knight in shining armor theme – the man who comes to save the woman in a difficult situation. Competitor Fabergé is even more direct with the throbbing lyrics "Macho, macho Brut! Brut, Brut,

macho!" repeated throughout an entire commercial.

Elca, No. 1 in the premium-priced cosmetics market and distributor for men's products including Aramis and Devin, takes a slightly more subtle approach with its in-office demonstrations of proper shaving and good grooming techniques called "barbershops." In another marketing program, Elca seeks to appeal to the athletic man with a "body spa" – a complete cleansing and skin-care product routine.

Clearly, regardless of sex, vanity and Venezuela have more in common than just the letter V.

Left, wheeling and dealing at the Miss Venezuela Academy, the local "boot camp of beauty." **Right**, the happy winner.

Venezuelans love a party, and their festival celebrations are among the continent's liveliest, be they led by devil dancers in Yare, the *Carnaval* revelers in Carúpano or the *tambor* players at San Juan.

As in other countries, the festivities are a hybrid of traditional Indian rituals, Roman Catholic pomp and Afro-Caribbean traditions. No two festivals are the same, although some contain the same elements: generous quantities of rum or *caña* (a sugar cane liquor), music and dancing. A religious procession is also standard.

Annual debauch: *Carnaval* – starting 40 days before Easter – is the most riotous festival celebrated nationwide. Although children dress up in Halloween costumes and paint their faces, adults are actually the serious *Carnaval* revelers. And the most authentic spot to celebrate a Venezuelan *Carnaval* in all its debauchery and madness is Carúpano, the cacao port and beach city on Venezuela's eastern coast.

A parade is central to the celebration. Giant plumed birds, Spanish characters from the conquest and monsters marching through the streets are actually revelers wearing elaborate oversized *papier-maché* masks and costumes. They parade through Carúpano acting out regional legends (especially those that involve magic and healing), engage in folk dancing and sing to accompany the bands that play around the clock for days. *Carnaval* merrymakers inevitably carry a bottle (or two or three); liquor recharges their flagging energy as they embark upon days of non-stop celebration.

The partying is contagious and it isn't long before tourists and townspeople alike are dancing like maniacs in the open air. The city's acoustic shell and outdoor dance floor are the focus for much of the frenzied dancing, but the spillover is great and there are few places where you will be able to find feet at rest or a moment's silence during the *Carnaval* celebration. Unless you plan ahead, there are also few places you'll find a spot to sleep. Tourists talk of having to sleep on park

benches (while the merrymaking continued all around them) because they could find no available hotel rooms.

Religious fiesta: Not far away, in Cumaná, the Cruz de Mayo folklore festival is another popular – albeit more subdued – celebration filled with Christian symbols. Starting May 3 and continuing to the end of the month, this tradition was apparently a way of honoring the Roman Catholic cross using local rites, songs, rhythms and dances. Music known as *joropo*, employing *maracas*, *bandolín*, guitar, the four-stringed *cuatro* and a type of accordion known as the *cuereta*, provides the background for the partying. It is believed this festival may date as far back as the Spanish conquest, when Franciscan monks arrived in Cumaná and the Dominican friars in Chichiriviche and Santa Fé carrying Christian crucifixes.

To prepare for the festival, altars of all sizes are erected in churches, arenas and private clubs around the city. Coconut tree leaves form the shelter, bouquets of flowers add color. At altars where there is no electricity to illuminate the finished product, bamboo tubes are perforated with holes and lit

Preceding pages: applauding fireworks at a fiesta. **Left** and **right**, jesters and high camp at *Carnaval*.

candles are placed inside. The altars are built on at least seven different levels, representing the Calvary of Christ, and a lottery determines which men and women are to be the godparents of each cross. The men must contribute money toward the altar construction and the women must provide flowers. The godparents will have the coveted job of placing the cross upon the finished altar.

The ceremony to erect the crucifix begins with Catholic prayers interspersed with songs about local customs, fishing, history, magic and even verses satirizing politicians. *Joropo* dancing, accompanied by a free flow of rum, follows. When the month of celebrating ends, the cross is taken down and the altar is

cated beats; *tambor* playing is not as simple as it looks. The drummers must know a variety of rhythms and they must be able to beat and drum non-stop for hours. *Tambor* skills are frequently passed down in families and the drummers at today's festivals most likely boast a grandfather or great-grandfather who was distinguished as a *tamborista*.

Women do not play *tambores*, but they usually lead the bump and grind action that comprises the festival dancing. Like their ancestors, black slaves brought to work on coffee and cacao *haciendas*, the women frequently dress in brightly-colored or stark white ruffled skirts, which they flounce as they shake hips and shoulders at breakneck

dismantled until the following year.

Power of the drums: Rum and religious icons are present, but it is a different kind of music that accompanies the three-day Fiesta de San Juan, or feast of St John the Baptist, celebrated in coastal towns. Arriving with the rains of June, this festival is a riotous one accompanied by frenzied beating on *tambores*, African drums made out of hollowed logs. Shirtless men, with their trouser legs often rolled up nearly to their knees, play the *tambores* by rapping on them sharply with open palms or by beating the hollow logs with sticks. Don't be deceived by the ease with which they thump out the compli-

speed. Generally, circles are formed and dancers enter the center in couples. A woman will try to impress her male partner with her gyrations until another woman enters the circle, bounces the original female dancer out with a powerful shove of her hips and wows the audience with her skills.

As the dancing progresses, it gets wilder – clearly not a festival for the timid. Men, too, enter the circle but less violently, to replace male dancers. Outside the circle, waiting dancers sway to the music and fuel themselves by tippling bottles of rum or cane liquor called *aguardiente*.

The most raucous day of the *tambores*

festival, as the feast is unofficially known, is June 24, the longest day on the celestial calendar and the shortest night of the year. This night – the evening of fire and water – is the epitome of the purification rituals that accompany the festival dedicated to baptism. Water would seem the logical liquid for dousing statues and festival-goers alike, but rum is usually substituted – which is no doubt why the conga line that winds through the host village that day almost certainly will take a quick detour into the nearest river at some point along the way. The statue may or may not be dunked but the rum and sweat-soaked revelers won't hesitate to take a quick plunge to cool off.

much chanting among the crowds at this point, the heavy-duty entertainment begins after the procession has covered its full path and the statue has been placed on a makeshift altar in the area where dancing will be held. Once in place, more rum is sprinkled on the statue and men, women and even children begin dancing themselves into a frenzy. In bigger towns, fireworks are set off. The dancing continues until dawn the next morning, when townspeople either retire to their homes or flake out on the beach for some shut-eye. The best spots to see this celebration are in the smaller towns such as Borburata near Puerto Cabello.

Bizarre cult: For outsiders, one of the most

On June 24, the church bells begin ringing at noon, followed by the *tambores*, signaling that it is time to remove St John's statue from the church and begin to parade it around the town. Villagers, many of them dressed in the patron saint's color – red – pass rum and *aguardiente* through the crowd as the procession weaves its way down the streets. Some of the liquor is sprinkled on the statue. Those who are not armed with libations carry flowers and lit candles.

Although there will be some dancing and

disturbing festivals may be that in honor of María Lionza. Whether this woman even existed is not clear; some say she was an Indian princess with blue eyes, others say she was the daughter of an Indian father and a Spanish noblewoman and that she disappeared in the mountains after she fled from marauders attacking her tribe. Since the turn of the century, tens or even hundreds of thousands of Venezuelans have worshipped her and sought her favors, making her perhaps the country's second most revered figure after Simón Bolívar.

Rituals honoring the mystical figure peak in October during the Día de la Raza celebra-

Left, Maria Lionza is center of a bizarre Venezuela cult. <u>Above</u>, animal sacrifice at a *santería* ritual.

tion (marked in the United States as Columbus Day). That is when pilgrims make their way to Sorte, a hill on the outskirts of Chivacoa east of Barquisimeto where altars and shrines to the pagan goddess are filled with Christian statues, bottles of perfume, liquor, cakes and offerings. Everyone from uneducated maids to presidential candidates travels to the forested area, designated as a national park in María Lionza's honor, to seek favors. These believers seek spiritual contact with the legendary figure, and claim they obtain it through possession by other, more minor, personages.

The pilgrims also believe in "courts," or a hierarchy of spirits of which María Lionza

in Venezuela (as well as the second most popular time to visit María Lionza's shrine), although most Venezuelans use the week's vacation to head for the beach. However, some towns still celebrate the Burning of Judas ritual on Easter Sunday. A life-sized figure is dressed in old clothes and exhibited in the village by day. The effigy usually represents some unpopular political figure which has tied to it a mock last will and testament listing the alleged abuses of the politicians. In the afternoon, the will is read and the figure is burned.

Devil dancers of Yare: Another Roman Catholic holy day, the Feast of Corpus Christi, is celebrated in San Francisco de Yare with

with her two bodyguards make up the highest tier, known as the celestial court. Followers say her powers can be used for good and evil. Many of the rituals are similar to those found in voodoo or *santería* and it can be unnerving to watch the devout, including children, fall into trances, convulse during rites and even walk on hot coals (*la baile de las candelas*) or chew glass. A statue of María Lionza as a powerful, muscular woman seated on a tapir and holding a man's pelvis above her head can be seen on the center median of the main highway in Caracas.

Christian celebrations: Semana Santa, the Holy Week leading to Easter, is a big holiday

elaborate performances by the continent's oldest devil dancing society. Devil dancing has been around since the Spanish conquest and is generally interpreted as a celebration in which good must conquer evil. The dancers make commitments to participate in the festival for a certain number of years; most make good their promise. Some also spend months, and considerable sums of money, preparing their dance attire.

In San Francisco de Yare, devil dancing carries with it an incomparable level of prestige. The chief dancer is revered: when he dies, his widow is taken care of by the dancers' society and the leadership of the society is often passed down to his sons. These men practise all year for the day when they will put on grotesque *papier-maché* masks and gaudy costumes, then dance to scare off the devil. Just in case God doesn't recognize them in their evil outfits, engaged in dancing that can only be described as diabolical, they carry rosary beads and other religious symbols for good measure.

Venezuela also has a number of local and regional festivals. Nearly every city has a patron saint and his or her day is celebrated with great pomp. Other regions customize their festivals to match their important industries, interests or pastimes. In the bullfighting city of Maracay, for example, the

Fería of San José in March fetes the city's patron saint with a series of bullfights featuring internationally-known *toreros*. Accompanying the display in the bullring is an agricultural exposition.

In Barquisimeto in January, on the other hand, the Fería de la Divina Pastora is geared more toward that city's nickname, "The Music Capital of Venezuela." The annual fair with handicrafts, sports events and folklore dancing offers an opportunity to hear the regional waltz, or *vals larense*, as it is known.

Left, high times with the batmobile. **Above**, a devil dancer unmasked at Yare.

In the cattle country of San Francisco de Apure, February marks the annual rodeo that includes everything from roping contests to beauty contests.

All over the island of Margarita, regattas are held in honor of the Virgin of Carmen during July. At the end of that same month in the city of Asunción, a civic holiday – the Batalla de Matasiete – honors the 1817 victory of the patriotic forces fighting against the Spanish. One of the country's biggest annual fairs is in San Cristóbal in honor of the city's patron, San Sebastián. Held in the month of January, this festivity attracts tens of thousands of merrymakers. Officials close off many of the city streets for dancing, there are five days of bullfights with *toreros* from Spain and Mexico and a number of sports events including an international bike race and various horse races.

Reversal of tradition: Venezuelans approach Christmas and New Year's Eve with customs that are the opposite of those of other countries. They socialize with friends and go out strolling or to the beach for the December 25 holiday, then spend the last day of the calendar year at quiet gatherings with family members. Fireworks will light up the sky both nights – usually shot off from backyards and apartment building rooftops all over Caracas and other major cities – but on New Year's Eve, in particular, don't expect to see any wild merrymaking in the streets. Restaurants are usually closed and the streets are quiet.

For Christmas, on the other hand, Venezuelans stock up on champagne, loaves of bread stuffed with ham and *hallacas*, traditional *tamales* served for the holiday – then, after a family meal early in the day, go out on the streets where they run into friends, rollerskate in front of the Cathedral or, in Caracas, stroll down Sabana Grande for coffee. This is the time of year when *gaita*, the folk music from Maracaibo, is heard.

Family gatherings and outings to the beach are usually on the schedule after the parades and military pomp that accompany the Fifth of July, the country's Independence Day. In Caracas, ceremonies with government and military officials usually focus on the spot known as Los Proceres, a park boulevard honoring the country's heroes. On this day, too, you'll find it difficult to locate a restaurant or shop that is open for business.

One word describes the Venezuelan palate: eccentric. Cosmopolitan Caracas boasts some of the most sophisticated restaurants on the continent, yet the preferred way of drinking 12-year-old Scotch is mixed with Coca-Cola. The national fast food is a nearly flavorless lump of fried cornmeal, while the Christmas specialty is a painstakingly prepared dish of three carefully spiced meats. Due to the size and geographical contrasts of the country, the range of cuisine is incredibly broad – from the mango *mousse* and other delicate French *nouvelle* delights in the capital to piranha, monkey meat and deep-fried ants in the Amazon.

Solid staple: For most Venezuelans, the staff of life is not bread but a flattened, fist-sized ball of fried corn or wheat flour called an *arepa*. As pervasive as the *tortilla* in Mexico, the cheap and filling *arepas* are gobbled in great quantities by the country's poor, but they also turn up in smaller, daintier versions in the bread baskets of fine restaurants, where diners slice them in halves and slather them with a light cream cheese called *natilla*.

While visitors may be hard-pressed to polish off even one *arepa*, Venezuelans might eat two or three for breakfast, and during the day stop in for more at fast-food stands called *areperas* (the best-known chain is Doña Arepa).

Seldom are *arepas* eaten plain. Usually they're slit and part of the inside is scooped out to form a pocket that's stuffed with virtually anything imaginable. Favorite fillings include *reina pepiada* (chicken with guacamole), *carne mechada* (shredded beef), *ensalada de atún* (tuna salad), *diablitos* (canned deviled ham), or simply grated *queso amarillo* (yellow cheese). At breakfast, a popular filling is *perico*, eggs scrambled with tomato and onion.

The *arepa* accompanies Venezuela's national dish, *pabellón criollo*. This large, tasty plate features a mound of shredded beef spiced with onions, green pepper, tomato, *cilantro* (coriander) and garlic, a mound of

white rice, a scoop of *caraotas negras* (black beans) and disks of fried plantain. Oddly enough, black beans are imported, mainly from Chile. It has been suggested that's why Venezuelan politicians traditionally maintain such good relations with this southern neighbor. During a recent Venezuelan presidential campaign, a national shortage of *caraotas negras* became one of the most hotly debated election issues.

Pabellón is not eaten on any particular occasion; rather it is part of the daily diet of

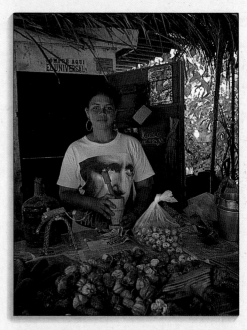

many working-class Venezuelans and a standard on many restaurant menus.

A more flavorful tidbit than the *arepa* is the *tequeño*, made of egg pastry dough rolled into rods as small as cigars or as large as cucumbers, wrapped around strips of cheese and fried. *Tequeños* are served as *pasapalos* (hors d'oeuvres) or eaten anytime as a snack. When fresh and hot, they are positively addictive. The name derives from the town of Los Teques.

Another Venezuelan standard is the *cachapa*, a thick, slightly sweet pancake made with maize. Munched at breakfast or for a snack, *cachapas* usually come with a slab of *queso guayanese*. They're eaten with a knife and fork, or rolled up as a finger food. *Empanadas* are fried cornmeal turnovers filled with cheese, meat or fish. They're often hawked on the street or at the beach from tin buckets.

Advice for carnivores: As for main courses, the country boasts fine meats, fish and *mariscos* (shellfish). Beef is produced in the Llanos, the central plains region, and menus feature cuts like *muchacho* (roast beef), *solomo* (sirloin) and *lomito* (steak). The *parilla* or mixed grill is a favorite choice of serious meat eaters.

Andean lakes and streams are abundantly stocked with *trucha* (trout), which is also

is a notorious fighter. Piranha is also caught for eating: its flesh is light and sweet.

Fruit paradise: Tropical Venezuela offers a cornucopia of fresh and natural foods that remain key parts of the diet despite the increasing presence of multinational processed-food companies. Exotic fruits are widely available and make succulent treats for visitors from cold climes. Street vendors sell amazing watermelon-sized *lechosa* (papaya), mangos, *guayaba* (guava), *guanabana*, *zapote* (sapodilla plum), *níspero* (the crabapple-like fruit of the medlar tree), oranges, pears, breadfruit, melons, pineapples, strawberries and coconuts.

You might see vendors with shopping carts

farmed for export overseas. Fishermen along Venezuela's 2,500-km (1,500-mile) Caribbean coastline haul in *pargo* (red snapper), *dorado* and shellfish like clams and oysters. You may be disappointed at the scarcity of lobster and conch – Venezuelan fishermen spirit this bounty away to the resorts of Aruba where they fetch a higher price.

In recent years, Venezuela has earned a place on the world's sport fishing map, and anglers flock from far and wide to test their skills against marlin and bonefish in the Caribbean, and *payara* and *pavón* (peacock bass) in Guri Lake and the Orinoco headwaters and tributaries. The feisty, fanged *payara*

full of what look like green ping-pong balls. They're *mamones*. Venezuelans buy them by the bagful, peel off the skin and suck on the pale pink flesh that clings to the pit.

Some fruits go by names unfamiliar in other Spanish-speaking lands: passion fruit is called *parchita* rather than *maracuyá*, watermelon is *patilla* rather than *sandía*, and limes are *limónes* (literally, lemons). Avocado is *aguacate* instead of *palta*.

Fresh juices are a thirst-quenching alternative to soft drinks. On a hot day, sip a tart, refreshing *limonada frappe* (lemonade with crushed ice) or a *papelón con limón*, lemonade sweetened with raw sugar. Street vendors do big business with *jugo de caña*, pale green sugar cane juice and coconut (*coca*) juice drunk straight from the shell. Just about any fruit can be whipped into a *jugo* (juice), *batido* (frothed with ice) or *merengada* (a milkshake). A scoop or two of sugar is always added, so if you don't like it too sweet, ask for *muy poco azúcar* (very little sugar) or *sin azúcar* (without sugar).

You'll find every kind of banana – from the stubby sweet *cambur*, ready for eating, to the large, starchy *platano* (plantain) for frying. A treat pedalled at the movies and on the beach are bags of crisply fried, lightly salted banana chips called *tostónes*. This snack also shows up in the Venezuelan expression

beef that's spiced with green pepper, onion, garlic, tomatoes, capers, sugar, cumin, black pepper, parsley, pork fat, olive oil, raisins and pimento-stuffed olives. Each *hallaca* is lovingly wrapped in banana leaves and steamed (the leaves aren't meant to be eaten). Needless to say, the preparation takes hours, even days.

This festive dish reputedly has humble origins – it supposedly began with servants recycling the jumble of scraps from the master's table. Yet the *hallaca* has grown so dear to Venezuelans that exceptions were made during the era of import restrictions for such key ingredients as olives. When items ran short or grew too pricey, people rioted.

comiendo tostón, which means getting caught in the act of committing a crime.

Holiday dining: Food takes on a special significance in Venezuela during the Christmas season when bosses throw parties for employees featuring *pan de jamón* (ham rolls), executives impress clients with lavish dinners at exclusive restaurants, and families gather for home-cooked feasts.

The most cherished holiday food is the *hallaca*. This packet of cornmeal dough is bursting with a filling of chicken, pork and

Left, caught in the act at a riverside restaurant.
Above, one of many Spanish *tascas*, Caracas.

Like many other Latins, Venezuelans relish sweets. Ever popular are *churros*, crispy fried pastry tubes sprinkled with sugar and usually served with hot chocolate. Dunking is allowed. Flan (*quesillo*), puddings, cakes, ice cream, coconut candies and other goodies are also craved, but the distinctive Venezuelan dessert is a dreamy sponge cake doused in coconut cream called *bienmesabe*. That translates as "tastes good to me," and to say it's rich is a colossal understatement.

Local tastes: Because Venezuela is a large country with many varied zones, distinctive regional cuisines have evolved. In coastal areas and on Margarita Island, you'll find various *hervidos de pescado* (fish soups). A favorite is *sancocho* (fish stew), a thick, steaming brew with chunks of red snapper, pumpkin, root vegetables, lemon and tomatoes. *Consomé de chipi chipi* is a thin broth laced with tiny clams that is reputed to be an aphrodisiac.

La tortuga marina (sea turtle) is a delicacy, but the species is endangered. Conservationists also advise steering clear of *pastel de morrocoy*, a pie made from land turtle. At Coro and the Paraguaná peninsula, *chivo en coco* (goat in coconut) is a specialty.

Andean cuisine is altogether original. In these high altitudes, *arepas* are made of wheat, rather than corn. The small white fed tropical beef has little fat, it is often larded by pricking it with small knives and filling the cuts with bacon or pork fat. One Venezuelan recipe calls for filling tough roast with large whole carrots and onions, plus bacon or pork and cloves of garlic. As the piece cooks, it may swell to double in size and when carved, it's a surprisingly tender mesh of meat and vegetables.

In the Amazon region, indigenous groups plant *yuca* (yucca or manioc), plantains, corn and beans. From *yuca* they make *casabe* (cassava), a dry, fibrous and rather tasteless flatbread that's somewhat like munching cardboard. The people also fish, catch turtles and hunt tapirs, monkeys and birds – but not

potatoes are remarkably sweet, and the tasty homemade cheese fried in cubes is not to be missed. Cured meats and sausages are sold by the roadside in many villages.

When the Pope visited Mérida, the Andean capital, in 1985, he was treated to *comida típica* (typical food), a dinner of rainbow trout. But while this trout is intimately associated with Mérida, it is not in fact native to the Andes. The Venezuelan government imported the fish from Europe and the United States between 1938 and 1941, and several trout hatcheries outside Mérida enjoy a thriving export business.

The Llanos are beef country. Since grass-parrots, whose meat is considered too tough.

Markets in Amazon towns may offer unusual meat like *peccary* (similar to stringy pork) and venison from tropical deer. Deep-fat-fried ants are considered a delicacy – especially the winged ones known as *culonas* (big bottoms). At the market in Puerto Ayacucho, you can buy typical Piaroa Indian food like *katara*, a spicy dish with water of yucca and *bachacos* (brown, ant-like insects). *Chichiguache* is a variation with cream of garlic and other spices, and is said to have aphrodisiac powers.

Cashews and *palmitos* (hearts of palm) are more mainstream treats from the rainforest, but conservationists advise against eating *palmitos* since harvesting kills the trees.

Foreign influences: While fried ants have not exactly caught on in Caracas, the impact of foreign cultures is obvious in restaurants of the capital. A sizeable Italian community ensures that pasta is a standard and well-prepared dish. If you see *pasticho* on the menu, that's lasagne. The Italian fruit bread *panettone* is all the rage at Christmas.

The Spanish influence shows up in the prevalence of *paella*, *tortilla española* (omelet with potatoes) and other Iberian specialties. Venezuelans prefer *paella a la valenciana* over other Spanish variations. French pastries, Swiss chocolates and Dutch cheeses are sold at delicatessens, and North American fast foods like pizza, burgers and fries are becoming all too prominent.

According to the National Restaurant Owners' Association, Caracas offers more than 600 fully-fledged restaurants and 2,000 secondary establishments or lunch counters. *Criollo* restaurants, *areperas*, hamburger chains and the ubiquitous *pollo en brasas* (grilled chicken) stands are interspersed with showy eateries devoted to cuisines including French classic and *nouvelle*, Swiss, German, Hungarian, Chinese, Japanese, Peruvian, Argentine and North American.

Such restaurants sprang up during the years when Venezuela was flush with petro-dollars, and foreigners swarmed to this cosmopolitan crossroads. Now splurging is a thing of the past. But due to the devalued currency, foreign visitors usually find that dining out in Caracas is delightfully affordable.

After lunch there's a siesta, so *Caraqueños* can enjoy a hearty noontime meal with a few hours to sleep it off before returning to work. Dinner tends to start late, and many restaurants remain open half the night.

A nation of coffee worshippers: More than just a drink, coffee is an integral part of the Venezuelan lifestyle. Rich, aromatic and always fresh, each *café* is brewed to order – Venezuelans would never dream of letting a pot languish on a heater. They enjoy *java* throughout the day – from big milky cups at breakfast to little heavily sugared shots from stand-up counters to glasses of cappuccino smothered in real whipped cream late at

night in the city's meeting place, the outdoor Gran Café in Sabana Grande. Coffee comes in about a dozen ways, and if you simply ask for *café*, the waiter won't know what you want. You must use finesse, specifying the size and exact degree of strength you desire.

Here's how you do it. Size is easy: *pequeño* (small) or *grande* (large). On the street, coffee is served in plastic cups without handles. A *pequeño* is about the size of a large thimble; a *grande* is close to a *demitasse*. Venezuelans often drink their coffee well-sugared – with a large cup you'll get at least two packets of sugar.

It's specifying the coffee strength that takes a little savvy. A black coffee is a *negro* – a

small one, using the Spanish diminutive suffix, a *negrito*. A watered-down black coffee, about the closest thing to North American coffee, is a *guayoyo*. Coffee that's half milk, which Venezuelans often drink at breakfast but almost never after a meal, is a *café con leche*. Order by asking for a *con leche grande* or *con leche pequeño*. It's not necessary to say "*café*."

Coffee with only a spot of milk is called a *marrón* (brown) – you would order a *marrón grande* or a *marróncito*. Coffee that's somewhere in between a *con leche* and a *marrón* is a *marrón claro*.

A taste for alcohol: In contrast to coffee,

Left, colonial-style restaurant near Mérida. **Right**, warming up *arepas*.

Food 105

there are few choices when it comes to beer, although Venezuelans joke that beer drinking is the national sport – and indeed, on the crowded beaches that may seem true. Venezuela has two main brands of *cerveza* – the best-selling Polar, which for several years has been exported with the gimmick of using refrigerated containers to ensure freshness, and Nacional, which has the reputation of being a slightly more working-class drink. There are a couple of regional beers, including Regional and Cardenal. Recent additions to the beer line-up are Polar Negra (a malt), Nacional Stout and Cristal (order this light beer by asking simply for a *solera*).

But Polar is such a big seller that several

years ago the company, in order to avoid anti-trust intervention, actually took charge of Nacional's advertising to boost its competitor's market share. A case of Polar always includes two bottles of Nacional. Venezuelans are good-natured about this – they accept it as a patriotic show of support for a national industry.

On a hot day, ask for a *cerveza vestida de novia* (dressed like a bride). That means you want it frosty.

Throughout Venezuela's heady oil-boom days, the country is said to have consumed the highest per capita quantity of fine whisky in the world. Waiters at society parties would carry trays of nothing but Scotch and guests would choose their favorite brand. At restaurants, hosts would order bottles placed at the center of the table and diners would help themselves. It may say something about Venezuelan taste, however, that the mixer of choice for aged Scotch is Coca-Cola.

During the import restrictions of the 1980s, the best restaurants managed to smuggle bottles in, but prices were exorbitant and most Venezuelans were forced to adjust their drinking habits. Nationally produced rum returned to the party table, much of it in whisky-looking bottles. Now rum can be bought cheaply everywhere.

Venezuelans drink rum with Angostura bitters (invented in the Orinoco port city of Angostura, now known as Ciudad Bolívar), on ice with fresh lime slices, with colas, *aguakina* (tonic) or with almost any fruit juice. A favorite – and delicious – mix is *ron con parchita*, rum with passion fruit juice.

Rarely do Venezuelans choose clear drinks like vodka and gin, nor are they noted wine connoisseurs. Wine is imported and tends to be expensive, but the selection is improving now that import restrictions have ended. *Sangría*, red wine with chunks of fruit, is popular in some bars and restaurants.

As with food, there are different regional spirits. *Llaneros* are known to swill the potent, clear *aguardiente*, made from sugar cane, until they slide out of their saddles. To take the edge off the chill mountain air, *Andinos* whip up a *calentadito* from the anise-flavored liqueur *miche* and warm milk. Or they sip the fermented corn drink, *chicha*. On the coast one finds *guarapita*, a deceptively innocent-tasting fermented sugar-cane derivative that's often mixed with *guayaba*, other juices or even rum (*ron con guarapita*). In the cities, a popular gift bottle at Christmas is *ponche crema*, a pre-mixed concoction similar to North American eggnog.

After a hard night, when Venezuelans groan, *Estoy herido* (I am injured) or *Tengo un ratoncito* (slang for "I have a hangover"), they don't take aspirin. There is only one cure – a steaming bowl of *mondongo* (tripe soup). If you're up early on a weekend, you'll probably detect this unmistakable aroma mingling with the scent of coffee.

Left, tropical spread. **Right**, a buffet lunch at Hato Doña Barbara in the Llanos.

Soccer may rule in the minds of sports fans in every other South American country, but in Venezuela baseball is king. Basketball, tennis, horse racing and *bollas criollas* all have their followings, yet nothing comes near the near-religious enthusiasm that a good game of *el béisbol* can inspire.

Uncle Sam's influence: Like many other features of Venezuela, the progress of baseball is related to the oil industry. When US oil companies traveled to Venezuela in the early 20th century, their staff brought the game with them. Initially played only in the oil camps, baseball's popularity slowly took off in the rest of Venezuelan society – especially in the 1940s when the professional winter leagues were started in the country.

Eventually, teams were built up throughout the country using American support and finances. As the level of play started to improve each year, major league teams, aware that Venezuelan players could possibly contend for jobs on rosters in the States, gradually started to give opportunities for promising Venezuelans to compete for jobs in "Las Grandes Ligas" (the big leagues).

And the powerful newspaper media of Venezuela began providing fervent coverage of the Venezuelan stars who made it big in the States. The first great Venezuelan player in the major leagues, Alfonso "Chico" Carrasquel, earned the starting shortstop job for the Chicago White Sox in 1950.

With Carrasquel in the limelight, many youngsters decided to follow in his footsteps. Thousands of Venezuelan kids tried to emulate Carrasquel by spending hours on the dusty diamonds throughout the country, dreaming of the day they too would line up at shortstop in a big league uniform.

Baseball stars: The result has been a long line of outstanding Venezuelan shortstops. The most famous is probably Luis Aparicio, who replaced Carrasquel in Chicago's starting lineup in 1956. Highlights of Aparicio's 18-year career included winning the American League "Rookie of the Year" award in

1956 and accumulating 2,677 hits, including 394 doubles.

Aparicio set the standard for how to turn the double play, and in general showed how the position of shortstop could and should be played. His style has been copied many times – but never equaled, according to most experts. Aparicio is the only Venezuelan ever to be inducted into the exclusive Baseball Hall of Fame in Cooperstown, New York.

Many North American players have honed their skills in the Venezuelan winter league

and gone on to major league stardom. Dozens of players have made it big in the US leagues after apprenticing in Venezuela, including the Los Angeles Dodger star Darryl Strawberry. *Caraqueño* old-timers still talk about the home run that current Dodger Strawberry, playing for La Guaira, launched to straight-away center field in 1983 at University Stadium. The ball almost cleared the stadium completely.

Venezuelan baseball today carries on this great tradition. While the Venezuelan winter league isn't what it used to be when the local bolívar was strong and big league players wanted to come down to Latin America to

Preceding pages: thumping a home run. Left, a baseball star laps up some attention. **Right,** fan and mascot.

make some extra money, winter baseball is still quite enjoyable for baseball fans. "I'd say watching the Venezuelan winter league now is somewhere between seeing Double-A and Triple-A ball in the States," says Rick Patterson, who managed the La Guaira club in the 1990–91 season.

Seven or eight "imports" from the United States fill the roster spots along with the Venezuelan players. Each winter league team has either a full or partial working agreement with a major league club, which provides some of its young prospects along with financing for equipment, trainer, manager and coaches to the Venezuelan teams.

Sport spectacle: For baseball fans or just

(another Zulia-state based team) and the Caribes of Puerto La Cruz. The eight clubs have been divided into two divisions – East and West – to save money on travel costs.

Baseball fans who would like to combine some nice beach time with a little Latin American winter ball will want to make the trip to Puerto La Cruz, about four hours by car from Caracas, which boasts some of the country's liveliest resorts and a busy baseball season. But there is also plenty of action in the capital. For people passing through Caracas during the winter season, which begins in mid-October and finishes at the end of January, it's relatively easy to secure game tickets to see the Caracas or La Guaira

those visitors to Venezuela who want to get a taste of the Latin American passion for sport, attending a winter baseball game is the perfect ticket.

Until the 1991–92 season, there were six teams playing in the league. The clubs include the Aguilas (Eagles) of Zulia (based in Maracaibo); the Cardinales (Cardinals) of Lara (from Barquisimeto); the Navegantes (Navigators) of Magallanes (Valencia); the Tigres (Tigers) of Aragua (Maracay); the Leones (Lions) of Caracas and the Tiburones (Sharks) of La Guaira (also Caracas). In the 1991–92 season, the league expanded with the addition of the Petroleos of Cabimas

teams in action. Just check the *Daily Journal,* Venezuela's English language newspaper, for the baseball schedule.

The atmosphere is terrific for baseball. The lights are good, the fields are in solid shape and the fans are lively. At times, La Guaira or Caracas followers have the added support of a little merengue band that keeps the fans up off their seats and rhythmically dancing to the beat during games.

Classic match: While each team has its great traditions and passionate *fanáticos* (fans), none can compare to the rivalry between Caracas and Magallanes. It's the equivalent of seeing the New York Yankees play the

Boston Red Sox in the US: the rivalry is quite simply the biggest sporting spectacle in Venezuela. And you don't necessarily have to love baseball to enjoy being part of the country's most emotional sporting event.

How the intense rivalry was established is not totally clear. In most views, the Navegantes of Magallanes from Valencia have the largest – and most rabid – following of any team in the country. One reason might be that the team has moved around a bit over the past 40 years, apparently picking up fans everywhere it went.

The club started in Caracas, hence the large following it still enjoys in the capital. The team – though not the name Magallanes – was then sold, renamed "Oriente" and sent to the eastern part of the country, playing "home" games in three or four different cities. It then got the name Magallanes back, and then was sold to the city of Valencia, where it remains.

Unfortunately, the team's popularity is more consistent than its playing standards. Some locals will tell you that Magallanes can't get its act together and succeed on the field consistently because it's the only team in the league run by a local government. The others clubs are privately operated.

Jesús Lezama, the most famous Caracas Lions fan for well over 40 years, disputes the notion that Magallanes is more popular than his club. Lezama can be seen at every Lions game in Caracas, wearing his baseball jersey and blowing a horn. He'll take his blaring instrument and waltz over to the opposing team's fan section and subject himself to the ridiculing comments of the Magallanes fans.

Wild scenes: The Caracas-Magallanes encounters are a sight to behold. In Caracas, the experience begins about two hours before game time when hoards of *fanáticos* jam against one another, jostling for one of the precious tickets that will get them into the 28,000-seat University Stadium.

The crowd is relatively tranquil for the first two or three innings. But "relatively tranquil" in Venezuela would translate to "rowdy" in, say, the States, with yelling, screaming and dancing. By the third inning or so, the thousands of cold Polar beers,

which retail for about 50 cents a pop, are starting to take effect and anything is liable to happen.

A fight, for instance between a loyal Caracas fan and a rowdy Magallanes supporter, who might have had the temerity to heckle the Leones fans in the home team's section on the third base side of the stadium, is just one example of the action. Bodies have been known to go flying before security guards – who carry swords as well as guns – reach the scene and escort the rowdies out.

Security is tight throughout the stadium both in Caracas and in Valencia. Attack dogs are placed on the field with the guards near the end of the games to prevent fans from

entering the field. If you didn't know about Caracas-Magallanes games, you'd think the President was expected.

By the end of the sixth inning, the crowd has become a little inebriated and perhaps a bit complacent. The fans need some excitement. So "The Wave" starts around the stadium. The Wave involves fans in a vertical section of the stand simultaneously rising to their feet, lifting their arms to the sky, then lowering their arms and sitting down. This may not sound so difficult, but the motion has to be passed on to those in adjacent seats, until the "Wave" has gone completely around the stadium; then it circulates again and

Left, "The Wave" makes the round, Venezuela-style. **Right**, windsurfing at the Morrocoy National Park.

again. The scoreboard indicates the old record for times around and awards recognition if a new record is set.

Fans at these games come in all shapes and sizes. One famous Magallanes supporter stands out, literally, because he's propped up by a pair of stilts that make him hover 6 meters (20 ft) in the air. You can only hope that he has taken out life insurance when you see him heckling in the Caracas section. He would be an easy target for an undercut by an incensed Caracas fan. The whole experience is enough to make you forget there's a baseball game being played out on the field.

The Caracas-Magallanes games are exciting enough at any time during the regular ers are turning to the game and kids are encouraged to play basketball since it's much cheaper and easier to practise than baseball. Sam Sheppard, who has been playing professional basketball in Venezuela since 1975, believes that basketball will be the most popular sport in this country – overtaking baseball – within the next 10 years.

The Liga Especial is Venezuela's top professional league. The league is made up of eight teams, two of which are based in Caracas and one each in Maracay, Valencia, Maracaibo, Guanare, Puerto La Cruz and Margarita Island. Each team is allowed two "imports" from the States. The US players are expected to put the ball in the hole, and if

season, which runs through the beginning of January. But they pale in comparison to the intensity of a game involving the two teams in the playoffs. The two top teams in each division play a round-robin series – two home games and two away – to determine the top two teams overall. They then fight it out in a best-of-seven series for the right to represent Venezuela against the champions of the Dominican Republic, Mexico and Puerto Rico in the Caribbean Series, which is held in early February.

Basketball boom: While basketball is still in its early stages in Venezuela, it's catching on around the country. More and more tall play-

Americans don't score effectively, management ships them home. "Sometimes I think they change American players more than they change their shirts," one American player said, referring to his Venezuelan bosses.

The 42-game regular season starts in early March and ends with the playoff finals in early July. Most experts agree that the talent level of players surpasses the quality of coaching in Venezuela at the moment. Consequently, basketball fans going to games will see a tendency for offensive emphasis at the expense of fundamental play and tough defense. But little by little, Venezuelan players are taking advantage of US college experience and improving basketball back home.

Fans pack the arenas. In La Asunción, the home court of the Margarita Island-based club, only about 2,000 fans can actually be seated. However, maniacal supporters of the club flood the facility, getting in any way possible including standing up during the whole game or hanging from the rafters.

An indifference to football: Soccer dominates the sports pages and fans' interest in every South American country except Venezuela. Without a serious tradition for the game, *fútbol*, as the sport is referred to in Spanish, never has generated an extreme amount of interest in Venezuela. The sport was first brought here by the influx of Italian,

does run from August until May. While crowds don't flock to see pro soccer players in Caracas, soccer is extremely popular in Mérida and San Cristóbal, both cities in the Andean region of Venezuela. The Andean people, much like their counterparts in Colombia, passionately follow soccer and pack the home-town stadiums in droves.

Similarly, Venezuela won't be confused with Argentina, Brazil, Peru, Uruguay or Paraguay for its tennis level when comparing South American countries. However, the sport is gaining ground. The Venezuelan Davis Cup team competes in the American Zone Group II and is trying to move up to the Group I level, just below the world group.

Portuguese and Spanish immigrants who moved to the country when the oil boom hit. However, soccer was considered an elitist sport, centered around these Europeans. Consequently, young kids from the *barrios* of Caracas area didn't start playing the game with the passion and fervor one sees in other South American countries' larger cities. In contrast to baseball, youngsters have never associated the sport of soccer with a means of escaping the slums for fame and fortune.

A Venezuelan professional soccer league

Left, a bullfight in Maracay. **Above**, *bolas criollas* **on a sunny afternoon.**

The sport of kings: It's safe to say that many Venezuelans are addicted to the horse track, evoking scenes of passion that may be second only to baseball. On average, US$2 million is bet every weekend at the races. The tracks in Valencia, Maracaibo and Caracas all draw well.

While Venezuelan horse racing is legitimate, it's different from racing in most other parts of the world. The quality of the horses running pales in comparison with the type of thoroughbreds running at tracks in the US or Europe. Even so, a visiting tourist might want to make a trip to La Rinconada, the horse track just outside of Caracas. The track is open Saturday and Sunday for competitions, with racing from 1pm to 6pm. La Rinconada was completed in 1959 while dictator Pérez Jiménez, a horse racing enthusiast, was in office.

At one time, La Rinconada was considered to be among the top tracks in Latin America, with stables for 2,000 horses. It's still a quality facility, but fiscal cutbacks have decreased the amount of upkeep on the track.

The stands at La Rinconada seat 48,000. A nominal entry fee is charged to people entering Section A or C. Those men wanting to sit in the classier Section B must wear coat and tie. A private Jockey Club is located on the top floor. Whatever the section, you'll notice

Cuadros can be officially stamped and entered into the computers in practically every little town in Venezuela. For Sunday's racing, bets can be placed up to 11am in metropolitan Caracas. While most of the streets are quiet early Sunday mornings, it's always amazing to see the gathering of mostly men frantically filling out their "sure-bet" *cuadros* at the last possible moment at the ticket windows. An average of US$6 million is bet for the 5 and 6 races on Sunday.

Bullfighting: Valencia, which features the second largest bullring in Latin America after Mexico City, is the key city for bullfighting in Venezuela. The bullring, named "Monumental," holds 27,000 people and was

that Venezuelans have a peculiar way of guaranteeing good luck: snapping their fingers while shaking their hands simultaneously to encourage their horse to speed up toward the finish line.

Off the track, the *Cinco y Seis* (5 and 6) betting game is extremely popular. Gamblers try to pick the winners of all six, or at least five, of the last six races each Sunday in Caracas, Wednesday in Maracaibo and Friday in Valencia. If only one or two *cuadros* (the official betting form in which the gambler indicates his choices) guess the six winning horses or combination of horses called *llaves*, the bet-maker can win a lot of money.

inaugurated in 1967 by the renowned Spanish matador El Cordobes and Venezuela's equally famous Curro Girón. The top bullfights are held in November and February in Valencia. However, the *corridas de toros* (bullfights) also take place in Caracas, Maracay, San Cristóbal, and Maracaibo.

Bullfights are generally held on Sundays and appear more frequently during the dry season, December through May. In addition to featuring the top matadors from Venezuela, bullfight organizers frequently bring in top matadors from Spain, which is still considered to have the most talented bullfighters in the world.

Venezuelan bowling: *Bolas criollas* is the Venezuelan variety of bowling on the green, played on dirt, grass or whatever surface is available. Although it is played in Caracas, the sport is much more popular in the country's interior. A sport for true athletes it is not, but more of an excuse for chums to get together and spend a day throwing balls, drinking some cold Polar beers and maybe placing a few bets on who can win. *Bolas criollas* has a certain blue-collar flavor to it and fits comfortably into the Venezuelan culture, which characteristically is never in a great hurry to get things done.

A target ball is tossed out 3–4 meters (12–15 ft) from the bowlers. Two teams of four

Venezuela. What could be a bigger life thrill than jumping to your death, yet, not actually jumping to your death? In a nutshell, that's what bungee jumping is all about.

It works like this. A bungee jumper attaches a harness to his or her ankles and jumps from a bridge or crane in a swan-like position. The elastic cord extends fully before the jumper actually hits the ground, pulling back up and down about three times. The jumper then hangs freely for several minutes.

Bungee jumping is becoming more popular every year, and not just for dare-devil types. In France and other parts of Europe, for example, executives are using the bungee

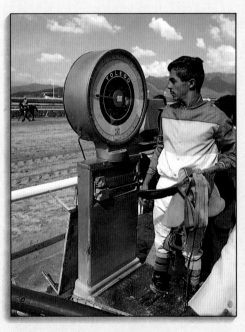

players compete. One team throws red balls and the other tosses green balls. The object of the game is to throw the ball closest to the target. The team that achieves that task each round earns a point. The teams continue to bowl until one team reaches a predetermined point total, usually 20 points.

Leaps in the void: The sport – or adventure – of bungee jumping began in New Zealand, spread to Australia and made its way to France and other European countries. Now, it's being established on a permanent basis in

jumping experience as a means to improve their decision-making skills.

"Once the executives do a jump, we've found the experience gives them a strong feeling of personal achievement and increased confidence that they can apply to their working world," says Ghislain Merviel, part of the group of French bungee experts who helped put together the program in Venezuela.

In Venezuela, bungee jumps have been done off two different bridges near Caracas, off the Teleférico cable car in the Andean city of Mérida as well as off a crane into the ocean in Margarita Island.

Left, La Rinconada race track in Caracas. **Above**, a jockey weighs in; some light entertainment.

On land, there's no denying that Venezuela offers it all to the tourist and explorer, from pristine beaches to the Andes mountain range and Amazon jungle. But for the adventurous snorkeler or scuba diver, there is a whole new world of life and breathtaking beauty to explore underwater.

Several of Venezuela's diving sites rate right up there among the top forms of marine viewing available in the Caribbean. *Aficionados* are beginning to discover that parts of the Venezuelan coastline can hold their own with Bonaire and the Cayman islands – considered two of the top diving sites in the world. The news hasn't caught on, and Venezuelan diving remains a diamond in the rough, with few tourists taking the time to discover its virgin offerings.

Anyone with a pair of goggles and a snorkel can enjoy a good deal of underwater life in Venezuela, but it should be noted that scuba diving can be dangerous if the right precautions aren't taken. There are only two compression chambers in Venezuela – one in Maracaibo and the other in La Guaira. Since quick transportation to the compression chambers may not always be possible, divers should already be relatively experienced before they come to Venezuela, or take lessons in the country with qualified instructors.

Choosing a site: Unlike many other Caribbean destinations, Venezuela's long coastline offers a whole range of diving areas, giving divers the opportunity to explore new and different marine life each time in the water. In addition to the underwater flora and fauna, divers can also explore the remnants of sunken ships, some of which have been lying dormant since the 17th century.

There are three marine-based national parks in Venezuela, all ideal for different types of diving: Los Roques National Park covers a group of over 350 tiny islands just off the northern Venezuelan coast; Morrocoy National Park is located on the state of Falcón, on the country's western coast; and Mochima National Park is in the Puerto La Cruz/ Barcelona area.

Amongst the coral, Venezuela's Caribbean coast.

As well as these National Parks, there are literally hundreds of potential sites scattered along Venezuela's coasts. Although it's possible to dive directly from the shoreline, the best underwater life is found around the plethora of islands nearby. That means that divers must make arrangements to get to the islands by boat – and off again!

The following is a rundown of what are currently considered the most exciting dive spots in Venezuela.

Chichiriviche de la Costa: One of the closest dive sites to Caracas, Chichiriviche de la Costa is a perfect place for divers to spot large groupers, angelfish and an occasional sea turtle. This bay, which also has a nice

sometimes limited here by the sediment dumped into the ocean by the river.

Puerto Cabello: Further to the west of Caracas and about a 45-minute ride from the city of Valencia is Puerto Cabello. Although this town is mainly known as an industrial port and a stopping-off point for container ships, it's possible to find some good diving on outlying islands. Isla Larga and Isla del Sapo are the major diving sites here, though the latter is more suited for snorkelers since the maximum depth around the island is 15 meters (50 ft).

The waters off Isla Larga are also home to one of the sunken ships off Venezuela – a World War II cargo ship. The rear of the boat

beach for non-diving companions, is about a three and a half hour drive west along the coast from Caracas. It's easier to get to this dive site in a four-wheel drive vehicle because of rugged coastal terrain.

In Chichiriviche, a coral wall along the sides of the bay drops down to a depth of 45 meters (145 ft), then a sand slope continues down to 90 meters (290 ft). The somewhat rocky bottom gives divers a good glimpse of rock-dwelling marine life such as lobsters and moray eels, while the shallow bay offers smaller fish, octopus and sea horses.

Although good diving and decent snorkeling can normally be expected, visibility is

sticks out of the water just off the island, while the prow is on the bottom at a depth of about 20 meters (65 ft). A coral wall has formed around the hull, giving an added dimension to the dive. In addition to the sting rays that can be seen roaming the sandy ocean bottom, many sponges, barracuda, lobsters, crabs and coral have taken over the hull of the 50-meter (165-ft) boat.

Another favourite dive spot, Los Aves, is accessible by boat from either Puerto Cabello or nearby Tukakis. Los Aves features some of the greatest variety of anemones (fish that look like flowers) that can be found in Venezuela. Another sunken boat – this one from a 17th-century fishing fleet – is located here. Exploring the wreck should be limited to experienced divers: the currents here are notoriously treacherous.

Morrocoy National Park: A three and a half hour drive west from Caracas, Morrocoy is considered the best area for beginners. The water is especially clear and divers can only go down to around 30 meters (98 ft). The sandy sea bottom is comfortable and less intimidating than the rocky bottoms found at places like Chichiriviche de la Costa and at islands in the Puerto La Cruz area. In addition, the water temperatures in Morrocoy are almost always pleasant so that a full wet-suit is not necessary.

Because of the clarity of the water, excellent snorkeling can generally be found within a short swim of these islands' shores. It's easy to spot brightly-colored angel fish, trumpet fish, needlefish and an occasional barracuda – all in water as shallow as 3 meters (10 ft) in some parts.

Night diving is a special attraction at Morrocoy. A swoop with an underwater flashlight can often reveal nocturnal creatures and colorful coral coming alive just when the sun goes down.

Higuerote: To the east of Caracas and about a 90-minute boat ride from the town of Higuerote (covering approximately 50 km, or 30 miles) lies Farallón Centinela. It and its

Perhaps the only drawback of diving in Morrocoy is that arrangements must be made in advance to take a group by boat to the islands (unless you are happy to stick to the less spectacular shore diving). But it's worth the choppy boat ride for divers wanting to get to untouched dive sites off islands such as Cayo Sombrero, Playa Mero, Cayo Norte and Cayo Sur.

The sandy sea bottom includes many species of coral, sea fans and sponges, all of which are growing out of the ocean bed.

<u>Left</u>, ready to dive; tube sponges and (above) pink anemone.

partner, Little Farallón (Faralloncito) are no larger than a couple of big rocks sticking up in the ocean. But upon entering the adjacent waters, divers can only marvel at the variety of underwater flora and fauna on display.

Farallón is actually the tip of an underwater mountain and is equipped with a lighthouse at its peak, 30 meters (100 ft) above the surface. The area is located on the continental shelf, where the ocean bottom begins a gradual drop off to a depth of over 400 meters. Amongst other attractions, an 8-meter (26-ft) long underwater tunnel approximately 27 meters (80 ft) below the surface of Little Farallón is home to sharks, large groupers, large schools of barracuda and many queen angelfish.

At Farallón, divers rarely have a clue as to what interesting creature might come creeping out of the ocean depths. Divers have even reported seeing whale sharks in the area. According to Marvi Cilli, a diving instructor for Subma Tur in Tukakis, "If you don't see a shark in Farallón Centinela, you'll never see one in your life."

The boat ride to Farallón can be hairy. But the incredible diving makes it all worthwhile. Since strong currents are the norm, divers should be experienced.

Puerto La Cruz/Barcelona: Further east – about five hours' drive from Caracas – lie the

occasional whale. It's advisable to go to the Puerto La Cruz area between July and November, when underwater visibility is at its very best.

Los Roques archipelago and La Orchila: Although they are probably the most difficult sites to dive in, for those underwater enthusiasts wanting an experience of a lifetime – one that rivals diving in Bonaire and the Cayman Islands – Los Roques and La Orchila are "musts" on the diving itinerary.

Divers who have visited Los Roques come back raving about the strikingly beautiful marine life at Gran Roque, including sharks, barracuda, jacks, spotted rays, black margates and the soft coral that inhabit the archi-

islands off Puerto La Cruz and Barcelona, including Mochima National Park, where there is some excellent deep-water diving. Unlike Morrocoy, divers in the Puerto La Cruz area can reach depths as great as 45 meters (150 ft). The currents are generally strong, and the water can be very cold so that full-body wet-suits are mandatory.

Still, divers who make the effort will be enthralled to see the greatest variety of anemones anywhere in the world. Anemones are prevalent in the Puerto La Cruz area because they thrive in the rocky terrain, which exists here instead of coral reefs. Divers have also reported seeing dolphins and an

pelago. There are also several caves at depths around 25–30 meters (80–100 ft) that will leave any underwater photographer spellbound. Just north of Los Roques lies another island, La Tortuga, which features a large underwater wall.

Since Los Roques is a relatively underdeveloped tourist site, there are some logistical problems. Because there is no compressor in Los Roques, divers must bring full tanks unless they can bring their own compressors. Although this wouldn't present a problem for those coming by boat, commercial airlines flying to Los Roques generally don't allow divers to board with full tanks.

La Orchila island is even more difficult to get to, since it is a Venezuelan military and government retreat. Although civilians are rarely allowed to visit, diving groups are sometimes invited for long weekends – which turn out to be unforgettable experiences. Since relatively few divers visit the virgin waters of La Orchila, its waters are teeming with fish and flora. Divers have reported spotting huge lobsters, moray eels, manta rays, large groupers and schools of hundreds of different fish species.

Preserving the world underwater: While it's safe to say that the environment has hardly come to the political forefront in this developing Third World country, some Venezue-

a boycott of the industry by the United States.

Other issues have received less publicity. Because they are classified as national parks, technically speaking the waters of Morrocoy, Los Roques and Mochima are off-limits to spear fishermen. Unfortunately, a large number of "poaching" spear fishermen have put them on their itineraries, not thinking twice about obtaining fish illegally at the expense of the underwater habitat. On rare occasions, a spear fisherman gets caught in the act and is reported to the authorities (the National Guard). However, it's rare for a violator to be severely punished.

Part of the problem is that there are simply not enough National Guardsmen adequately

lans in the diving community are working assiduously to make sure its pristine marine areas stay that way. It's not an easy job. "The Venezuelan people are going to ruin all that they have before they realize how lucky they were to have it," laments Marvi Cilli of Subma Tur.

One of the most long-standing environmental issues in Venezuela has been the killing of dolphins by tuna fishermen who use the archaic "purse seine nets," leading to

Left, a school of fish in Morrocoy National Park. **Above**, coral in the archipelago Las Ares de Sotavento.

to patrol the vast amount of waters that make up the national park areas. And once someone is nailed in the act of breaking the law, he can generally avoid criminal prosecution by paying the underpaid guardsmen a bribe.

Environmental damage is also done by boat owners who decide to dock on the coral. Many boaters drop their huge anchors without forethought, possibly killing entire colonies of coral. Scuba divers and snorkelers in Venezuela must be certain not to touch coral because it's easy to kill the vegetation just from slight contact. "We teach our students never to touch anything when they are diving," Cilli says.

PLACES

Despite its enormous size and some spectacular physical barriers to land travel, Venezuela is not a difficult country to explore by air. Thanks to cheap petroleum, air services are affordable and well developed, making Venezuela's domestic hub, the capital Caracas, a logical base for most travelers.

The city is certainly a pleasant, if somewhat characterless, choice: sprawling around a mountain valley like a South American version of Los Angeles, it offers an international range of modern hotels and restaurants, as well as a subway system that puts New York and London to shame.

But it is the Venezuela outside Caracas that most travelers come to see. First and foremost are the 2,500 km (1,550 miles) of Caribbean coastline, with stretches to suit every taste. The most luxurious resorts are found east of Caracas, including Venezuela's most popular tourist destination, Margarita Island.

Less developed is the coastline to the west: Choroní is a small fishing village with a colonial heart, while Chichiriviche and the Morrocoy National Park offer serenity and seclusion. For a glimpse of the most truly pristine Caribbean beaches, however, a day trip to the islands of Los Roques is a must.

Second in popularity to the beaches is the town of Mérida in the Venezuelan Andes, jumping-off point for cable car trips to snow-capped heights and horseback rides to isolated villages. The Llanos or plains area is Venezuela's Wild West, where local cowboys still work at cattle ranches and the countryside is one of South America's greatest bird-watching areas. Further south, Puerto Ayacucho is the gateway to the Amazon area, although tourism here is not as well developed as in other parts of the Amazon basin in Brazil, Ecuador and Peru.

Perhaps Venezuela's most unique experience is a visit to the Gran Sabana, also dubbed the "Lost World" after a novel by Sir Arthur Conan Doyle, who imagined the flat-topped mountains of the area to be populated by dinosaurs. Day trips now run from Caracas and Margarita into the heart of this mysterious region, which includes Angel Falls, the world's highest waterfall.

Extended journeys to the Gran Sabana often include stop-overs in the colonial city of Ciudad Bolívar, gateway to the Upper Orinoco area. And although it has little to recommend it touristically, some travelers schedule a short trip to Maracaibo – the Texan-style oil city that is crucial to Venezuela's wealth.

Preceding pages: a holiday weekend in Choroní; siesta hour in the Llanos; a young mule train leader in the Sierra Nevada de Mérida; vendors at the Caracas bus terminal. <u>Left</u>, checkpoint Carlos.

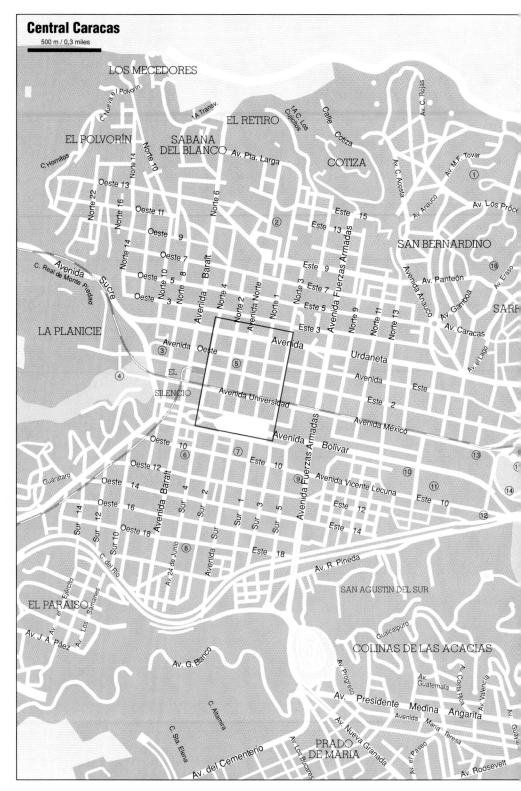

Central Caracas

500 m / 0,3 miles

LOS MECEDORES

EL POLVORÍN

SABANA DEL BLANCO

EL RETIRO

COTIZA

SAN BERNARDINO

SARF

LA PLANICIE

EL SILENCIO

EL PARAISO

SAN AGUSTIN DEL SUR

COLINAS DE LAS ACACIAS

PRADO DE MARIA

C. Nueva e I Polvorín

1A Transv.

1A C. Los Cujicitos

Calle Cotiza

C. Hornitos

Norte 14

Norte 10

Av. Pta. Larga

Av. C. Acosta

Av. C. Rojas

Av. M. F. Tovar

Av. Los Próce

Oeste 13

Norte 22

Norte 16

Oeste 11

Norte 6

Este 15

Este 13

Av. Arauco

Oeste 9

Baralt

Norte 14

Oeste 7

Este 9

Avenida Fuerzas Armadas

Avenida Sucre

C. Real de Monte Piedad

Oeste 10

Norte 5

Norte 8

Norte 3

Oeste 5

Avenida

Norte 4

Norte 2

Avenida Norte

Norte 1

Este 3

Este 5

Este 7

Norte 9

Norte 11

Norte 13

Av. Panteón

Avenida Anauco

Av. Eraso

Av. Gamboa

Oeste 3

Avenida

Oeste

Avenida

Av. Caracas

Av. el Lado

Avenida Oeste

Avenida Urdaneta

Este

EL SILENCIO

Avenida Universidad

Avenida

Este 2

Avenida México

Oeste 10

Avenida Bolívar

Este 10

Avenida Fuerzas Armadas

Avenida Vicente Lecuna

Este

Guarataro

Oeste 12

Oeste 14

Baralt

Sur 4

Este 12

Este 10

Oeste 12

Oeste 16

Sur 2

Sur 1

Sur 3

Sur 5

Este 14

Sur 14

Oeste 10

Oeste 18

Avenida

C. del Río

Avenida Sur

Este 18

Av. 24 de Junio

Av. R. Pineda

Av. el Ejército

Av. Los Samanes

Av. J. A. Páez

Av. G. Blanco

C. Altamira

C. Sta. Elena

Av. del Cementerio

Av. Los Bjcares

Av. Nueva Granada

Av. el Paseo

Av. Progreso

Av. Presidente Medina

Avenida María Teresa

Angarita

Av. Guatemala

Av. Costa Rica

Av. Valencia

Av. Guay

Av. Roosevelt

Guaicaipuro

① ② ③ ④ ⑤ ⑥ ⑦ ⑧ ⑨ ⑩ ⑪ ⑫ ⑬ ⑭ ⑱

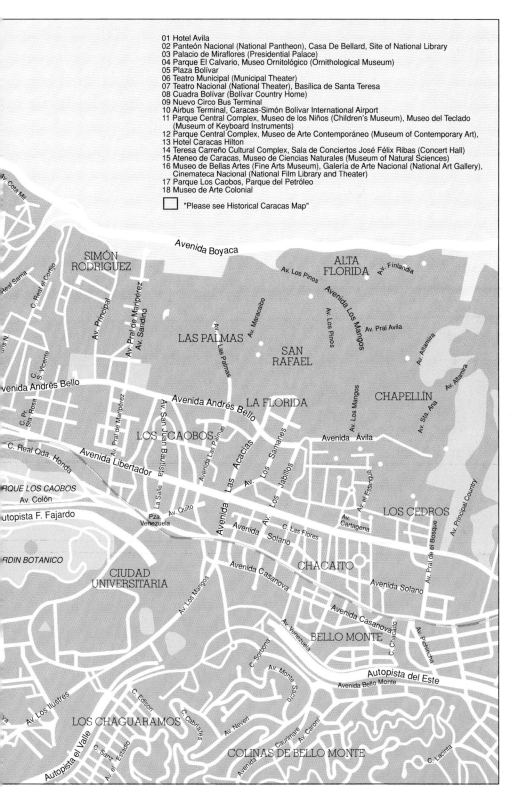

01 Hotel Avila
02 Panteón Nacional (National Pantheon), Casa De Bellard, Site of National Library
03 Palacio de Miraflores (Presidential Palace)
04 Parque El Calvario, Museo Ornitológico (Ornithological Museum)
05 Plaza Bolívar
06 Teatro Municipal (Municipal Theater)
07 Teatro Nacional (National Theater), Basílica de Santa Teresa
08 Cuadra Bolívar (Bolívar Country Home)
09 Nuevo Circo Bus Terminal
10 Airbus Terminal, Caracas-Simón Bolívar International Airport
11 Parque Central Complex, Museo de los Niños (Children's Museum), Museo del Teclado
    (Museum of Keyboard Instruments)
12 Parque Central Complex, Museo de Arte Contemporáneo (Museum of Contemporary Art),
13 Hotel Caracas Hilton
14 Teresa Carreño Cultural Complex, Sala de Conciertos José Félix Ribas (Concert Hall)
15 Ateneo de Caracas, Museo de Ciencias Naturales (Museum of Natural Sciences)
16 Museo de Bellas Artes (Fine Arts Museum), Galería de Arte Nacional (National Art Gallery),
    Cinemateca Nacional (National Film Library and Theater)
17 Parque Los Caobos, Parque del Petróleo
18 Museo de Arte Colonial

"Please see Historical Caracas Map"

CARACAS

When the conquistador Diego de Losada founded Caracas on July 25, 1567, he thought he had found an ideal location: the city would lie in a narrow valley with refreshing breezes, few mosquitos and days that were sunny and warm – but never too hot – all year round. Naturally, de Losada did not dream of the explosive growth the city has seen in recent decades. He certainly did not foresee that more than four million people would one day squeeze into the farming hamlet named for the fierce Caraca Indians.

Today, Caracas is a city with growing pains, some spectacular. Shanty towns spread up the slopes of the mountains boxing in this glitzy, glittering city. But, for the most part, the solution to overcrowding has been to build vertically, making Caracas the high-rise capital of South America that city architects love and hate. Except for the crumbling streets of the La Pastora neighborhood and Plaza Bolívar, most of the old pastel-colored colonial houses are gone, their razing mourned by few.

Colonial backwater to chaotic capital: Caracas was never an important Spanish viceroyalty and Venezuela did not have the gold, the sophisticated Indian civilizations or even the strategic importance of other South American countries. Because of this pale history, *Caraqueños* (as city inhabitants are called) worship the modern. Their petroleum wealth gives them enough money to follow that philosophy of buying new rather than repairing or restoring the old.

Colonial Caracas is difficult to imagine, looking at the Caracas of today. The Guaire River is still there, though now murky, but you'd have to strip away highways, flatten the mirrored skyscrapers and insert farm fields and palm trees before you come close to picturing the original city. If the task requires too much imagination, you can always head downtown to the Concejo Municipal, the town hall, and take a look at the

painting of *Nuestra Señora de Caracas* (Our Lady of Caracas) hanging there. Much of the canvas is occupied by the white-clad virgin, but tucked into the center bottom of the painting is the city first known as Santiago de León de Caracas as it was in the 18th century: nothing more than a collection of adobe houses with red tile roofs and courtyards. While Lima was filled with mansions for Spanish viceroys, Quito graced by more than 80 colonial churches and Potosí basked in the wealth of its silver mines, Caracas was a small malaria-ridden outpost where nothing happened except for the occasional earthquake or pirate raid.

The Concejo Municipal painting dates to the 1700s, but as recently as a century ago Caracas was still a plain dotted with trees, farmers' fields and one-story whitewashed houses. The tallest structure was the Cathedral spire, visible for miles. Within a generation, the city was transformed: by 1955 Caracas's population had swollen to 1 million and high-rises hid the spire. Since then, the popu-

lation has skyrocketed fourfold, explaining why Caracas's reservoirs are inadequate and water is rationed in the dry season, why its highways are bumper-to-bumper and why its phone and mail services – overtaxed and undermaintained – are more symbolic than useful.

Superb subway: The one exception to flagging public services is the Caracas Metro, a glistening subway system that is the envy of other developing countries and the best friend of tourists wishing to explore the city. The Metro opened in 1983 following a year of public education advertisements aimed at teaching normally unrestrained *Caraqueños* that graffiti, pushing, yelling, eating and a long list of other infractions would not be permitted. Against all expectations, the advertisements were a success. The Metro is clean, quiet, well-maintained and calm – astonishingly different from the above-ground scene of commuters who enter buses with blaring music, sometimes uncooperative drivers and pushing passengers.

Since its inauguration, the French-built subway has extended its original east-west line and added a short north-south spur. But, although a raging success, the Metro could never accommodate the city's entire demand for public transportation. That's why, above ground, Caracas is utter chaos. The streets are jammed with slow, fume-spewing buses, honking mini-buses (known as *por puestos*) and tens of thousands of taxi-cabs, along with the private vehicles of any *Caraqueño* foolish enough to drive in the city. And, like Los Angeles in the US – another car-loving city built in a basin – air pollution is at crisis level.

Air quality is so poor, in fact, that officials some years ago started the *día de parada*, a pollution-cutting policy barring every car from the roads for one day a week. The banned day was determined by the numbers on license plates. However, *Caraqueños* circumvented the law and worsened the smog by buying a second car. Studies show there are about a million vehicles in Caracas and more than 40 percent of the city's residents

Left and **right**, Caracas is Venezuela's business heart.

spend at least two hours in cars and buses daily, not because they travel long distances to work but because of traffic congestion. Another 37 percent commute for an hour.

Parking is another problem, and cars end up everywhere, including on the sidewalks, making walking tours of the city a challenge in some neighborhoods.

Unplanned expansion: There are no easy solutions to the city's problems. Already overtaxed, Caracas is still growing. Immigration to the city continues, fuelled by poor Peruvians, Ecuadorians, Colombians and other South Americans who find it easier to buy visas or forged papers into Venezuela than to continue north to the United States. The homeless and the mentally ill sleep on cardboard in shop doorways. And Caracas's footpaths are clogged by street vendors offering everything from laundry detergent to shoulder pads.

Even so, experienced South American travelers will find the Venezuelan capital empty of the abject poverty rampant in other countries. There are fewer beggars and panhandlers. The shanty towns of the poor are not built of discarded cardboard and tin sheets but of brick and cement; some squatter neighborhoods, or *barrios*, even have running water, electricity and sewage systems. Still, millions of *Caraqueños* live on the fringe of poverty and are surrounded by crime. Their work day begins long before dawn when they begin the walk from their hillside homes, where there is no public transportation, down to the closest main street or avenue. From there, many commute hours to work; the closer they live to the city center, generally the more expensive the housing is.

And housing can be expensive, in part because land is at a premium and in part because Caracas also has its share of astoundingly wealthy residents. Some are high-society families who have second homes in Miami and spend much of their free time throwing lavish parties that are eagerly reported in the local newspapers.

But Caracas is also a city for the

The efficient Caracas Metro shames New York and London.

socially mobile. Lower and middle class *Caraqueños* inevitably have more than one job; secretaries may sell cosmetics on the side, bank executives may be part owners of clothing stores, hair salon owners may dabble in real estate in their free time. The goal in every case is to stash away enough bolívars to allow them to buy VCRs, microwave ovens, new cars and other status symbols – considered more important in Caracas than having a bank account to match.

Colonial Caracas: Although Caracas prides itself on being a modern metropolis, it retains its historic corners. The best place to begin exploring the city is at the colonial center, **Plaza Bolívar**. In a country where nearly every city and town has a plaza named after Independence leader Simón Bolívar, it is some honor to be *the* Plaza Bolívar – which this Caracas square is.

Lush palms and tropical plants shade the equestrian statue of the Liberator at the plaza's center. After nightfall, lighting makes this a dramatically lovely spot. But it is during the day that the plaza hops. Children chase pigeons and squirrels around its edges, the disabled hawk lottery tickets and camera-wielding tourists snap photos. Aged *Caraqueños*, dressed as in the 1950s with white hats and light-colored suits, sit on shady benches and reminisce about a smaller, quieter capital. Less than a decade ago, their day's entertainment would have included watching the three-toed sloths sluggishly moving in the trees above. But animal-lovers successfully pushed to have the sloths, long a fixture in the plaza, moved to Parque del Este away from the youths and children who tormented the creatures.

Just as Plaza Bolívar is a hub of activity now, it was the scene of spy rendezvous, political forums, concerts, public executions, theater and even bullfights in past centuries. The plaza is flanked by Venezuela's symbols of power: the Cathedral, Archbishop's Palace, Concejo Municipal, Capitolio Nacional where the Congress meets and the so-called Casa Amarilla housing the Foreign Ministry.

The Casa Natal, Bolívar's birthplace, overshadowed by the modern city.

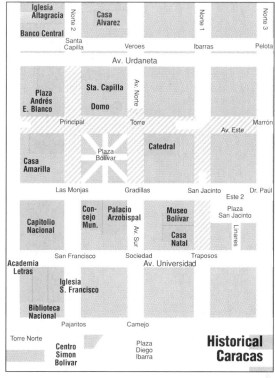

Historical Caracas

The **Cathedral** sits at the corner called La Torre – the tower – in recognition of the church spire's former lofty status. It is a curious *Caraqueño* custom, a holdover from colonial days, to identify addresses not by street or number but by the nicknames of intersections and buildings. Like La Torre, many corners have logical names, but others are frivolous or linked to now-forgotten anecdotes. "Hospital", self-explanatory, was the name of the corner where medical treatment was dispensed; "Pelota" (Ball) is the corner where ball games were once played; "Péle el Ojo" (Keep Your Eye Peeled) was once a seedy part of town; but few remember how names like "Cola de Pato" (Duck Tail) or "Aguacatico" (Little Avocado) made their way onto the Caracas scene.

Rubens and roller skating: Although rebuilt after earthquakes and modified to accommodate new architectural styles over the centuries, the Cathedral is modest by Latin American standards. But its collection of religious art is outstanding. The painting of Christ's Resurrection is said to be a Rubens donated by a French admiral who escaped harm during a storm off the coast of Venezuela. The unfinished *Last Supper* is a work by beloved Venezuelan painter Arturo Michelena while Murillo's *Purgatorio* is a haunting canvas. The crucifix in the church is a model of the cross Columbus took to the Dominican Republic in 1514; the copy was given to Venezuelan Cardinal Jose Alí Lebrun during a visit by Pope John Paul II. At Christmas, the Cathedral hosts one of Venezuela's more bizarre rituals: Yuletide roller skating in front of the church.

A side chapel in the Cathedral is dedicated to the Bolívar family. Here, under a Moorish ceiling painted to represent the Holy Trinity, lie the remains of the Liberator's wife and parents. After Simón Bolívar's death in 1830, he too was interred in the chapel, but his remains were moved to the National Pantheon in 1876.

The more than 350-year-old **Palacio Arzobispal**, remodeled yet again in recent years, is one of the few structures

SI SE OPONE LA NATURALEZA LUCHAREMOS CONTRA ELLA Y LA HAREMOS QUE NOS OBEDEZCA

SIMON BOLIVAR

AFIRMACION DE FE EN EL FUTURO POR EL LIBERTADOR FRENTE A ESTE SITIO SOBRE ESCOMBROS DEL CONVENTO DE SAN JACINTO AL CESAR EL TERREMOTO DEL 26 DE MARZO DE 1812

on the plaza to have survived earthquake damage. From 1637 to 1803 it was the bishop's residence before it was upgraded to its present status as the home of the archbishop. Next door is the **Concejo Municipal**, a structure that may have had more functions than any other in the downtown area. The original building, a seminary dedicated to Latin America's patron saint, Rosa of Lima, was destroyed by an earthquake and had to be rebuilt in 1641. Fifty-five years later, it was converted into Venezuela's only institute of higher education. In 1725, Spanish King Felipe V ordered it renamed the Royal University – a center for learning open only to young men with the proper lineage and Christian morals. In the structure's chapel, a holdover from the building's original purpose, Venezuela's Declaration of Independence was written.

It was not until 1870 that the complex became the seat of the city government. Rebuilt and modified through the years, much of the present building dates only from the turn of the century. In the Raúl Santana Museum within the Concejo Municipal is an exhibition on old Caracas, much of which is dedicated to the area around Plaza Bolívar.

On the opposite corner from the Concejo Municipal is **Edificio La Francia**, a gold-lover's paradise in the form of a historic building that houses floor after floor of tiny jewelry shops. Here exquisite earrings, necklaces, cuff links and brooches of 18-carat gold are sold by weight. Some designs incorporate now hard-to-find Margarita pearls and Venezuelan gemstones.

Convent turned Capitol: The gold-domed building at the southwest corner of Plaza Bolívar is the **Capitolio**, or Congress building. When Antonio Guzmán Blanco, one of Venezuela's string of 19th-century dictators, booted the Catholic Church out of his country, the exiled included the nuns from the Concepción convent which, once located on this spot, was notorious for its wealth. It is said that the nuns managed to escape the country with the cache of jewelry collected as dowries from the blue-blooded

Pigeons and Polaroids at the Plaza Bolívar.

women who joined the cloister. With the nuns gone, 114 days of furious construction turned the 15th-century convent into El Capitolio, opened in 1874.

The walls and ceilings of this legislative building are covered with patriotic works by Venezuelan artists, including Tovar y Tovar, whose scene of the Independence War's decisive battle of Carabobo was painted in sections in Paris then shipped to Venezuela to be fitted into the building's cupola. Here, too, is Peruvian painter Gil de Castro's famous painting of Bolívar standing on an orange and black checked floor.

The black marble box displayed in the Capitolio holds the gold key to the urn containing the Liberator's remains in the **Panteón Nacional**, the national monument half a dozen blocks north near the base of the Avila mountain. Guarded around the clock, the Panteón is the mausoleum for Venezuela's most venerated heroes. A good time to visit is just before closing at 5pm, when guards parade through the building.

Although he died alone and penniless, shunned by his fellow Venezuelans, Simón Bolívar today is one of the continent's most revered heroes and a reproduction of his childhood home has been turned into a museum. Two blocks east from the Capitolio at the corner known as Esquina de San Jacinto, the stone **Casa Natal** marks where the Liberator was born to María Concepción Palacios y Blanco and Don Juan Vicente de Bolívar, a wealthy businessman 32 years her senior. When Don Juan Vicente died at age 70, he left a young widow with four children, Simón being the youngest.

The home was destroyed by an earthquake and rebuilt, remaining in the Bolívar family until the 19th century when it was taken over by strongman Guzmán Blanco, who rented it out. Later it changed hands repeatedly for use as a commercial outlet, stable and storage space until reconstructed as a national monument. In the patio of the Casa Natal is the stone font where Simón Bolívar was baptized.

It was not far from the Casa Natal that

Inside the Bolívar museum.

the Liberator met one of the biggest challenges to his campaign to free the country from Spanish rule. Painter Tito Salas captured in oil the moment when Bolívar, on the plaza at the corner of San Jacinto, addressed the priests and people who claimed an 1812 earthquake that destroyed the plaza was God's message for him to stop his seditious talk. "If Nature opposes us, we will fight against her and we will make her obey us," Bolívar exclaimed, and the famous quote is recorded in huge letters on a side of the building at this corner.

A few blocks to the west of the Casa Natal is Caracas's most misnamed neighborhood, **El Silencio**, The Silence. Even the oldest *Caraqueños* don't remember a time when the title was appropriate for the traffic-clogged area where boisterous sidewalk vendors abound.

Slum renovation: Years ago, this working class neighborhood was designated as the guinea pig in the city's boldest experiment in urban planning. Under President Isaías Medina Angarita, the miserable slums of El Silencio were flattened and replaced with Venezuela's first urban project – the model El Silencio *bloques*. The whitewashed apartment buildings were designed by architect Carlos Raúl Villanueva to allow sun and air to enter and, even today, their blue shutters and window grilles give them a colonial touch.

Although this neighborhood is far from the eastside *barrios* of the rich, it once boasted the most opulent home in the entire country: **Miraflores**, the colonial mansion now used as the working office of the Venezuelan President.

In 1880, when President Joaquín Crespo began to construct the house for use as his home, rumors flew. Some claimed the walls were reinforced with iron to make the building earthquake-proof, that it was the most expensive house ever seen in the country, that the initials of Crespo and his wife were incorporated into designs all over the home. The rumors were true and when the house was finished, it was magnificent. Unfortunately, in the eight years it

Late nights at L'Attico bar and restaurant.

took to construct the mansion, Crespo died in battle; the man whose name is most associated with Miraflores never had the chance to live there.

Since the turn of the century, when the government purchased the home, Miraflores has been used by every president as a work-place. It is decorated with European tapestries, damasks and French and Italian furniture. Sometimes it opens to the public; check with the National Tourism Office (Corporturismo) for security clearance and visiting hours. Atop a steep hill to the west of El Silencio is Caracas's oldest park, **El Calvario**, built in the 1870s. A Greek Orthodox church at its base and the smell of eucalyptus, carried on breezes from the trees at the peak, mark the start of the uphill trek to the park. Named for the stations of the Cross once found at its summit, this was a gathering spot for pilgrims who, with lit candles in hand, followed curving paths up the hill past the crosses that marked each station.

Now the pilgrims and candles are gone. The few crosses that survive are in

museums, and the paths have been replaced by steep stairs. Still, a chapel remains at the top of the hill, a leftover from one dictator's campaign to transform the park into the replica of a spot that impressed him in France.

The view of the city is outstanding from these hilltop gardens, which are interspersed with marble busts of venerated Venezuelans, including Bolívar, pianist Teresa Carreño, composer Pedro Elías Gutiérrez and Bolívar's teacher, Simón Rodríguez. Because of robbery reports, however, trips to El Calvario are not recommended after nightfall and, during the day, should only be made in groups.

High-rise living: A century ago, *Caraqueños* went to El Calvario to get a bird's eye view of the city. Now many get the same view out the windows of their highrise apartments. Except for the very wealthy who live in large homes (*quintas*) surrounded by exuberant flowers, mango trees and bougainvillea, and the poor, who live in small hillside shanties called *ranchitos*, *Caraqueños* live

Chess on the Sabana Grande boulevard; tropical Gothic at Santa Capilla.

in skyscrapers (or "sky crappers" as one city guide, struggling with English, proudly proclaims). By law, the sky-scrapers in this earthquake zone are erected according to strict seismic sensitive plans. The last big quake, in the late 1960s, confirmed that the majority of buildings were tremor-proof.

Though high above the ground, *Cara-queños* haven't lost their farming roots. Green vines trail down the sides of buildings, bright flowers spring from window planters and, inside apartments, potted plants thrive in the warm and humid climate despite worrisome pollution from automobile exhausts.

But Caracas is not all high-rise concrete jungle. The biggest outdoor gathering place for pedestrian fun is **Sabana Grande**, a trendy car-free boulevard that stretches 2 km (1 mile) from Plaza Venezuela to the Chacaíto subway station, the latter unmistakably marked by a giant yellow kinetic sculpture of acclaimed Venezuelan artist Jesús Soto. Upscale boutiques, shoe stores, perfume shops, bookstores and outdoor cafes line one side of the sidewalk while informal vendors lay out their goods on tables and plastic sheets on the other. Sabana Grande is the glittering side of Caracas, its playground for the well-heeled and its corner of conspicuous consumption.

This is very different from the Indian markets of other countries, where handicrafts are proffered amidst cut-rate clothing, tires and dog leashes. Caracas is sophisticated. There may be discount clothing and tacky home decorations, but there are also sturdy hammocks, finely crafted avant garde jewelry and fashionable shoes mixed among the untaxed sales items. Their buyers are young couples strolling hand-in-hand down the mall, families out for ice cream, businessmen who stop at Sabana Grande's bars for a cold Polar beer or shot of Pampero rum after work and fashion-setting women who, in mini-skirts, Spandex slacks and spiked heels, come here to be seen.

The top gathering place in Sabana Grande is the **Gran Café**, its green and

Guitar session on the Sabana Grande boulevard.

white striped canopy signaling it as Venezuela's favorite outdoor coffee shop. Cappuccinos generously topped with cinnamon and whipped cream compete with the more traditional range of coffee offerings and elaborate ice cream concoctions while guitarists, Andean flute players and mime artists vie for attention and tips.

Gran Café patrons lounge for hours, often hidden behind dark glasses, as they discuss politics, music, prices or, inevitably, the latest development in the petroleum industry. And this is the haunt of sports enthusiasts seeking betting updates on the popular *5 y 6* horse racing cards. Not far away are the checkerboard tables occupied by chess *aficionados*, serious players oblivious to the stares and comments of passers-by.

Sabana Grande has a little bit of everything, including record and tape shops with the latest in Caribbean music, bookstores, T-shirt shops and the ubiquitous *perfumerías* or perfume and cosmetic shops that are so popular here. (Both men and women in Venezuela are heavy cologne users and getting stuck in a packed elevator in Caracas can wreak havoc on a tourist's olfactory glands.) Upscale inns like **Hotel Lincoln Suites** sit just blocks from the "hot sheets" hotels, as they are known by gringos in the city, with rooms at hourly rates available for frustrated lovers. Top-notch restaurants are tucked in among bakeries and budget-priced ethnic cafes offering Middle Eastern *falafels*, Spanish *tascas* and egg rolls. And one of the city's best shops for local handicrafts, **Artesanía Venezolana**, is found across from the **Plaza Venezuela fountain** at the western edge of the pedestrian mall. The huge circular fountain is a lure at night, when multicolored lights turn the spray of water into a visual show.

While pedestrian traffic in the Sabana Grande mall runs all day and most of the night, there is nearly as much activity under the ground. The Caracas Metro line runs directly below this popular boulevard, with subway stops at Plaza Venezuela and the mall's end, Chacaíto, as well as an intermediary station called

A friendly disagreement.

Sabana Grande. In imitation of life above ground, these subway stations sport their own collections of shops.

Shopping paradise: Serious shoppers may head off to some of the other commercial areas, including **Central Comercial Ciudad Tamanaco** – better known as CCCT (pronounced: *say-say-say-tay*), the continent's largest shopping mall and one of the Venezuelan capital's most exclusive collections of boutiques. Mixed in with the designer stores and hair salons are ice cream shops, movie theaters and bistros.

Another shopping option is the **Paseo Las Mercedes**, an older but also exclusive shopping mall in the upscale Las Mercedes neighborhood, where the bluebloods of Caracas high society have homes. Among its stores and restaurants, Paseo Las Mercedes also has a bookstore run by the continent's oldest Audubon Society branch. Its offerings include specialized volumes on flora, fauna and Indian cultures, in addition to good coffee table books on Venezuela. The main street leading to Paseo Las

Mercedes is lined with informal vendors selling hammocks, baskets and other local handicrafts (as well as goods from Peru and Ecuador).

Las Mercedes, like other commercial neighborhoods, is busy day and night. *Caraqueños* unwind in a big way, especially on weekends when nearly every kind of live music is available, from Mexican mariachis to Latin jazz to salsa. Pitch-black discos are where energetic couples take control of the dance floor while illicit trysts take place in the shadows; these clubs are so dark that doormen literally lead patrons to their seats with flashlights. Some allow only couples; others allow groups regardless of the gender but single women may find themselves turned away at the door. For conversation, the city abounds with excellent restaurants and cozy jazz bars.

However, if you have never seen Caribbean dancing, you're missing a golden opportunity if you don't dress up and stop by a discotheque. Venezuelans take their music seriously (*see Pop Culture Paradise, pages 77–81*) and their danc- **Classical notes.**

ing is amazing. Keep in mind, though, that the music may be extremely loud; bring some earplugs.

Some older *Caraqueños* will say the now cacophonous city was better off as a rural enclave where nightlife was non-existent and troubles were few. But most proudly note that Caracas has made a name for itself, not only as a place where money – rather than class – buys social status, but also as an oasis for the theater, arts and museums.

Museum Mecca: The city's loveliest museum is the **Quinta Anauco**, a re-stored coffee *hacienda* converted into a showpiece of colonial art and furniture; its slave quarters contain a reference library dedicated to colonial art and history. Located on Avenida Panteón in the San Bernardino neighborhood, this home with Andalusian and Moorish touches was built in 1797 by a well-connected military official. The owner fled to Curaçao with others loyal to the Spanish Crown during the revolution and the home was confiscated and rented to the Marqués del Toro, a friend and collaborator of Simón Bolívar. A bust of del Toro sits amid the orchids and citrus trees in the tropical garden outside the museum. Bolívar was a frequent guest at the house, which he loved for its view, and he spent his last night in Caracas at the Quinta Anauco before heading to Colombia – where he died.

For other museums, you must head to **Parque Central**, rising tall and glittering from a tangle of downtown highways. Parque Central consists of 44-story towers that, when started in 1966, were designed to meet the city's housing needs. Fraught with delays, funding problems and construction setbacks during the two decades it took to complete, Parque Central is now the crux of the city's arts center and home to the **National Tourism Office** (Corpoturismo) headquarters.

On the ground floor of the complex is the **Museo de los Niños**, a children's museum with everything from a giant keyboard upon which youngsters walk to a radio studio where they can broadcast their own shows. The museum is

Caracas has a vibrant theater scene.

easily identifiable by the shrieks and laughter of grade school students inside. Nearby is the **Museo de Arte Contemporáneo** with a collection featuring the finest of Venezuela's contemporary artists, including sculptor Marisol, painter Alejandro Otero and kinetic artist Jesús Soto. Joining the native sons' work is an international collection including paintings by Léger, Matisse, Miró and Picasso and the sculptures of Henry Moore and Fernando Botero.

In this area, known as Bellas Artes, Caracas's best museums are within walking distance of the **Ateneo** and **Teatro Teresa Carreño**, a massive arts and music complex featuring everything from stage plays to jazz concerts. Venezuela's Symphony Orchestra and its Youth Orchestra perform at Teresa Carreño while avant garde theater performances, dance classes and chamber music recitals can be found at the Ateneo.

A block east of the Ateneo are the **Museo de Bellas Artes** and **Galería de Arte Nacional**, sharing a classical-style building where swaying ferns and palms lend shade to a peaceful courtyard. The Fine Arts Museum proudly displays the works of Mexican muralists Diego Rivera and Rufino Tamayo and the distinctive bloated figures of Colombian artist Botero. The National Gallery exhibits only the works of Venezuelan artists, among them Armando Reverón with his sea scenes, Tito Salas (who dedicated much of his work to the life of Simón Bolívar), Arturo Michelena with his epic and heroic paintings and Herrera Toro, known for his religious themes. Across from the Museo de Bellas Artes sits the **Museo de Ciencias Naturales** with exhibits on anthropology, archaeology, mineralogy and other sciences.

The great outdoors: Like the Venezuelans in the countryside, who would just as soon sleep outside in hammocks as under a roof, the *Caraqueños* continue a love affair with nature as evidenced by the numerous parks dotting the city. **Parque Los Caobos**, planted with the mahogany, or *caobo*, trees that inspired its name, is a huge public park near the

Swotting at Caracas University.

entrance to the Art and Science Museums. Here mimes and puppeteers gather at midday, little girls dressed in tulle and white patent leather shoes come with their parents on Sundays and older children skateboard and bike along concrete paths that cut among fountains, palm trees and bamboo.

Across the highway from the north side of Parque Los Caobos is the **Jardín Botánico**, a verdant and exotic botanical garden where tropical trees, vines and flowers of every type imaginable are found. For a more intimate brush with nature, try the tiny park called **Los Chorros** tucked against Caracas's northern hillside. Neighborhood children come here to collect the mangos that drop from its shady trees or float homemade boats down the skinny stream that runs through the park. After wading in the same stream, families dine in the open air over a *parrilla*, sizzling grilled meats sold at the park's restaurant. And lovers stroll through along the paths, past the park's mountain waterfall, at sunset. Although pretty all year round,

Los Chorros breeds some ferocious mosquitos during the rainy season, so repellent may be in order for any visits to this park.

The favorite park for many youngsters is **El Paraíso** with its zoo, the city's oldest. However, the variety of animals on view is much greater at **Parque Zoológico Caricuao**, at the end of the subway line. Opened in 1977, the Caricuao zoo has hundreds of animals displayed in their natural habitats; a petting zoo of domestic animals allows children to get close. There are food kiosks to sate hungry and thirsty visitors and a small train to transport zoo-goers around the facility.

There is also a zoo at the massive **Parque del Este**, designed by Brazilian landscape architect Robert Burle Marx and recently connected to the subway system via a Metro stop named for the park. Military inductees sweating in their uniforms jog along the paved roadways that cut the park while the more sedentary make their way around on the motorized train that winds past the zoo,

The open spaces of the Parque del Este.

near the lagoons where paddle boats can be rented and not far from the planetarium. Outdoor concerts and dance performances are frequently held at the acoustic shell just inside the park entrance. A fixture in the park, the replica of Christopher Columbus's ship the *Santa María,* has been spruced up.

Lofty landmarks: From inside Parque del Este, the view of **Mount Avila** – rising up on the city's north side – is an impressive one. The Avila is the symbol of the city, the green wall of mountain that separates Caracas from the Caribbean sea and the port of La Guaira. On sunny days, fluffy white clouds nestle at the Avila's peak; dark clouds gathering above it signal the inevitability of the drenching rain that floods city streets in minutes, mercilessly pounding pavement and pedestrians alike until, quickly, the sun returns.

In the foothills of the Avila is the asphalt ribbon known as the **Cota Mil**, a 1,000-meter (3,280-ft) high freeway with parking areas where motorists can pull over and watch storms roll in over

the city or, in the evenings, see the hovels of the poor transformed into lights that dot the valley like thousands of stars. Also after sunset, the Cota Mil's lookout points, or *miradores*, become an extended lovers' lane crowded with parked couples.

An even better spot for a view of the city is the **Teleférico** (cable car) – when it works. After it opened in 1957, the Teleférico was a sparkling example of modern technology and it regularly carried *Caraqueños* and tourists from the city up to the **Avila National Park**. At the summit is the Humboldt Hotel, a white elephant built by the dictator Marcos Pérez Jiménez, which is nearly inaccessible when the cable car is out of service. The same cable car was idle for nearly a decade in the 1970s when it was closed for repairs.

Hiking trails and roads, best approached by jeep, lead up the 2,765 meters (9,070 ft) to the top of the Avila, where the novelty of an ice-skating rink, cascades of water, fields of flowers and a nature paths are lures. Eucalyptus, juniper and even pine trees form the backdrop for this park where yellow and white *querre querre* birds flit among the trees and noisy *guacharaca* birds stuff themselves on ripe mangos and mulberries. If you need directions, ask the volunteer park rangers or the residents of **Galipán**, a town of Canary Island immigrants who raise flowers and fruits to sell in Caracas's markets.

Although it is actually at the base, not in the park itself, a well-loved landmark of the Avila is the hotel that carries its name. Built by the Rockefellers from North America half a century ago, the **Hotel Avila** has not aged as well as it might. But Caraqueños still speak with fondness of the days when it was *the* spot for top-flight musicians to perform for the hotel's guests, among them movie star guests and diplomats. Despite its slightly faded charm, big-name performers like unchallenged salsa king Oscar d'León still wow audiences here from time to time. And there is no more romantic outdoor swimming pool in the city than the Avila pool, hidden among tropical foliage.

Left, jammed traffic, mobile market. **Right**, forever ready to swing at Caracas cemetery.

COLONIA TOVAR

A cool mountain breeze wafts into the restaurant where blond, blue-eyed waiters in *lederhosen* serve up *sauerkraut* and *wienerschnitzel*. The meal might be washed down with a cold stein of German beer, and afterwards the guests might stroll out to their Alpine hotel. But this is not the Tyrol or Bavaria; the scene is Colonia Tovar, a mountain village near Caracas that was first settled by German immigrants and maintained many of its traditions during generations of total isolation.

Venezuela's 19th-century war of independence stripped the countryside of its slave workers and farmers. To ease the labor shortage, immigration laws were rewritten to entice European farmers. In 1843, 145 men, 96 women and 117 children from the Black Forest community of Kaiserstuhl boarded a French vessel to begin their ocean crossing to Venezuela where they had agreed to farm virgin land owned by a wealthy creole named Martín Tovar. Smallpox aboard ship claimed 70 lives and put the vessel in

quarantine when it finally reached Venezuela. After 40 days of isolation, the confused colonists were allowed on shore in Choroní, down the coast from Caracas.

But news of the disease had spread and there was no welcoming committee, no fanfare, not even transportation. Accompanied by their own priest, tailor, teacher, druggist, carpenter, printer and blacksmith, the colonists trudged 30 km (20 miles) up the mountains to Tovar's lands, burdened by their farm implements, fruit trees, seeds and the barley that would make their beer.

A second boatload of Germans arrived soon after but Venezuela's cold reception of the first immigrants was never forgotten. The ill-will was further fueled when the Germans were told they would need signed permission from the government bureaucrats each time they wanted to leave the town. In response to this demand, the colonists set up the most closed community the country had ever seen.

Isolated, Colonia Tovar residents recreated the Black Forest community they had left. They ate German-style sausages, drank beer produced at their brewery, kept traditional customs and married their blond-haired children off to one another. Venezuela's many 19th-century conflicts passed them by nearly unawares and for more than a century they survived, excluded and excluding, in the cool, sunny clime of their highland home.

But with the end of World War II came the fad of outdoor treks, which lured Venezuelans to the peaceful town. Robust walkers made nine-hour weekend trips from Caracas 30 km away, while those with less stamina mounted mules and sauntered up the hills surrounding the Humboldt Valley. Many stayed in the Hotel Selva Negra (Black Forest Hotel), now more than a half-century old. They drank coffee grown by the colonists, ate barley bread and bartered over bouquets of brilliantly-colored flowers raised in fields around the town. Gradually, Colonia Tovar's walls of isolation began to crumble.

With the arrival of a paved road in 1963 came regular visitors who bought baskets of strawberries and blackberries, handcrafted cuckoo clocks and local beer. With the outside contact, the German language began slowly to disappear. There is still a preponderance of fair-skinned, light-haired Tovar

Descendants of German immigrants...

residents but their grandchildren have dark hair and Spanish names. And the once traditional Black Forest costumes are now donned more to appease tourists than because of local custom.

Seen from a distance, Tovar buildings look like they have been culled from the pages of a European magazine. On closer inspection, however, the dark wood cross-beams that cut their exteriors and seem to support their ceilings are just painted on. And the quaint shops and handicrafts exist for the busloads of tourists that arrive each weekend, not for local residents.

Picturesque Tovar has its dark side, too. Locals refuse to talk about what is rumored to be a disproportionately high incidence of birth defects among families, owing to decades of intermarrying. *Caraqueños* claim handicapped residents are kept out of sight. Still, the village – inspiration for the fictional town in Isabel Allende's contemporary bestseller, *Eva Luna* – is a curious and anachronistic escape from Caracas. Travelers winding their way up from the smoggy capital see palm trees and pines side by side. By day, the air is brisk but at night it gets downright cold. The streets are steep but they make for pleasant strolling. At the main plaza is the L-shaped Catholic church, drawn from the plans of a chapel in Germany. The interior is simple, its most valuable possession being the organ made by a local craftsman. On the bell tower you can see inscriptions in German.

Behind the church are the town's three mills – for coffee, wheat and corn. And a walk downhill on the main roadway from the church is the cemetery, hidden among pine trees at the side of the road. The graves of the first German immigrants are marked by checkerboard patterns of ceramic tiles. Burials continue in the old-style way, with lines of black-clad mourners following the pallbearers – all on foot – down the hill from the church and into the graveyard.

Fine local potters and woodworkers display their goods in shops around the town. Hot breads, bowls of fruit or chilled glasses of strawberry juice sold at outdoor cafes and kiosks sustain visitors until they work up enough of an appetite for German sausage and *strudel* – always, but always, washed down with a beer. ∎

...still populate their village in the Andes.

Caraqueños get up early to go to work. They get up even earlier to go to the beach, and the closest stretch of sand and ocean is over the mountains at the coastal strip known as **El Litoral**. On weekends, the highways are filled with beach-bound mini-buses carrying bathing-suit clad families, women with coolers of food and young men armed with cold Polar beers. Family groups mostly head for **Balneario de Camurí Chico**, a full-service beach with change houses, bathrooms, restaurants, outdoor cafés, and beach chairs and awnings to rent. Its shallow, peaceful waters are usually lined with splashing toddlers.

Other *balnearios* in the area are **Los Caracas**, **Caraballeda** and **Naiguatá.** Weekend lifeguards are on duty at the beaches designated as *balnearios* and, during the peak seasons of Holy Week, Carnival and summer vacations, helicopters also patrol El Litoral in search of swimmers and boaters in trouble as well as surfers who find themselves drifting too far out with the current.

At intervals, some of these beaches along the Caribbean near La Guaira, Caracas's port, are so polluted that swimming is banned, although many Venezuelans ignore the warnings and dive in anyway. For the more prudent, beaches farther along – including some with imaginative names like **Playa Pantaleta** (Panty Beach) and **Todosana** (All Healthy) offer cleaner waters. When swimming is out, there is still yachting, surfing and windsailing.

The **Macuto Sheraton** and **Meliá Caribe** hotels on the waterfront rent watersports equipment. Those who prefer sunning beside a freshwater pool with an ocean view can check into the hotels and escape El Litoral's broiling sun. Or you can just stroll up to one of the many outdoor cafés, order fresh fried fish and a beer and then people-watch from under an awning.

Play is what draws *Caraqueños* to El

The secluded hideaway of Todosana beach.

Litoral, but work is what keeps this area bustling. **La Guaira**, known as Huayra by its original inhabitants, the Tarma Indians, is Venezuela's most important port with modern wharves and contemporary buildings that contrast sharply with the small colonial homes lining its streets. Two forts here, **El Vigía** and **La Pólvora**, were for long the only means of defense against pirates and buccaneers who knew Caracas awaited them just beyond the mountain.

From 1734 on, the defense of the port and the commercialization of Venezuelan goods fell under the direction of the controversial Guipuzcoana Company, located in the **Casa Guipuzcoana** – one of the loveliest restored colonial buildings in the country. This import company, under the mandate of the King of Spain, built roads, introduced new crops (including cotton) and exported the harvests of local farmers. But as its monopoly grew, so did its underhandedness. The company created false shortages to manipulate prices, underpaid cacao farmers and fueled the hatred of local residents. Despite boycotts, armed revolts by growers and even complaints to the Crown, Casa Guipuzcoana ruled the port for 58 years.

Just down the block and across the street from Casa Guipuzcoana is the **Museo Fundación John Boulton**, an 18th-century colonial home now housing a rich collection of documents, maps and plans dating from the city's foundation as well as antique weapons and furniture. The tall house with its ample balcony was built in 1720 by John Boulton, a young Englishman and exporter of coffee, cacao and tobacco and an importer of flour, oil and brandy. When ships returning to Venezuela from Great Britain were not full, stone from Scotland was used for ballast. That stone makes up the floors of the house.

Before being converted into a museum, the house remained for 140 years in the hands of the Boultons, who grew to be an influential family in Venezuela. Today in the society pages of Caracas's newspapers, the Boulton surname surfaces with regularity.

Three km (2 miles) east of La Guaira is **Macuto** – although the distinctions between towns are now clear only to local residents, for the beachfront villages all seem to run together with no clear borders. This town, named for the Indian chief Guaicamacuto, was the beach station for the Teleférico (cable car) in its early years when it not only went up the Avila from Caracas but came down again on the coastal side.

Along the beach in Macuto is the **Paseo Macuto**, a concrete walkway bordered by seagrape and almond trees along the beach called **Balneario Macuto**. Here, too, along the waterfront, is the wonderful and wacky **Museo Reverón**, the whimsical home-workshop built in 1921 by artist Armando Reverón. Called the Castillete de Las Quince Letras when he was alive and now a museum, it provided the inspiration for Reverón's main artistic themes: the beach and the sea. Its eclectic design hides the dark side of Reverón, a man plagued by nervous breakdowns. He died in a sanatorium during one period of hospitalization.

Left, "jungle juice" for sale. **Right**, La Sabana beach.

LOS ROQUES

"Heaven on Earth" is how Christopher Columbus described the archipelago of Los Roques, lying some 128 km (80 miles) north of La Guaira. These 60 *cayos* (cays, or reef-formed islands), boast Venezuela's most pristine beaches and are rapidly becoming one of the country's hottest tourist destinations.

Despite this new-found popularity, Los Roques remain tranquil and unspoiled. That's thanks partly to their remoteness, and partly because they have been protected as a national park since 1972. The archipelago is flung across an area of more than 225,000 hectares (556,000 acres), making it one of the Caribbean's largest marine preserves.

Wildlife sanctuary: While the archipelago bakes under a blazing sun all day, at night it is caressed by cooling trade winds that help keep annoying insects at bay. Most of the *cayos* are low, their pure white sands barely rising above the surface of the turquoise and emerald waters. A few have rocky outcroppings. Clumps of mangrove trees, cactus and seagrass add splotches of green to the arid landscape that is home to iguanas and lizards. Marine turtles lumber ashore to lay their eggs.

Frigate birds, brown boobies, scarlet ibises and herons abound. The tiny western island, **Selesqui**, has the largest bird population, earning it the nickname "Cayo Bobo Negro" (Black Booby Cay). Flocks of gulls nest on **Cayo Francés** (French Cay).

Snorkelers and divers will be delighted by schools of rainbow-colored parrot fish, royal blue angelfish, puffy porcupine fish and slender trumpet fish. There are molluscs, sponges, sea urchins and many varieties of coral including gorgonia, brain and fire. Occasionally you might see a barracuda or moray eel.

The islands of Los Roques have been known for centuries – by people on both sides of the law. But because they have no fresh water, they have not supported

Testing the waters.

permanent settlement until recently.

Long ago, the archipelago may have held some mystical significance. Prehispanic ceramics, possibly used in sacred or magical ceremonies, have been found on four islands. Cayo Estación Sur has yielded a number of squat human figurines, including a man with "doughnut" eyes, and women with tiny arms and hands and large rectangular heads that have been pricked or incised.

More recently, Los Roques have been a secret haven for Venezuelan sun-worshippers, who flew in by private plane for a day's amusement or sailed their yachts over for a long weekend. During his first presidential term in the 1970s, Carlos Andrés Pérez came here for sybaritic get-aways, anchoring his yacht offshore while he enjoyed an early-morning jog on the beach.

In the 1980s, when the Venezuelan currency crashed and the country imposed import restrictions, *contrabandistas* (contraband runners) found Los Roques to be a convenient stopping-off place. Restaurateurs in Caracas had a secret pipeline from the Caribbean for obtaining duty-free liquor, crystal and fine china.

Foreign invasion: Today Los Roques are being discovered by sailors and sport fishermen from abroad. The islands are reputed to offer some of the world's best bonefishing – both in numbers and size. Schools of hundreds average 1.4 to 1.8 kg (3 to 4 lb), while trophy size is over 3 kg (7 lb).

Two small airlines, CAVE and Aerotuy, have instituted the first regular, scheduled services to the archipelago. They are also among a handful of companies operating live-on boats for cruise, fishing and dive programs.

The only permanent settlement is on **Gran Roque**, the largest island. At 3 km (2 miles) long and scarcely more than 1 km wide, that is none too big. It has the only paved airstrip in Los Roques, a small *pensión* and the homes of about 150 families of fishermen. Their colorful wooden boats are beached on the sand, not far from hungry pelicans dive-bombing fish in the shallows.

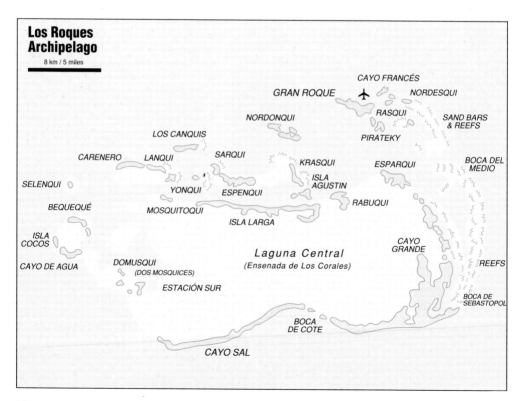

Los Roques Archipelago

8 km / 5 miles

Everything except fish is imported from the mainland. There's a desalinization plant, but the Navy sometimes has to supply fresh water.

Fishermen haul in *pargo* (red snapper), *mero* (grouper), lobster and shellfish. Their main market is La Guaira, but since the currency was devalued in the 1980s, many catches of lobster and crab have been spirited away to restaurants in Aruba, where they command a higher price. From time to time, moratoriums on the harvest of queen conch have been instituted to preserve their waning numbers, but as visitors can testify, the piles of empty pink conch shells on the beaches continue to grow.

Yachtsmen can sometimes buy their evening meal direct from passing fishermen. On Gran Roque, the favored dish is *sancocho de pescado* (fish soup). *Consomé de chipi-chipi* is also savored. The little clams that go into this pot are said to be an aphrodisiac. They're found mainly around the island of **Crasqui**.

Biological research: Researchers at the **Los Roques Scientific Foundation** on **Cayo Estación Sur** (formerly Dos Mosquises) have been trying to farm lobster and crab, which are being dangerously overfished. So far the lobster experiment has failed, but the crab shows promise. The foundation also studies marine turtles – you can see tanks of them at the station – and investigates a range of other ecological issues.

Launched in 1963, the foundation is supported by grants from the government and private industry. Lab courses in marine ecology are open to small numbers of qualified students. The Navy helped build the laboratory, and there's a dirt landing strip.

About 40 islands in Los Roques are large enough to have names. Hundreds of other tiny sand cays, rocks and coral reefs surface only at low tide.

Over the years, many names in the archipelago have changed due to fishermen writing phonetic spellings on their charts. North East Cay is now Nordisqui, Sailors Cay is Selesqui, Domus Cay (Home Cay) is Dos Mosquises (now Cayo Estación Sur).

The pristine cays of Los Roques.

THE EAST COAST

The Caribbean coastline east of Caracas – often referred to as the Gold Coast – may be Venezuela's best kept secret. Its apparently endless succession of secluded, palm-fringed tropical hideaways has made this a paradise for sun-worshippers and beach bums of every age and inclination. It has long been a favorite destination with Venezuelans, but only now are foreign travelers discovering the region's hedonistic joys.

But the lineup is more than just the golden sands and crystal waters always associated with the Caribbean. Some of South America's oldest cities lie along the Gold Coast, and their colonial buildings, slow-paced charm and unique folkloric customs remain intact.

Gateway to the east: The stretch of sandy seaside starts with **Barcelona**, a city on the west banks of the Neverí River, just 5 km (3 miles) from the ocean. Two centuries ago, this was an important port for food shipments to the nearby Dutch Antilles, and commerce remains the mainstay of the local economy today.

Barcelona, formed in 1671, is actually the union of two older villages – Nueva Barcelona del Cerro Santo and San Cristóbal de Cumanagota; the site for the new town center was a point equidistant from the two. Although a bustling commercial city on the surface, Barcelona is actually rich with colonial architecture. Most notable are the ruins of the **Casa Fuerte** on Avenida 5 de Julio at the **Plaza Bolívar**.

The Casa Fuerte was originally a Franciscan monastery but independence forces booted out the friars in 1811 when they publicly supported the Spanish Crown. Five years later, the structure was fortified to make it a military facility and it proved its worth when it successfully held back the first attack by Royalist soldiers. However, in April of 1817, the Crown forces destroyed the facility and killed at least 1,600 people inside, including women, children and the elderly who had taken refuge there.

Construction of the **Iglesia San Cristóbal** on the Plaza Bolívar started in 1748 but delays and setbacks caused by earthquakes dragged out work on the building for nearly another 25 years. In the small chapel connected to the cathedral is a crystal container with the remains of Italian martyr St Celestino, brought from Rome in 1777.

Also on the plaza is the **Museo de la Tradición**, on Calle Juncal diagonally opposite the **Casa del Gobierno**. This, Barcelona's oldest colonial home, was erected in 1671. Although seriously damaged in an earthquake more than 150 years ago, the house has been restored and offers a fine example of a colonial kitchen. When slavery was legal, it was outside this structure that slave sales were held every weekend. The museum contains everything from colonial art to furniture. It also has a number of statues of saints, brought from Spain with early colonists, and once displayed in the cathedral. Look for the *posaderas* – huge rounded boulders that were placed outside the front

Preceding pages: the palm-fringed Playa Colorada (Red Beach) between Puerto La Cruz and Cumaná. **Left,** a leap in the deep. **Right,** a jewelry range, Puerto La Cruz.

doors of homes and used by night-time visitors who sat on them and drank coffee with their hosts.

The museum is also home to a set of silver spurs that allegedly belonged to José Tomás Boves, the renegade fighter who terrorized Bolívar's forces and became known as the Spanish "butcher". The route from Caracas along the east coast is the same one that, more than a century ago, 20,000 Venezuelans took to escape the bloody wrath of Boves. He and his fierce troops of Indians and escaped slaves came down upon Caracas with such a vengeance that 75 percent of the population fled – many of them on foot – in a fearful migration that continued all the way to Cumaná. Barely more than half survived the long journey plagued with disease, starvation and Indian attacks.

Booming resort: From Barcelona there is a 47-km (28-mile) road to the northeast to **Higuerote**. From Monday to Friday, Higuerote is a peaceful town with several thousand residents. But on weekends the population swells 20

times, with beach goers and yacht owners flocking to this resort town with docks, a ferry service to nearby islands and countless weekend homes for rich *Caraqueños*. Although Higuerote was once a clean and appealing town, its proximity to Caracas has brought it more visitors than local services can handle and the water along the coast here is polluted. Motor boats have infringed upon the once quiet atmosphere, too. However, there is still decent swimming at the small islands off shore.

But if isolation is what you seek, then turn off the road just 12 km (8 miles) before you reach Higuerote. This is the way to **Tacarigua de Laguna**, a national park containing the incomparable Club Miami. Years ago, when the Venezuelan government declared all beaches public land, Club Miami already existed as a rustic private resort for the wealthy. Its owners were allowed to continue operating the facility, consisting of a line of small guesthouses with running water and electricity, as well as a restaurant and bar, but they were for-

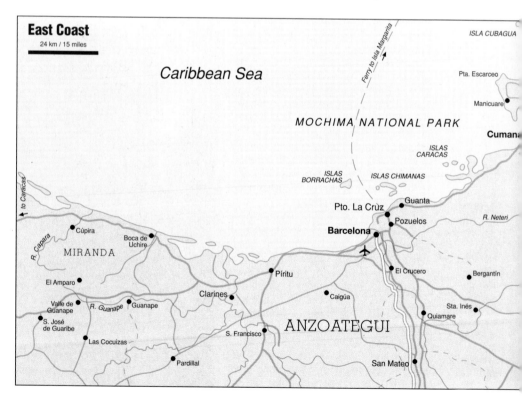

bidden to make any improvements. The latter restriction has been bent, but not much, and the club is one of the country's best escape spots. Some Venezuelans pack up their four-wheel-drive vehicles with food, water, tents and hammocks and go camping along the beach near Club Miami but, generally, the difficulty in reaching this spot and the lack of facilities (except for the club, which is overpriced by Venezuelan standards) mean that crowds are rare.

Almost as marvelous as the club is the fascinating journey to get there. During the dry season, all-terrain vehicles can drive across the dry river bed at the edge of the town of Tacarigua de Laguna. But when the water is high, the vehicles must be ferried across the narrow and shallow river on makeshift rafts. Better yet, pay one of the local fishermen to take you through the mangrove lagoon to the back entrance of the club. (If you don't see them around, go to Poleo's restaurant at the waterfront and ask for Señor Remigio or Señor Uchire.)

As the boat zips through the eerie mangroves, you'll pass fishermen netting fish and collecting shrimp, as well as some of the exotic wildlife that lives here. Most prominent are the *coro coros*, brilliant red ibis which feed in the lagoons. The boat drivers will drop you off at a flat open field that once served as the club's private landing strip during its heyday. Both with the raft ferry and the boat service, make arrangements for your return to the town of Tacarigua. (The transportation should be paid for on the return trip; travelers who pay in advance have found themselves stranded when it came time to go home.)

At Club Miami, you can string up a hammock between two coconut trees, join in the weekend beach barbecue and feast on roasted seafood at the club or thrash around in the shallow waves that wash onto the silvery sand here. Sunsets are fast but spectacular, and club goers often head out for midnight swims. The chances of finding an unoccupied *cabaña* at the club are usually good, although if you're traveling during a holiday period or want to stay several

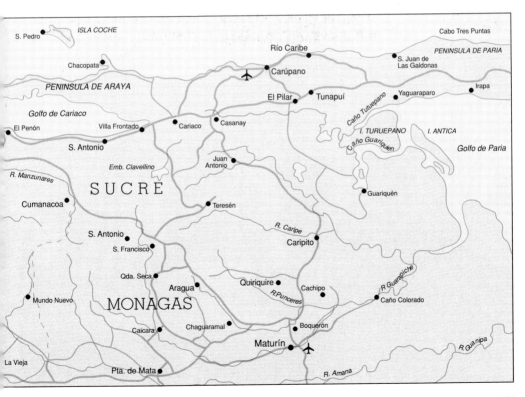

days during the week, you might want to call in advance.

Following the Sun Route: Officially, the east coast beach zone begins at **Puerto Píritu**, where the stretch of roadway known as the *Ruta del Sol* – Sun Route – begins. The most popular city along the road is energetic **Puerto La Cruz**, the region's main oil industry port. Located on the Pozuelos Bay between Barcelona and Guanta, this once sleepy fishing town has been transformed in recent decades into a thriving commercial center and resort city with nearly 200,000 residents. The change came with Venezuela's oil boom when petroleum companies began to look for a coastal spot where they could pipe oil from their southern fields for refining and export; Puerto La Cruz was chosen, a refinery was built and the local fishermen were left open-mouthed while a city grew up around them.

The gathering spot in Puerto La Cruz is **Paseo Colón**, a 3-km long boulevard along the seashore, bordered by restaurants, soda fountains, hotels and nighttime entertainment. At one end of the *paseo* is the ferryboat to Margarita Island, four hours away, and at the other are seaside *marisquerías*, as the seafood restaurants are known. After sunset, Puerto La Cruz residents leave their stuffy homes to stroll in the cool breezes that wing in from the ocean. Children play ball or ride bikes along the concrete walkway, adolescents come to flirt and vendors set up displays of locally made handicrafts, including well-made hammocks. The beach along the *paseo* is lovely to look at, especially from an outdoor café at sunset, but don't go in the water; it is badly polluted.

Luckily, there are a number of good beaches on the outskirts of Puerto La Cruz. Be wary of Venezuelans giving you advice on what beaches to visit because they say a beach must have *ambiente*, which is usually another way of saying it will be loud and crowded. Or they may recommend a beach simply because it is quickest to reach, such as the popular but unpleasant **Isla Plata**. This small island is accessible via a

Colonial mannequins at the Anzoátegui museum.

quick ferry service that operates every 10 minutes from the far east side of Puerto La Cruz. The water is clear and calm but the beach is small and crowded and the roped-off swimming area is tiny. Beyond the ropes, speed boats zip back and forth, making it unsafe to swim out in deep water. Worst of all is the view from Isla Plata, which faces another rocky, arid island where an ugly oil refinery rises up. Alarms and bells from the facility interrupt the otherwise calm setting.

Vendors sell beer and soft drinks on the island, but many beachgoers bring their own picnic supplies. Also, there are no facilities for changing clothes so you must change in the bathrooms at the ferry dock or come already dressed in a bathing suit. And bring plenty of sunscreen because shade is at a minimum.

Other islands, like **Las Borrachas**, **El Faro** (also known as La Chimana) and **Monos** are more secluded and enjoyable. All have small coral reefs where snorkeling is possible. Since fishermen generally go out at night or before dawn,

Fishermen set out.

their boats are idle during the day and they are glad to arrange to take you out on island-hopping expeditions. Take protection for the unrelenting rays of the sun and something to drink. You can also check with Puerto La Cruz travel agencies for planned island expeditions in which beverages and food are usually provided.

Beach facilities near Puerto La Cruz are expected to become more widespread as tourism grows. Already, US-based cruise line Carnival, one of the world's biggest, is building a combination resort and port in Puerto La Cruz to serve as the company's base of operations for the southern Caribbean. The project includes plans for a 496-room hotel and is expected to anchor the city as one of the country's top tourist spots.

The Carnival project is not the first time Puerto La Cruz has been singled out as a potential tourism paradise. **El Morro**, the most notorious project of its kind when it started, lies on the edge of the city. The project was expected to cost nearly half a million dollars when it

was initiated in 1971 as a complex with lagoons, Mediterranean-style houses, golf courses and 1,500 floating *cabañas* designed to function as a hotel. In total, it was to have 35 hotels, 40 motels, 2,000 vacation homes and facilities for 60,000 tourists. The ambitious plan was bogged down by a number of construction and funding delays and some of it remains unfinished.

For tourists who seek the secluded beauty of Venezuela's undeveloped beach areas, El Morro is somewhat of a nightmare – a massive self-contained development designed to bring together tens of thousands of beach seekers.

Ideal getaways: But Venezuela's best beaches – and most spectacular scenery – are found east of Puerto La Cruz on the 80-km (50-mile) stretch of highway that runs to Cumaná. This is where you'll find the fabulous beaches known as **Playa Arapita** and **Playa Colorada**. The latter, a long blue stretch of water with reddish sand and shady coconut trees, is the country's most photographed stretch of coast. Camping is permitted

here and you can also hire small motorized launches for trips to other, less accessible beaches in the **Mochima National Park**.

The park designation has been given to a stretch of waterfront territory and islands known for their coves, coral and color. Here, wild orchids grow from the sides of trees, ferns and exuberant flowers peek out from the shadows of tropical trees. Some parts of the national park even include mangroves and, in the dry forests of the lower zones there are iguanas, black lizards, snakes, wild rabbits and deer. Gulls, pelicans and frigate birds take to the skies while mammals such as ant-eaters, jaguars, sloths and armadillos stake out their territory on the ground.

On the far eastern edge of Mochima, just outside the borders of the park, are **Balneario Los Uveros** and the beach known as **Playa San Luis**. This more than 3-km long stretch of coast has been turned into a full-facility beach area with changing rooms, restrooms, showers, restaurants, camping areas, small

Hand-made dolls at Barbacoas.

174

hotels and a pleasant lit beachwalk along the waterfront.

Continuing down the coast toward Cumaná lies the town of **Barbacoas**, a handicraft town best known for its rag dolls, usually black with wild-colored hair. The dolls, known locally as *muñecas de trapo*, are frequently sold along the roadside. Woven baskets and delicate bird cages from reed and bamboo are also made here.

Beyond Barbacoas is **Cumaná**, the first Spanish city in the New World. In 1515, Franciscan friars began a settlement at what would be, six years later, declared by conquistador Gonzalo de Ocampo as the city of Nuevo Toledo. Its name was changed to the present one in 1569 when the city was rebuilt following several attacks by Cumanagota Indians. The first Spanish conquistadors were received fairly well but after the Spanish began to enslave the Indians of the area, forcing them to dive for pearls off the coast and subjecting them to severe punishment if they did not bring back enough, the Indians rebelled. There were several massacres, although the Spanish retained control of Cumaná.

This fishing center is not as electric as Puerto La Cruz, but its colonial architecture is far more fascinating. Low and hot, Cumaná is kept green by the Manzanares River flowing through it, kept shady by coconut groves and kept cool by breezes blowing off the Caribbean. Its population is black, descendants of slaves, and its flavor is Afro-Caribbean, from the music to the homemade remedies and "white magic" practised here. This is also a city where people are proud of working with their hands and fine crafts can be purchased.

Colonial fortress: Located at the mouth of the Cariaco Gulf, Cumaná also has a history of war, piracy and earthquakes. The newer section of town, closest to the airport, is nondescript but the older section of town with its colonial buildings is amongst the best preserved in Venezuela. This area is clustered around the foot of the hill where the fortress, **Castillo de San Antonio**, is found. This strategically-located military fort was

Luxury boats at Puerto La Cruz.

built in 1678 to protect the city from the English, French and German corsairs that plied the coast. It was erected using classic plans for military fortifications: a four-point star with four cannons at each point. Through the centuries, the facility was rebuilt several times after earthquakes caused serious damage.

During the independence wars, Bolívar's General Paez was imprisoned here for raising arms against the Spanish governor. The fort is located on the hill known as **Cerro Pan e Azura** and is beautifully floodlit at night. Across the gulf is the arid **Araya Peninsula**, the source of Venezuela's salt.

Tunnels, long since closed by earthquakes, once connected Castillo de San Antonio with the older, smaller complex known as **Santa María de la Cabeza**. Visible from the fort but now in ruins with no monies to restore it, this was the 17th-century residence of the Spanish governor. The fortified building was also the province's second military defense during colonial times. Once occupied by 250 soldiers and 50 cannons, it has been destroyed by time and tidal waves and sits abandoned not far from the church of Santa Ines.

The **Iglesia de Santa Inés de Fuerte Araya** is named for the saint who has been Cumaná's patron since 1572 when she was credited with saving the city from an Indian assault. This church was built upon the ruins of the Church of the Virgin of Carmen, destroyed by an earthquake in 1853, and its possessions include books and religious images brought to Venezuela by some of the country's first European missionaries. Some say a small statue of Saint Inés came to the city with pirates and that it was kept in this church for many years. However, the 400-year-old statue in the sacristy now is not Saint Inés, but the Virgin of Candelaria.

Cumaná also contains the ruins of the **Convento de San Francisco**, once home to a university. The monastery, built from 1669 to 1673, is a mute witness to much of the city's history. The first University of Cumaná operated here starting in 1812; after the country's in-

Spanish ramparts at San Antonio fortress, Cumaná.

dependence it was converted into a national public school. Located on Calle Sucre in front of the **Plaza Ribero**, the former monastery was damaged by an 1853 earthquake and left in ruins after a second quake in 1929. Cumaná is now the seat of the Universidad de Oriente with programs in marine biology, oceanography and ecology.

Cumaná's **Cathedral** contains the **Cross of Pardon**. Legend has it that a sinful woman, repentant, embraced the cross and begged for pardon. Onlookers were unable to separate her from the cross and took this as a sign that she had been forgiven. It is now believed that anyone who manages to embrace the cross will automatically be pardoned of their wrongdoings. Unfortunately, there was no heavenly intervention in the early 1800s when José Tomás Boves stopped by. Three months after he had routed Caracas, Boves reached Cumaná and started a new round of bloodshed, starting out with massacre of 200 people who took refuge in the Cathedral.

Poet's home: One of the city's most popular native sons was poet Andrés Eloy Blanco, best known for his poem *Píntame Angelitos Negros* (Paint Me Little Black Angels) which has been set to music and made famous by a number of singers including North American Roberta Flack. The poem urges a painter, working on a canvas of a fair-skinned Virgin Mary, to paint the angels black. Eloy Blanco's birthplace on Calle Sucre just off the Plaza Bolívar has been converted into a museum where visitors can obtain copies of his verses and see how Cumaná residents lived at the turn of the century. **Casa Natal Andrés Eloy Blanco** is open weekdays.

From Cumaná, it is possible to drive to the Araya Peninsula or take a short motorized boat trip (leaving from the Hotel Cumanagota) to the **Royal Fort of Santiago de Araya**, built by Royal Spanish decree in 1625 to protect the nearby *Araya* salt fields from Dutch incursions. During the whirlwind construction to erect this fort as protection against Dutch ships that secretly stole valuable salt from the barren and arid

Caribbean sunset.

flats, workers were forced to work at night because the daytime sun was unbearable. All the materials used by the laborers, as well as their food and water, had to be brought to the peninsula by boat because there is nothing – not even a plant – on this plain.

When the Spanish began to mine the fields of salt, the doomed workers they sent there labored naked; when dressed, the salt ate away the fabric of their clothing. Although still stunningly beautiful, the salt fields are dangerously hot and unshaded. If you wish to visit, you must obtain permission from Ensal, the government-run company that manages the salt production in Puerto La Cruz, and take a parasol for shade.

Von Humboldt's cave: Highway Routes 9 and 2 south from Cumaná lead to the **Guácharo Cave**, not far from Caripe, after just over 100 km (60 miles). **Caripe**, the so-called "Eastern Garden of Venezuela," is a pleasant country town where orange trees, fruit farms and coffee production abound. Four km (2 miles) from Caripe is the Alexander Von Humboldt National Monument, the Guácharo Cave, in El Guácharo National Park. This cave has 1.5 km of exotic geological formations and rings with the amazing cries of the blind nocturnal oil birds called *guácharos*.

It is illegal to enter the cave without authorized guides and only about a third of the cave is open to the public; the rest is entered only by scientists. The cave and its rare, fruit-eating occupants were recorded by German explorer Alexander Von Humboldt, who gave the *guácharos* their scientific name: *statornis caripensis*.

Inside the entrance to the cave is a brook fed by the Cerro Negro stream; from there the huge tunnel known as Humboldt Hall, with its dream-like stalactites and stalagmites, awaits visitors. The formations have been given nicknames such as *Virgén del Valle* (Virgin of the Valley), *Angel de la Guardia* (Guardian Angel) and *Cabeza de Elefante* (Elephant Head). Continuing forward to an area where rocks partially block the tunnel, you'll begin to hear the

Colonial splendor, Cumaná.

cries of the sightless birds inside. Like the formations, the caves you'll pass through have also been given whimsical names including *Cuarto de los Enamorados* (Lovers' Hall) and *Pila de Agua Bendita* (Holy Water Fountain). Eventually you'll come to the enormous cone-shaped stalagmite called La Torre and another rock obstruction. A commemorative plaque indicates that this is as far as Humboldt went.

You can go further – there are three caves to the east (Los Monjes, Las Velas de Calvario and Mataquero) and one to the west – before coming to the Salon de Baile (Dance Hall). That is followed by the Hall of Silence because the sounds of the *guácharos* can no longer be heard here. A narrow passage leads onto Precious Hall, then Dog's Hall and the Hall of Bells. Just past the cave with multi-colored stalactites is the Cuarto de los Pechos and the end of the passageways open to the general public.

Fisherman monument at Cumaná.

Straight east along the coast road about 115 km (70 miles) from Cumaná is Carúpano, known for its Carnaval, the most colorful in the country. It was in this town that Bolívar decreed the abolition of slavery (once the slaves agreed to fight with his independence forces against the Spanish troops). This city has always been the hub of intense commercial activity and presently has about 150,000 residents. Midway through the 1800s, it was the country's biggest and most important port.

Here you'll find the **Santa Rosa de Lima** church, an 18th-century church that was destroyed by an earthquake in 1797 and, 32 years later, was rebuilt on the spot where it now stands on Avenida Independencia in the Santa Rosa neighborhood. That new building collapsed in 1959, however, and yet a third church had to be erected. The original site for Santa Rosa is now where you'll find **Parque Suniaga**, a public park. The **Santa Catalina** church in front of Plaza Colón was built only 60 years ago.

From the mountain of **Maturincito**, just a few minutes outside the city, there is a fantastic view of the region's beaches and savannahs. The best of these include **Puerto Santo** about 10 km (6 miles) east of Carúpano; it is lined with coconut trees and has a strong surf. **Balneario Los Uveros** has food and washroom facilities, while other good beaches include **Playa Copey, Playa de Oro, Playa Caribe, Playa Grande** and **Caracolita** in Río Caribe, about 20 km (12 miles) from Carúpano.

Río Caribe, named for the river that runs through it, was once a cacao-growing region; it is still a farm area but coffee and sugar-cane fields now flourish here and fishing is an important industry. This town of 25,000 has preserved the colonial charm of its old homes, complete with the elaborate interior patios that the Spanish favored. When cacao was a chief export product, the so-called "Cacao Lords" lived here and traces of that opulent past remain.

At Río Caribe's nearby beach of **Macuro**, a monument marks where Columbus first set foot on the South American continent. Another good beach, accessible by way of a dirt road, is **San Juan de las Galdonas** with its crystalline waters and fishing skiffs.

MARGARITA

North of the Venezuelan mainland is a sun-kissed island where pearls the size of pigeon eggs were once found, where sunsets slowly explode into Technicolor shows and where rare birds feed on the shellfish clinging to the roots of mangroves. This is Margarita, the island whose name comes from the Greek word for "pearl".

This spot of land where Columbus set foot during his third voyage to the Americas in 1498 would actually be two islands if it were not for an 18-km (11-mile) isthmus that joins the pair. Venezuelans – inveterate shoppers – have long flocked to Margarita on weekends and vacations because its duty-free status makes it an inexpensive spot to buy imported cheeses, perfumes, liquors, electronic goods and clothes. Foreigners may dish out bolívars for beautiful hammocks, baskets and pottery but their main bargain is the beach, miles and miles of it. Since the mid-1980s, the island has become the Caribbean's budget destination for Europeans and North Americans who want to enjoy sun and surf without seriously denting their wallets.

Mangroves and mountains: Despite its reputation, there is more to Margarita than just sun and sand. History buffs can wander through restored 16th-century colonial forts and churches. Nature *aficionados* get their fill of exotic birds and marine life, especially at La Restinga mangrove lagoon.

Margarita, as well as the tinier islands of Coche and Cubagua off its coast, had strong ties with the fierce Caribe Indians and the peaceful Aruaks and Guaiquerís before the Spanish conquest. The Caribes were relentless warriors who gave their name to the hurricane-besieged Caribbean as they pushed through it, overpowering everything in their path.

Despite the Caribes' conquering ways, they too fell victim to an even more ruthless foe: the Europeans. After Columbus's voyage, the Spanish colonization of the island began, fueled by the discovery of rich pearl-bearing oyster beds off the island. News of the pearls spread, as did word that the Spanish galleons carrying gold from Mexico and Peru would pass Margarita, and it wasn't long before pirates began raiding the island – prompting the construction of the forts which still stand today.

Then, as now, the first things the buccaneers would have seen as they approached the island were the two rounded mountain peaks officially named the **Tetas de María Guevara** (María Guevara's breasts). Although the history books do not back the claim, some Venezuelans say María Guevara was a 19th-century independence movement heroine who was none too well endowed, and that it was local facetiousness which immortalized her in the naming of the two impressive humps which cut the Margarita horizon. More likely is the story that María Guevara was a local madame well known to the lusty sailors who docked here. Either way, the mountain bustline is one of the

Preceding pages: fishing boats near Porlamar. **Left,** maximum exposure. **Right,** colonial clock tower in Asunción.

island's best-loved local landmarks.

Visitors reach the island on ferries that leave from Cumaná and Puerto La Cruz and dock at the Margarita town of Punta de Piedras, or they fly into the General Santiago Mariño Airport. Either way, it isn't long before they make their way into **Porlamar**, once a quiet fishing town and now a dynamic city with 150,000 residents, wide boulevards of shops, plenty of fine seafood restaurants and hotels in every price range. The city's original name was Puerto de la Mar but, in true Venezuelan style, the words were run together and shortened. Dress here is casual – shorts and sandals are the common uniform – and everything worth visiting is found in a six-block square grid running south of **Plaza Bolívar**.

Porlamar lives on tourism and commerce and streets like **Avenida Santiago Mariño** are filled with stores that sell everything from French perfume to locally produced T-shirts. Most stores on the island open at 9am, close from 1 to 3, and open again until 7pm. During peak holiday periods like Christmas, Easter and the month of August, enterprising *Margariteños* keep their shops open during the lunch hour, foregoing the traditional siesta in order to add bolívars to the cash register.

Porlamar was founded March 25, 1536, by a priest, Francisco de Villacorta. Although its once-famous pearl beds are gone, exhausted by too much harvesting, commerce is still the main attraction here on the island where Venezuelans go to stroll and shop. The city's most impressive historical landmark is the century-old **Faro de La Puntilla**, a lighthouse at the end of Calle Fajardo. Its most interesting stop is the **Museo de Arte Contemporáneo** featuring Venezuelan artists, including more than four dozen works by Margarita-born sculptor-painter Francisco Narváez. Those who miss the museum at the corner of Calle Igualdad and Calle Fraternidad can still see his work; the ring of pigtailed girls around the fountain at the Hotel Bella Vista just down the street from the museum is a Narváez sculpture and a

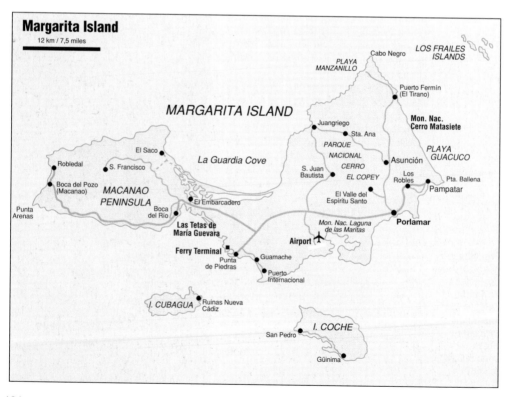

local landmark. It is called **La Ronda**.

Pregnant prisoner: Porlamar may be the island's most important city, but **Asunción** was its strategic center. Founded in 1561, it was placed just far enough inland to make it inaccessible to most pirates – and harder for the still rebellious Caribe Indians to attack. Even today, it is the political seat of Nueva Esparta state consisting of Margarita and the islands of Coche and Cubagua.

Little more than a century after Captain Pedro González Cervantes de Albornoz founded Asunción, the **Santa Rosa Fortress** was built to guard the town. Santa Rosa was the scene of important battles and it was here that the pregnant 16-year-old wife of Juan Bautista Arismendi, a well-known hero of the War of Independence, was held hostage in one of its dungeons.

A special plaque marks the cell where the young woman gave birth to a daughter who died in the fortress; Luisa Cáceres de Arismendi herself survived the imprisonment and was later reunited with her husband.

In front of Asunción's Plaza Bolívar is the **Nuestra Señora de la Asunción Cathedral**, the oldest church in Venezuela. Construction on the church began in 1571 but it wasn't until 46 years later that the building was completed. Visitors are welcome when mass is not in progress. But the island's most renowned religious spot is outside the city in what was once called the Charaima Valley but has now been renamed the **Valle del Espíritu Santo** (Holy Spirit Valley). This is the sanctuary of the Virgin of the Valley, patron saint of the island. Legend says a Guaiquerí Indian found a beautiful image of the virgin in the Piache Cave here.

A small colorful chapel has been constructed at the cave where fishermen and sailors leave valuable offerings, including pearls, silver and gold, in payment for favors granted. The road to the sanctuary is lined with vendors offering good bargains on hammocks, straw hats, baskets, rag dolls, sandals and the island's four-stringed guitars known as *cuatros*.

Colonial defences at Pampatar fortress.

Back to the coast again, but north of Porlamar, is the fishing town of **Pampatar** and the fort known as the **Castillo de San Carlos Borromeo**, the island's most important pirate defense when it was built by order of a royal Spanish decree in 1663. The massive structure in which a historical museum operates is not the original fort; that was destroyed when Dutch pirates burned Pampatar in 1662. During the Independence War, the Spanish soldiers fleeing the fort tried to destroy it yet again but revolutionary troops discovered the 1,400 pounds of explosive powder hidden in the complex.

Trapped ship: Across from the fort is the **Iglesia del Santísimo Cristo del Buen Viaje** (Church of the Holiest Christ of the Good Voyage). Sailors claim that the crucifix over the altar was brought on a passing ship that found itself unable to lift anchor and leave Margarita until the religious statue was left behind. Nearby, **Casa Amarilla**, the neoclassical custom house, has been restored. At **Playa Pampatar**, the local

beach, visitors can watch the grizzled fishermen take out their boats, dry and repair their nets or return to shore with their catches. These same fishermen can also point out the way to **Cueva El Bufón**, an underwater cave that is popular with swimmers; locals say this is where ancient pirates hid their loot.

Anyone who finds themselves in Pampatar on Thursday, Friday or Saturday should hang around until 8.30pm, when the townspeople head over to the **Canódromo**, a greyhound racing arena. Admission to the track is free and, during the Christmas, Easter and summer vacation seasons, racing cards are presented nightly.

Between Porlamar and Pampatar is **Los Robles** (also known as **El Pilar**), a small town that proves the adage "You can't judge a book by its cover." Inside the town's modest whitewashed colonial church is the solid gold statue of the Virgin of Pilar. The statue was sent to the colony in 1504 by Spanish Queen Juana La Loca, Isabella's daughter.

On the main road northeast of

Taking it easy...

Asunción lies **Santa Ana**, a city with not much tourist value but plenty of historical importance. The simple white **Santa Ana Church** is where, on May 6, 1816, Simón Bolívar signed the decree abandoning the war and proclaimed the formation of the Third Republic. The so-called Assembly of Notables met at the church and formally recognized Bolívar as Supreme Chief of Venezuela and its armies. Outside the town is the village of **El Cercado** where the best pottery on the island is found.

Sunsets, skiffs and seafood: If a piña colada at a seaside café at sunset sounds appealing, then **Juangriego** should not be missed. Located on one of the island's most spectacular bays, with clean waters, brightly-colored fishing skiffs and explosive sunsets, this fishing village also boasts dozens of restaurants along the waterfront that serve up fabulous seafood meals. Local residents claim the best place to see the sunset is from **La Galera Fort**. Spanish General Pablo Morillo slaughtered the patriot forces here when he retook Juangriego

from the independence army in 1817. Behind the fort is the **Laguna de Los Mártires** (Martyr's Lagoon) where legend says the waters turned red with the blood of 200 political prisoners who were executed by Morillo.

At the **Cemeterio**, graveyard buffs will find the headstone of James Towers English, an Irish Legion commander who died far from his homeland while helping Venezuelan independence forces in 1819. Born near Dublin, Ireland, in 1782, English was contracted by Bolívar to organize an expeditionary force of 1,092 men to aid in the war against Spain. During a battle in Margarita, the young officer died of a cerebral hemorrhage but his troops went on to fight in the battle of Carabobo, the decisive victory battle in the Venezuelan revolution.

(Visitors considering a trip to Juangriego should take note of recent problems with renegade cabbies who rob their passengers. Although the incidents are isolated, there have been reports of unlicensed taxi drivers badly beating

resisting victims. Officials recommend that tourists take *por puestos*, the inexpensive mini-buses that take passengers all over the island, taxis that work through Porlamar hotels or cabs that have the driver's registration and license in plain view of passengers.)

Although Margarita is a treasure chest for history buffs, most of its visitors are sun seekers and there are more than 50 beaches to choose from. The island is not as tropical as the Venezuelan mainland, where green foliage abounds, but many of the beaches have palm trees for shade and the soft white sand and Hollywood sunsets are worth the trade-off in greenery. For the most part, the calmest waters are on the island's southern shore but Margarita offers something for everyone: gentle shores for families with children, protected bays for swimmers and wild waves for surfers.

The most popular beach is **Playa El Agua** with soft waves (although a powerful undertow) and kiosks serving fried fish, lobster, oysters, local sweets and drinks. Natural shade is at a minimum but beach-chairs and awnings (called *toldos*) are for rent and should be used, even by the most dedicated sun-worshippers, because the rays here can be fierce. Waiters with drinks and snacks will serve you right at your chair.

Playground for a dictator: There are restrooms and changing rooms along the walkway parallel to the roadside and parking. At the south end of the beach is a concrete wall, beyond it is the house that served as the Margarita retreat of Marcos Pérez Jiménez, the last Venezuelan dictator. A few years ago the residence was converted into a small guesthouse.

Playa El Agua may be the island's most popular beach, but **Playa Puerto Cruz** is undoubtedly its most spectacular. Following a long, gently curving bay, this is the whitest, widest and windiest stretch of sand on the island. Swimmers must stay close to shore because of the powerful undertow, even though the waves make surfing tempting. For those who shy away from rough seas, this is best for an intimate day of lounging on

Left, even the pirates like Spanish *tascas*; **Below**, the Caribbean.

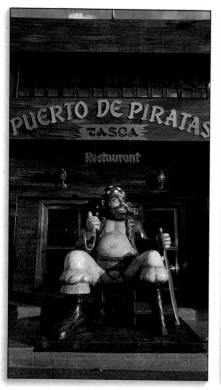

the sand. The government has planted palm trees to provide shade and a number of kiosks catering to hungry and thirsty beach bums have sprung up; a cold Polar beer or icy soft drink is never far away. Playa Puerto Cruz is farther from Porlamar than Playa El Agua, but it's a straight shot from Juangriego.

Next to Playa Puerto Cruz, at the base of the mountain pass that joins the towns of Pedrogonzález and Manzanillo, is **Playa Puerto Viejo**. The beach can be reached on foot by walking to the far northeastern end of Playa Puerto Cruz, scaling a small rocky hill and descending. Although this is a narrow strip of sand, the surf is calm and the water is shallow – heightening its appeal for swimmers and children. Early beach-goers should try to stake a claim on the small sandy area, set off by a group of rocks, in the middle of the beach. This is difficult to reach at high tide but if home-steaded early in the day it remains the only sure bit of sand that won't be claimed by the rising tide. The view here toward Playa Puerto Cruz is the Margarita landscape most frequently captured by painters. It's best to pack a picnic and plenty to drink when heading to Puerto Viejo because all that's guaranteed is soft sand, clear Caribbean water and shady coconut trees.

Cab drivers' retreat: The beach closest to the airport, and the one nicknamed "Taxi Driver Beach," is **Playa El Yaque**. This has long been the spot to which cabbies slipped away for a nap and a beer between meeting flights. In recent years, it has become popular with windsurfers who praise its steady breeze and shallow waters; this is where Margarita's windsurfing competitions are held. For sunbathers, though, this is not a choice spot. The sand is sparse, there is little shade and winds blow stinging sand.

Just as windsurfers have their beach, so do surfboard fanatics. Elliptically-shaped **Playa Parguito** has the island's highest breakers thanks to an offshore shelf of rocks. This is a pretty beach some distance south of Playa El Agua, with a handful of food kiosks and palm

Strumming up a storm in Porlamar.

and seagrape trees, but reaching it requires traveling through an unattractive lagoon. Bring sandals to this surfing spot because pebbles, not sand, dominate the beach. It is never too crowded.

About 5 km (3 miles) east of Asunción, **Playa Guacuco** is more popular with locals than tourists and development projects are marring its appeal. The fine sand beach is narrow and shaded by palm trees, but when the surf comes in during the late afternoon, the water rises up to the tree line. A number of construction projects are ruining the once peaceful appeal of this strip of Caribbean coast.

Arid peninsula: Adventurous travelers who have exhausted the beaches and forts of the island can cross the isthmus to the **Macanao Peninsula**, the largely uninhabited arid terrain that locals call "the other island." Void of most vegetation, the most the peninsula has to offer are cacti, rock mountains and a handful of fishing towns. Linked to the rest of Margarita by a bridge at the mouth of Mangle Bay, residents of **Boca del Río** – the peninsula's largest city – live from commercial fishing. Their town is also home to the Agriculture School connected to Venezuela's Universidad del Oriente. Fish are raised experimentally at the school. In Boca del Río and some of the smaller fishing towns, there are shipyards where visitors can watch the construction of the small boats called *peñeros*.

Boca del Río is close to one of Margarita's main tourist attractions, **La Restinga Lagoon and National Park**. Visitors can hire boats to take them through the 15 km (10 miles) of mangroves where pelicans, cormorants, frigate birds, great blue herons, egrets, flamingos, gulls and rare scarlet ibis live. The lagoon is about 40 km (25 miles) from Porlamar and can be reached in a rented car, cab or in a *por puesto*. The *por puestos* leave from Calle Mariño near Porlamar's waterfront and drop travelers off not far from the boat dock where launches set out through the lagoon. Tourists who want to take a *por puesto* back to Porlamar later in the day

Touring the mangrove swamps of La Restinga.

should mention this to the bus driver. There are also a number of travel agencies that offer guided tours – an option recommended for travelers who speak little Spanish.

The small, motorized wooden launches leave the dock as soon as they fill up, gliding through the dark green waters of the salty canals. Oyster beds cling underwater to the tentacles of mangrove trees and the boat drivers will answer questions – in Spanish.

On the far side of the lagoon is **La Restinga Beach**; sometimes you can make arrangements with the boat owner to drop you off on the beach then pick you up later. Usually an hour or so is enough time to stroll over the crushed seashells that make up the beach, wade into the surf or get a snack or drink at one of the bayside kiosks. If you make such a pick-up arrangement with the boat owners, do not pay your full fare in advance – most won't expect full payment until the end of the trip anyway. You can tip if warranted.

Obsession with pearls: Offshore from Margarita are the tiny islands of **Coche** and **Cubagua**, both populated in the 16th century by colonists who fished pearl beds, and now largely uninhabited. Cubagua was the site of **Nueva Cádiz**, the first town in South America and a settlement rich in history and legend. The town sprang up in response to the feverish pearl exploitation of the 1520s and 1530s on this 33 sq. km (13 sq. mile) island lying between Margarita and the Venezuelan mainland.

The Indians on Cubagua found the Spanish obsession with pearls – which they themselves viewed simply as adornments – amusing and they gladly traded them for knives and supplies. But the amusement wore off when the conquistadors began to force them to dive for oyster-bearing pearls, and beat them when they came back empty-handed and forced them – bleeding – to enter the salty sea again. Some died in the jaws of sharks and others were, as Spanish priest Bartolomé de las Casas recorded in his journal, victims of hunger, cruelty and desperation.

Columbus's stop in Margarita netted him 80 pounds of fine pearls and made his 1498 voyage one of his most profitable. But by 1533 the pearl beds of Cubagua were exhausted; eight years later an earthquake and tidal wave flattened what was left of Nueva Cádiz. The ruins of this historic city were buried under sand for centuries until archaeological excavations began in 1949.

Since then, the island has been largely ignored. The 28 resident families live off fishing, stocking up on other necessities during frequent trips to Margarita. But a new $4.9 billion tourism project has put Cubagua once again in the spotlight. In 1990, a 99-year lease was granted a Venezuelan investment group that plans to turn the island into a tourist mecca. The plans include several hotels, including one with 1,500 rooms, pools, nautical clubs, spas, cottages and recreation areas.

The fate of the archaeological remains of Nueva Cádiz remains unsettled and the fishing families still on the island will have to be relocated so as not to hinder the worship of the sun.

The dry Macando peninsula.

THE GRAN SABANA

In the late 1880s, the novelist Sir Arthur Conan Doyle attended a series of lectures given in London by the botanist Everard Im Thurn, the first man to scale the tabletop mountain Roraima in Venezuela's vast, uncharted Gran Sabana region. Im Thurn held the audience spellbound with the news that this high plateau was populated by plant and insect species that had been cut off for millions of years from the rest of the world. Conan Doyle's imagination was captured. In 1912, the creator of Sherlock Holmes published *The Lost World*, a novel about a Roraima-like *mesa* (high plateau) in South America inhabited by giant dinosaurs and "missing link" ape men who had escaped the course of evolution.

The book has not aged well, with its breathless *Boy's Own* plot and righteous imperialist tone, but the image of Venezuela's isolated peaks that inspired Conan Doyle has had an enduring fascination. So much so that the Gran Sabana region – covering some 500,000 sq. km (200,000 sq. miles) of Venezuelan territory – is now routinely referred to in tourism circles as *El Mundo Perdido*, "the Lost World."

Ancient formations: Mt Roraima is only the tallest and most symmetrical of dozens of tabletop mountains – called *tepuis* from the local Pemón Indian word for mountain – that dot the area. They form part of the Guyana Shield, one of the globe's oldest geological formations. The sandstone of the *tepuis* is estimated to be at least 1.8 billion years old, predating even the most primitive ocean-going life forms.

When the super-continent Gondwana split into South America and Africa some 135 million years ago, the Guyana plate became riddled with fissures. Millions of years of cataclysmic thunderstorms eroded the gaps within the sand-

Preceding pages: the haunting *tepuis* or tabletop mountains. **Left**, the Indian-style village of Kavak.

stone, leaving only the sheer-cliffed *tepuis* as they are today – some as high as 1,500 meters (5,000 ft) rising from a thick green bed of tropical rainforest.

Most *tepuis* are almost permanently shrouded in clouds, even in the dry season which extends from June to November. Some, like Auyan-tepui, have swamp-like surfaces, while others, including Roraima, have been washed by rainfall to almost sheer sandstone. Yet even on barren Roraima, unique plants survive: lichen, moss and hundreds of varieties of orchid, some with flowers almost as small as the heads of pins, exist in the cracks. Tough clumps of bromeliads cling to the rock, often feeding on insects lured into their funnel-shaped flowers. And each *tepui*'s insects are as unique as the flora: having adopted to their chilly mountain-tops, none would be able to survive the journey through the tropical lowlands to one of the other *tepuis*.

While Conan Doyle imagined the surface of each *tepui* to be a world frozen in time, these species have in fact evolved in isolation. They have been forced to adapt separately to their harsh environments in a fashion similiar to life forms on the Galapágos islands (indeed, the modern Venezuelan explorer Charles Brewer-Carias has dubbed the *tepuis* "islands in time.)"

Exploring the Lost World: Following the last Ice Age, the Gran Sabana area was settled by the Pemón Indians, many of whom still live in the area. Very few *criollo* settlers arrived until around World War II, when diamonds were discovered. Today there is a large military presence thanks to the sensitive border with Guyana and Brazil, making the region's towns an odd mix of young soldiers, hard-bitten miners, yuppie dropouts from Caracas and wide-eyed foreign tourists.

Although day trips to the Gran Sabana can now be made from Caracas and Margarita island, it's worthwhile spending a little time soaking up the region's almost mystical atmosphere. Most visitors start off from a base in **Ciudad Bolívar** further to the north and take one of the new passenger flights directly

into the area on small, propeller-driven planes. Travelers with more time and a four-wheel drive jeep at their disposal can follow the dirt highway south, through the town of **El Dorado** (where the famous French escapee from Devil's island Papillon ended up in jail on one occasion) and down to the Brazilian border. It should be noted that most roads in the Gran Sabana are truly dismal, usually sheer sandstone exposed by the rains, and two cars should travel together in case of breakdowns.

However, the main tourist center of the Gran Sabana, **Canaima**, is almost always reached by air. Located on a plain at the northern fringe of the Gran Sabana, the small village was created in the 1950s as a service center for tourism and gateway to the **Canaima National Park** – with some 3 million hectares (7.4 million acres) the sixth largest in the world.

The setting for Canaima could not be more spectacular. Here the **Río Carrao** broadens into a lagoon with a pink-sanded *playa* (beach) and palm trees.

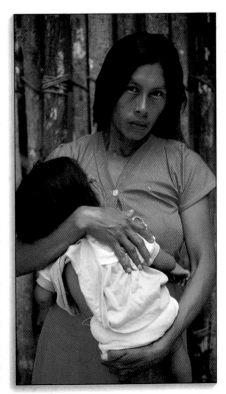

THE TALE OF JIMMY ANGEL

The accidental discovery of the world's highest waterfall by the Missouri-born bush pilot Jimmy Angel has become a part of the mythology of the Gran Sabana. It's a story fit for Indiana Jones.

In 1935, Angel was working as a pilot in Panama City, hiring out his Flamingo monoplane to anyone who would pay. Things were not going well. Speaking to an interviewer many years later, Angel recalled that he was completely broke, sitting in a hotel lobby and wondering what to do next when, out of the blue, he was approached by an old Mexican engineer. He offered Angel US$5,000 – an huge sum in those days – to fly him onto a *tepui* in the heart of Venezuela's uncharted Gran Sabana region.

Angel jumped at the chance, and took the man onto a 1,000-meter (3,300-ft) high plateau. It was "a hell of a place to land a plane," as Angel said later, but he managed it, right next to a small stream. Then they started digging. "In three days we took 75 pounds of gold out of the gravel," said the aviator. "We could have taken out more, but I was afraid to put too much extra weight in the plane."

A year later, Angel tried to find the spot again, taking with him his wife, a geologist named Gustav Heny and Heny's gardener (presumably to do some digging). Predictably, Angel couldn't recognize the spot. After a few fly-overs, he landed successfully on top of Auyan-tepui – but the plane became mired in the *mesa*'s swampy surface.

Luckily Heny had recently scaled Auyan-tepui from the south side, so knew the way down. It took 11 days of strenuous walking before they made it to human settlement.

As we now know, the journey hadn't been a total disaster. Not far from where they had landed, the group found the free-falling pencil of water that was dubbed, in the aviator's honor, Angel Falls. At the time, immortality seemed a poor consolation. Not only had Angel not found any riches, he had lost his plane, *El Río Coroní*. In fact, the monoplane stayed sitting on top of Auyan-tepui until 1970, when it was replaced with a replica. The original can be seen outside the airport in Ciudad Bolívar. ■

Jimmy Angel's monoplane.

Into the lagoon pours the wide **Hacha Falls**, and looming above them are several *tepuis*, including **Auyan-tepui** (devil mountain) – some 700 sq. km (270 sq. miles) in area and 2,460 meters (8,070 ft) in height.

Accommodation at Canaima is offered by two rustic jungle-style lodges, the large and rather expensive **Avensa Canaima Camp** and **Jungle Rudy's** (Ucaima Camp) up-river from the falls. The latter is a small and intimate collection of wooden huts, set up and run by a Dutchman named Rudy Truffino, who first came here in the mid-'50s. Responding to Canaima's growing popularity, a number of families have recently begun offering basic accommodation in their houses, usually with hammocks to sleep in.

Although it has become more commercial of late, Canaima is still a good place to spend several days enjoying the views of the *mesas*, or taking short walks to the waterfalls like **El Sapo** and **Yuri**. The National Park is also home to a range of exotic birds like the golden cock of the rock, and to wild jaguars and tapirs, but they have become increasingly difficult to spot.

On the southern side of the huge Auyan-tepui is another comfortable and remote lodge, **Kavak**, operated by Aerotuy airlines in conjunction with the local Pemón Indians, who own the land here. The *indígenas* built Kavak in the style of a traditional village and largely look after its day-to-day running, while Aerotuy brings travelers here on tours from around Venezuela.

The day trip is one of the most exciting in all of South America: after a flight through the valleys between *tepuis*, there is a short walk from the airport to a series of three waterfalls where visitors can swim in warm jungle grottos or take a natural shower. The climax is swimming through a 50-meter (160-ft) canyon to the last waterfall, which plunges into a secluded, cliff-rung lake that can become as choppy as the open sea. Those with more time can also overnight at the rustic lodge.

The world's highest waterfall: Spilling

Angel Falls, the world's highest.

into a canyon on the flank of Auyan-tepui is the thin plume of **Angel Falls**. Its waters drop 979 meters (3,212 ft) from the top of the *tepui* to the jungle below, of which around 800 meters (2,600 ft) is free-fall – making Salto Angel, as it is known in Spanish, some 15 times higher than Niagara.

The falls were only discovered in 1936 by the legendary bush pilot Jimmy Angel (*see page 198*). These days, light aircraft make the fly-over of the falls several times every day from both Canaima and the lodge Kavak.

The only problem is visibility: during the rainy season, the falls are often covered by clouds. During the dry season, visibility may be good but there is often little water. Still, you may be lucky, especially flying early in the morning. From Canaima, it is possible to follow the river during the wet season and walk to the base of the falls – the camping trip takes four to five days and you need to be reasonably fit.

For hikers, organized expeditions are also mounted to climb Auyan-tepui, taking around nine days. Although it is higher, the trek to the summit of **Mt Roraima** is actually less strenuous. The mountain lies outside the National Park, on the border with Guyana (which Venezuela actually claims). Because this is a sensitive border, expeditions to Roraima are theoretically forbidden by the military, although they regularly go ahead, taking some 12 days return from the nearest habitation.

Diamond mining outposts: Since the 1930s, settlement has been going ahead in the lush rainforest area between Canaima National Park and the Brazilian border. Towns like **Santa Elena de Uairen** and **Icabarú** have grown to include several hundred people: most are gold and diamond miners who head off to fossick in the hundreds of streams that wind through the region.

It was near Icabarú that the 154-carat Bolívar diamond, Venezuela's largest, was found in 1942 by a miner looking through the off-cuts. Apparently it had been tossed aside by miners looking for more "normal" sized rocks. These days miners can still be met trudging along with their shovels and equipment on their backs, or in small *bodegas* (stores) buying groceries and alcohol with tiny diamonds and grains of gold – the latter are valued by shopkeepers on the spot, using miniature scales. Miners are happy to sell larger nuggets directly to travelers.

Most recently, this border area has also lured many young, professional families from Caracas who have tossed over their old lives for a new start, building rustic accommodation in particularly isolated spots. Typical of these "yuppie pioneers" are Mauro and Elsa Segulin, trained architects who dropped out of their city jobs to design and operate **Kawaik Lodge** near the village of **El Pauji**. Communication with the outside world is largely by radio, and getting there on the twice-weekly light aircraft can be unpredictable. But with the *tepuis* visible on the horizon, a stream running through the property and jungle rivers within striking distance, there are few more idyllic spots in Venezuela to get away from it all – and, for a few days at least, stay lost in the Lost World.

Left, a low river level reveals rich plant life. **Right**, a gold miner weighs his day's find at Kawaik lodge.

AMONAS

Amazonas – home to exotic plants, rare animals and 20 different Indian cultures – is a federal territory stretching over nearly 180,000 sq. km (70,000 sq. miles) in the southernmost region of Venezuela. Bordered to the west by the Orinoco River and Colombia, and to the south and east by Brazil, it includes lush rain forest, hundreds of rivers and broad savannahs. Like the rest of the Amazon basin, Venezuela's Amazonas Territory is a frontier land where dramatic conflicts are being staged, environmental tragedy is always threatened – and a place where travelers can enjoy one of the world's great wilderness adventures.

The last frontier: Everything about Amazonas is extreme. The Sierra de La Neblina (Mountains of the Mists), which skirt the southern end of the territory, are second only to the Andes as the highest range in Venezuela. Yet they are so remote that La Neblina, the highest peak of the range, was not discovered until 1953. Its elevation is 3,014 meters (9,888 ft).

Even the rivers are remarkable. The mighty Orinoco exhibits a rare phenomenon here: during certain times of the year, instead of receiving waters from the smaller Río Casiquiare, it feeds part of its own volume into this inferior channel. The Casiquiare then runs in the opposite direction from the Orinoco's main course, empties into the Río Negro and on into the Amazon. German naturalist Alexander von Humboldt documented this curiosity when he came to the area in 1800, and it amazes engineers even today.

About 8,000 species of plants grow in Amazonas – 7,000 of them indigenous. Orchids, bromeliads and mosses drape the rain forest, with a canopy so thick and immense it seems impenetrable. Jaguars prowl deep in the jungle, along with ocelots, deer, tapir, giant ant-eaters, peccaries and half a dozen species of monkeys. The fearsome bushmaster snake grows up to 4 meters (12 ft); the deadly fer-de-lance and the better-known anaconda are not quite so long.

There are 680 species of birds, including magnificently colored toucans, parrots and macaws. And there are insects galore – a hundred different families with all their various relations – including brilliant, neon-colored butterflies, six-inch cockroaches and more disease-carrying mosquitos and biting flies than most travelers would care to know about. Scorpions and bird-eating spiders are found on the rain forest's floor, while its rivers swarm with electric eels, piranha, caiman, *pavón* (peacock bass), freshwater dolphin and marine turtles.

Endangered ecosystem: Although Amazonas is teeming with life, the rain forest ecosystem is extremely delicate. If the land is cleared for large-scale farming, the shallow nutrients are quickly leached out and washed away by the rains, leaving a barren, desert-like landscape. Miners leave behind rivers contaminated with mercury and holes that fill with rainwater to become breeding grounds for mosquitos.

Unfortunately, the Venezuelan gov-

Preceding pages: bridge across a jungle river. **Left,** Yanomami Indian children. **Right,** a screeching macaw.

ernment launched an ill-considered program for settling and populating Amazonas in the late 1960s. *La Conquista del Sur* (The Conquest of the South) quickly proved to be a giant bust, and the focus was shifted from cultivation to research and conservation. About the only thing to endure from this fiasco was a research center established in 1971 by the Corporation for Development of the South in San Simón de Cocuy, the southernmost town in the country.

Scientists from the center have shown that Amazonas contains a wealth of lumber, medicinal plants, dyes, resins, gums and fibers, and the many rivers hold unlimited hydroelectric potential. But such riches have been only marginally exploited. Unfortunately, the Amazonas has proven to have the largest gold deposits in South America and in recent years has drawn thousands of miners – with many coming illegally over the border from Brazil. While Venezuela has not suffered the same sort of environmental catastrophe from devel-

opment as its southern neighbor, the situation is volatile.

The region has some legal protection. Besides three national parks – Yacapana, Serranía La Neblina and Duida-Marahuaca – certain areas are off-limits to both mining and tourism. Bioma, the Venezuelan counterpart of The Nature Conservancy, plans to launch a drive to buy at least 9 percent of Amazonas to preserve as virgin territory.

The invasion begins: Despite the difficulties, the area has attracted explorers for centuries. The Orinoco was probed as early as 1531 by Diego de Ordaz, who dreamed it would lead to El Dorado. Dozens of other explorers combed the 2,700-km (1,700-mile) river and its tributaries, but the source of the Orinoco remained a mystery until 1950.

In that year, a team of Venezuelans, French and North Americans traced the last 190 km (120 miles) of the Orinoco's course to the Sierra Parima at the Brazilian border. The origin of the seventh largest river in the world is a stream that trickles from a mountain the expedition

A forked tongue.

members named Delgado Chalbaud (elevation 1,047 meters/3,435 ft).

The majority of travelers to Amazonas will be satisfied with jungle tours operated from Puerto Ayacucho, the capital of the territory. Non-Venezuelan citizens who wish to leave the towns and venture into Indian lands must get a permit from the Office of Indian Affairs at the Ministry of Education in Caracas. Technically, it's granted only to scientists, and the application process is slow and grueling. But since the government's recent push to stimulate tourism, permits are available through some tour operators in Puerto Ayacucho.

Transportation in this remote region is mainly by aerotaxi and dugout canoes called *bongos* or *curiaras*. The only paved road runs from Caicara at the border with Bolívar state to Samariapo, south of Puerto Ayacucho. Jeeps or four-wheel-drive vehicles are needed to navigate the bumpy dirt roads.

Settlers' towns: The *criollo* towns are clustered along the Orinoco, Atabapo and Guainia rivers, bordering Colombia. **Puerto Ayacucho** is by far the biggest, with a population of about 20,000. The place where most travelers begin their journeys, it was founded in 1924, and was originally the base camp for workmen building the road south to Samariapo. That paved highway links the two ports along a section of the Orinoco that cannot be navigated due to rocks and the treacherous Atures rapids.

The average temperature in Puerto Ayacucho is 27.6°C (82°F). During the dry season (December through April), the town gets very dusty, and when the rain comes, it's extremely humid. The climate contributes to the lingering atmosphere of lethargy.

A river port and a border post, Puerto Ayacucho has a heavy military and navy presence. Many Indians live here or come to the market to trade. The airport offers daily service to Caracas and other cities, while several charter operators fly tourists, scientists and missionaries to outlying areas. Everyone seems to have a hair-raising tale about their airplane's petrol gauge running low as

A red howler monkey.

they desperately search for an airstrip in the sea of trees below.

The poolside bar of the **Gran Hotel Amazonas** is Puerto Ayacucho's unofficial nerve center and a great spot for people-watching. The eclectic crowd might include hungry-eyed uniformed men, distracted scientists trying to track down equipment that strayed en route to the town, missionary families with well-scrubbed children and shady types who just seem to be hanging around waiting for something to happen.

In the **market**, which is most active at dawn, you can bargain for woven baskets, *wapas* (trays), blowpipes, feather adornments and other Indian handicrafts. At his small shop, the well-known local character Pascual Silva sells *katar*, spicy sauce famed far and wide as an aphrodisiac. You might also sample some local treats like deep-fried ants. (Get 'em while they're hot.)

Interesting exhibits on the various indigenous groups of the Amazonas are displayed downtown at the **Museo Etnológico del Territorio Federal Amazonas** (Amazonas Ethnological Museum).

Combatting tropical disease: On a hill just outside Puerto Ayacucho is CAICET, the Amazon Center for Research and Control of Tropical Diseases. Malaria is staging an alarming resurgence. Up to the 1930s, the disease manifested in fevers and chills claimed 10,000 lives a year from a population of some three million. By 1960, it had been eradicated from most of the country except for certain residual areas, mainly in the Amazonas. But starting in the 1980s, the cases again were in the thousands and doubling almost annually – with scientists particularly concerned that local mosquitos have become resistant to insecticides.

For visitors, malaria is not likely to be a problem except in the remoter jungle areas, but you may wish to take anti-malarial tablets as a precaution. Be sure to pack long-sleeved shirts, trousers and insect repellent. Try to stay inside at dusk when the insects are at their worst, and be prepared that chiggers and flies are also a major annoyance.

Jungle pleasures: But don't let these concerns ruin your enjoyment of Amazonas. There's much to see in this wild corner of the country. Roughly 35 km (22 miles) north of Puerto Ayacucho is **Pozo Azul** (Blue Well), a deep, clear lagoon fed by a little stream. It's safe to swim here, and there are many animals and birds to spot in the surrounding forest. The same distance in the opposite direction from the capital and just off the road to Samariapo, is the popular **Tobogán de la Selva** (Jungle Water Slide). This 20-meter (60-ft) granite rock forms a natural slide and is set in a recreational area with nature trails and refreshment stands. The **Canturama tourist camp** is nearby.

Samariapo is a small river port at the end of the paved road from Puerto Ayacucho. South of town are the impressive **Maipures rapids**.

And about 20 minutes by boat is **Isla Ratón** (Rat Island), the largest spot of land in the Orinoco River. It's also surely one of the hottest places on Earth. The sun beats down on its rocky red shores

Hiking through the rain forest.

and bakes its flat fields a toasty brown. Clusters of multi-colored houses stand bare to the burning rays, like clay models being fired in a kiln. There's a **Salesian mission** with a school, where Piaroa girls in cotton dresses sit embroidering in the shade of the courtyard. A small hospital tends Indian families. One major problem is keeping vaccines chilled. There's no permament electricity – only a kerosene-powered generator that runs for a few hours each night.

The legendary **Autana**, sacred mountain of the Piaroas, is located on the mainland, to the east. This 1,220-meter (4,000-ft) column has a labyrinth of caves near the summit. During certain times of the year, the sun's rays shine in one side of the mountain and out the other. In the same region, **Cerro Pintado** (Painted Mountain) boasts the largest known petrogylphs (rock carvings) in Venezuela, including a 50-meter (150-ft) snake that is said to represent the Orinoco.

Deep in Amazonas, along the Upper Orinoco, **La Esmeralda** rests in the shadow of Mount Duida (elevation 2,400 meters/7,900 ft). This settlement has the dubious distinction of being the only place in South America where Humboldt couldn't keep his diary because he was busy batting off the tenacious bugs. Some 128 km (80 miles) upstream lies the mission **Platanal**, with basic accommodations for travelers.

Yutaje, in the rugged highlands due east of Platanal, features a comfortable tourist camp with fishing, canoeing, swimming and birdwatching. *Yutaje* in Piaroa means "twin falls," and the falls themselves are about 10 minutes by boat. **Campamiento Camani** is a fishing resort on the Río Ventuari, hundreds of miles away from any road. Opened in 1990, it offers accommodation in *churuatas* with plumbing, a swimming pool and bar. *Pavón* (peacock bass) weighing up to 12 kg (26 lb) have been caught here, along with the ferocious *payara* and many other species – some of which can only be fished at night. About 250 kinds of birds have been sighted near the camp.

Baby crocodiles opening wide.

PEOPLES OF THE AMAZON

Only about an estimated 80,000 people live in the Amazonas territory – a third of them are members of some 20 distinct indigenous groups with their own languages and cultures. Only the most isolated, like the Yanomami, who live deep in the jungle near Brazil, have been able to resist the encroachment of the outside world. In 1991, in a precedent-setting decree, President Carlos Andrés Pérez reserved a large stretch of Amazonas as a permanent homeland for the group.

The Venezuelan Indians have not faced the same systematic decimation as their counterparts in Brazil, but many have been contacted by missionaries, suffered invasion of their lands by miners and ranchers, been poked and prodded in the name of science and urged to assimilate into *criollo* society by the government. Only a few groups are starting to become politicized.

In 1984, after a rancher tied two Piaroa Indians to his horse and dragged them into captivity, the community of Caño Grulla called Venezuela's first ever Amazon Indian conference, summoning the governor of Amazonas and other officials. The summit ended with the governor advising the Piaroa not to expect protection from the state but to try to integrate themselves with the *criollos* – a major blow to Indians struggling to maintain their traditional culture against attacks from all sides.

The Yanomami and other Indian groups have been endangered by the white man's gold fever since the days of the conquistadors. In the late 1980s, thousands of gold miners invaded the Amazon Territory looking for a latter-day El Dorado. These are not just individuals staking a claim for themselves, but also sophisticated technicians backed by large multinational companies. Occasional violent clashes have occurred.

Amazonas is also a battleground for souls. Catholic missionaries have been working among the different Indian groups for years. The Salesians came in the 1930s, establishing schools and clinics in Puerto Ayacucho and other communities. In the 1940s, the Protestant, charismatic New Tribes missionaries entered the picture, sending families to

Left and right, Piaroa Indians.

live in Indian villages. They learned the indigenous languages and have put five of them into written form. The government has taken advantage of this to communicate with the groups by printing booklets on health issues and other concerns.

Travelers are likely to see Indian villages sprinkled throughout the rain forest. The Piaroa live mainly along the Sipapo and Cataniapo rivers, which branch off from the Orinoco south of Puerto Ayacucho. Their traditional homes are thatched conical buildings called *churuatas*. As their contact with the outside world increases, more and more Piaroa are abandoning their traditional loincloths, beads, feathers and body paint for T-shirts and trousers.

They raise animals and farm in round plots called *conucos* that look chaotic, with a jumble of crops. Actually, this method is ideally suited to the environment for many reasons, including the fact that it prevents a disease occurring in one plant from spreading through an entire field.

The semi-nomadic Yanomami (also called Yanomamo) live very deep in the rain forest, traveling back and forth across the border with Brazil. Anthropologist Napoleon Chagnon, who lived among the Yanomami for years, wrote a controversial book called *The Fierce People*. He focused on their vicious tribal warfare using long arrows tipped with deadly *curare*, concluding that they were perhaps the most violent social group on earth. The Yanomami believe in evil spirits and spells, and any unfortunate incident fuels their drive for vengeance.

The Yanomami are hunter-gatherers. Communities live in a *shabono*, a large circular compound. They string hammocks under the outer ring and the use the open center for public events like ceremonial dances. Yanomami shamans snort *yoppo*, a powerful hallucinogenic powder blasted into the nostrils from a long pipe. They believe this allows them to receive supernatural visions. The Yanomami cremate their dead, then grind the bones into a powder which they consume in a special brew. In this way, they keep alive the spirit of the deceased.

Other groups indigenous to the Amazonas include the Maquiritare (also spelled Makiritare), who live on the Upper Orinoco and are noted builders of dugouts. ∎

Left, Yanomami Indians. Right, boa for breakfast.

SIERRA NEVADA DE MERIDA

Mérida is known as *el techo de Venezuela* – the roof of Venezuela. The highest state in the country, capped by perpetual snow. Pico Bolívar, at 5,007 meters (16,427 ft), is the mightiest of them all, while you can visit the frosty summit of neighboring Pico Espejo (4,765 meters/15,634 ft) on the world's longest and highest cable car.

The people of this harsh Andean terrain are hard-working, resourceful and religious, and Mérida is an enclave of tradition. Peasant farmers eke out a living on steep terraced plots and cart their potatoes and carrots off to market by mule. Villages with Indian names like Moconoque, Mucuchies and Timotes are strategically situated about a day's mule trek apart. Often these settlements are little more than clusters of crooked, red-roofed, single-story houses built flush against the narrow road. There may be a stand selling woollen ponchos and blankets to combat the damp, chill air, and probably a shop offering smoke-cured hams and homemade cheese. Otherwise, life centers around each town's Plaza Bolívar with its colonial church.

Even the metropolitan capital of **Mérida**, which shares the state's name, lacks skyscrapers (this is an earthquake zone). But it is impressive in other ways. Besides the cable car to the clouds, the city boasts an abundance of parks, one of the country's largest and oldest universities, a cathedral with a portrait of God Himself, and an ice cream parlor offering quite possibly the most bizarre flavors in the world (anyone for a double dip of garlic and tuna?).

Andean center: Mérida is about a 45-minute flight from Caracas, and the landing on a short, narrow strip surrounded by jagged peaks is a heart-pounding experience. Rather than flying, you might prefer to drive to Mérida along the Transandina highway. The 160-km (100-mile) stretch from Valera in Trujillo state to Mérida city is incredibly dramatic, with hairpin turns, switchbacks and a few sheer drop-offs.

The Transandina traces part of the trail that Simón Bolívar braved on his campaign to liberate Nueva Granada (Colombia). In 1819 he led 2,000 *llaneros* (plainsmen) and a foreign legion of English and Irish troops over the Andes to victory at the decisive battle of Boyacá.

The first stop in Mérida state is the little village of **La Puerta**, "The Door" to the Andes. From here it's a 22-km (14-mile) zigzag of a drive to **Timotes**, legendary among trout fishermen. Casting for brown and rainbow trout is a popular sport in the streams and lagoons all over Mérida. The season is mid-March to the end of September. Permits are available from any hotel.

Some 45 km (28 miles) from Timotes, you'll reach the freezing **Paso del Aguila** (Eagle Pass), just below Pico Aguila. This is the highest point in the Venezuelan highway system, at an elevation of 4,007 meters (13,146 ft). Bolívar and his troops marched through the pass in 1813 on the Admirable Campaign that concluded with his triumphant entry into Caracas. The bronze statue com-

Preceding pages: mule trains through the mist. **Left,** a roadside ice grinder. **Right,** cable car to Pico Espejo.

memorating his courage is actually a condor, not an eagle. A nearby snack bar sells steaming hot chocolate that you can sip around a crackling fire.

The chill of the Andes may come as quite a shock in tropical Venezuela. If you aren't prepared with warm clothes, you may want to stop at a roadside stand to purchase a *ruana*, the woollen poncho of the region. The most distinctive style is made of double-sided cloth – one side red, the other blue.

Desolate heights: In Mérida, the desolate area above the treeline – at about 3,500 meters (11,500 ft) – is called the *páramo* (high plain). The Venezuelan expression "to end up in the *páramo*" is used to describe someone at death's door. Life is hard here, for the climate is cold, windy and wet. Little grows at these altitudes. In some places, scrawny children press against cars to beg.

But it's not all bleak. The poverty is not as widespread as in the Andean regions of other countries. And the terrain has its own peculiar, somewhat eerie beauty. If you visit from October through December, you will see the yellow blossoms of the *frailejón*, a plant with fuzzy, spiked leaves that can grow up to 2 meters (6 ft) high. Some 45 varieties of these "tall friars" grow on the *páramo*. *Andinos* use *frailejónes* in 101 ingenious ways. They wrap home-churned butter in one type to impart a delicate flavor and stuff another type in mattresses. They fry the pith of the stems of yet a third kind for munching.

Bird watchers will find the *páramo* a rewarding challenge. Mérida boasts nearly 600 species. In the rainy season from May to October, when the wild flowers bloom, the high plain positively buzzes with hummingbirds. *Frailejónes* attract the incredible bearded helmet-crest.

The Transandina highway winds through the *páramo* to **Apartaderos**. From there you can backtrack, along the road to **Barinas**, to visit **Sierra Nevada National Park**, the legendary **Hotel Los Frailes** and **Santo Domingo**, with its trout farm, Truchicultura El Baho. The Andean cock-of-the-rock can be found

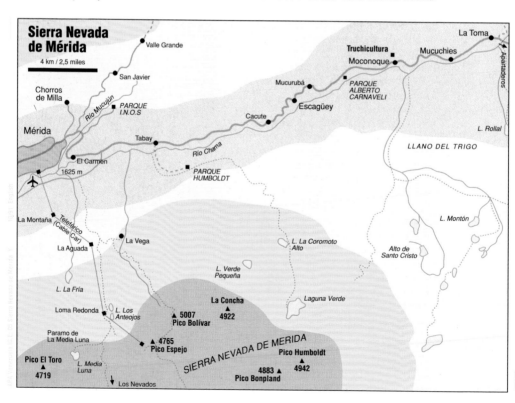

in the country around Santo Domingo.

Colonial escape: Los Frailes (The Friars) is probably the most charming and popular resort in Mérida. The hotel is built on the site of a 17th-century monastery and offers comfortable rooms with wooden beams set around a cobblestone courtyard with fountain. If you ask ahead, you can hire horses to ride across the *páramo*. The hotel offers a fine, rather elegant restaurant. Even if you find no room at the inn (reservations must be made well in advance), be sure to visit the dark, cozy bar where a fire roars in the hearth. Try one of the local drinks, like *calentadito*, hot, spiced milk spiked with the anise liqueur *miche*.

The nearby **Parque Nacional Sierra Nevada** (Sierra Nevada National Park) protects the Andean ranges of Serranía de Santo Domingo and the Sierra Nevada de Mérida. Besides mountains, the park encompasses *páramo* dotted by *frailejónes*, pine forests and the haunting black waters of 170 glacial lagoons. The largest, Laguna Mucubaji, seems bleak at first but offers a surprising abundance of birds including the speckled teal, black-chested buzzard-eagle and the páramo pipit. Snows from Pico Mucuñuque, the highest mountain of the Santo Domingo range, melt into streams that feed the enchanting **Laguna Negra** (Black Lagoon), an hour's hike from the park entrance. **Laguna Los Patos** (Duck Lagoon) is a hard, 2.4-km (1½-mile) trek past Laguna Negra. Fishing, camping and horseback riding are allowed in areas of the park.

Back at the intersection of the Transandina and the Barinas highways lies **Apartaderos**, famous for its cold, cured hams, which hang from the rafters of roadside *charcuterías* (delicatessens). The meat tastes like Italian prosciutto. Cold, smoked sausages are another local specialty, and many Venezuelans wouldn't consider a visit to Mérida complete without bringing home the bacon, so to speak. *Charcuterías* also stock the local white cheese, *queso del páramo*, which is available smoked (it's called *queso ahumado*). Many people fry cheese as part of a hearty Andean break-

Highway through the Andes.

fast that also includes *arepas* made of wheat, rather than cornmeal. Other *charcutería* staples are *mantecada*, the region's sweet white bread, and bottles of *miche*.

Lush valleys: As you come down from the *páramo*, you'll notice sweeping green valleys, fields of yellow mustard, bright carnations (destined for markets around the country), orchids, lilies and dahlias. Most farms are still small, labor-intensive operations, but there are a few large *haciendas* dating back to colonial times. Farmers grow potatoes, carrots, onions and all manner of vegetables, along with garlic, and in places, coffee and sugar cane. In the valleys you'll find every kind of fruit tree, including mango, orange and avocado. Berries are gathered from bushes in the wild as well as cultivated.

You'll note that fields are apportioned off by stone walls. All that rock was painstakingly pulled from the soil to make the land tillable. Some of the walls at Apartaderos are said to date back to the Timoto-Cuica Indians, and the fields

are still called by their traditional Indian name, *poyos*.

When the Spanish arrived in the area during the 17th century, they found a civilization of skilled farmers. The Indians were growing more than 30 crops, including maize, potatos, squash and beans. The conquistadors killed many of the men and married the women, so today there are hardly any pure Indians. But the indigenous culture has survived in the foods, the folklore and to a degree, the place names. Most celebrations honoring Catholic saints feature dancing to the beat of drums and dressing in costumes with masks. Nearing Mérida city, you'll notice several names with the prefix *mucu*, an Indian word meaning "place of."

Further along the Transandino at San Rafael de Mucuchies is a curious little chapel made of thousands of stones. It was pieced together by the enigmatic Juan Félix Sánchez, an artist who is also revered locally as a mystic. He finished the project in 1984, when he was 83 years old. The chapel is actually a small

Mountai
village
Mérida.

218

replica of the one Sánchez built at his isolated homestead in El Tisure, high in the Andes.

The next town, **Mucuchíes**, has a tidy little plaza dominated by the blue and white San Benito Church. A big local celebration is the Vasallos de San Benito (Vassals of Saint Benito), held in late December to express gratitude for favors granted by the saint. His image is taken from the altar and paraded through the streets amid much revelry.

In the Mucuchíes plaza is a famous statue of the Indian boy Tínjaca and his dog, Nevado (Snowy). The story goes that Bolívar stayed in the area in 1813 and his host gave the boy and the dog to *El Libertador* as a sign of allegiance. Supposedly they both stayed faithfully by Bolívar's side until they were shot down and killed in battle.

The dog Nevado was a Mucuchíes breed – seen usually only in the Andes and the closest thing Venezuela has to a national canine. You'll probably see children selling large, cuddly balls of fluff – Mucuchíes pups – on the road-

Harvesting.

side. When fully grown, the dog resembles a Saint Bernard and has a white coat splotched with brown and black. The Mucuchíes was developed in the early 18th century, when Spanish brethern established a monastery in the Andes and began raising sheep. They imported Great Pyrenees dogs from Europe to guard their flocks, which mixed with local mutts to eventually create the Muchuchíes breed.

Although the Great Pyrenees were prized for their loyalty, obedience and strength, Mucuchíes dogs have an added characteristic: ferocity. They are often used as guard dogs on Andean farms.

On the Transandina highway several kilometers from the town of Mucuchíes is **Moconoque**, which is really only a couple of houses and a trout farm, closed to the public. The house at the entrance to the farm is said to be where Bolívar was staying when he was made a gift of Tinjaca and Nevado.

Exploring the capital: The regional capital of **Mérida** is not a physically beautiful city, but its setting is spectacular.

Nestled in a lush valley thick with trees draped in Spanish moss and flowering plants, Mérida boasts a dramatic backdrop of five of the highest peaks in the Andean chain. The locals call the mountains *Las Cinco Aguilas Blancas* (The Five White Eagles). They are La Corona, La Concha, La Columna, El Toro and El León. La Corona is actually two peaks, Humboldt and Bonpland, while La Columna is comprised of Espejo and Bolívar. All tower over 4,700 meters (15,420 ft); Bolívar, at 5,007 meters (16,427 ft), is the highest.

About 130,000 people live here, including more than 30,000 students of The University of the Andes. The community definitely has a university flavor, making for both lively intellectual life and nightlife. *Merideños* appreciate nature and sports – they enjoy at least least 22 parks, including one with an orchid nursery, one dedicated to local writers, one with waterfalls and one with a clock that plays Beethoven tunes on the hour.

The climate at this altitude (1,645 meters/5,400 feet) is pleasant and moderate. It's usually warm in the daylight hours – from 21–31°C (70–80°F), but at nightfall the mercury drops and it gets nippy – about 5°C (40°F).

Mérida may seem a tranquil place today, but its foundation involved scandal and bloodshed. Juan Rodríguez Suárez, an officer who was supposed to be exploring the Sierra Nevada with a party of soldiers in 1558, apparently got it into his head to found a town, which he named it after Mérida, Spain. In those days, towns were founded only by royal proclamation, so Rodríguez Suárez found himself in serious trouble. He was branded a criminal, tried and sentenced to an absurdly gruesome death. But sympathizers intervened and helped the rebel officer flee to Trujillo, where he was granted the first political asylum in the New World.

Rodríguez Suárez had founded Mérida on the site of present-day Lagunillas. Hostile Indians forced the settlers to pack up and move some kilometers to the east, to a place now known as La Punta. Finally, Juan Maldonado y

A Tyrolean touch.

Ordóñez, the man who had arrested Rodríguez Suárez, established Mérida once and for all at its present site, giving it the grand name, La Ciudad de Santiago de los Caballeros de Mérida. *Caballeros* means gentlemen, and for many years Mérida was known simply as "the gentlemen's city." Even today, Mérida remains perhaps the most polite metropolitan area in Venezuela. *Merideños* tend to be well-mannered, but also reserved and conservative – particularly compared to boisterous and fun-loving *Caraqueños*.

Power of tradition: In Mérida there is great respect for the Church. When Pope John Paul II visited the country in 1985, he drew his largest crowds here. There is also respect for Bolívar. Mérida was the first place to proclaim him *El Libertador* – on May 23, 1813. It is considered disrespectful to Bolívar's memory to pass by his statue in the plaza wearing sloppy clothes or carrying suitcases or large bundles. Police have even reprimanded students with backpacks. Finally, there is respect for the siesta –

from noon until 2pm each day commerce grinds to a halt as shops, banks and offices close to allow workers a snooze after lunch.

Siesta hour is a good time to head to one of the city's many parks. **Parque La Isla** features hundreds of orchids, while **Parque Beethoven** has two clocks – one made of flowers and one with wooden soldiers that march around a chalet to the tune of Beethoven compositions when the hour strikes. Across the street is the city's **Museo de Arte Moderno** (Modern Art Museum), with works by contemporary Venezuelan artists. **Parque de las Cinco Repúblicas** (Park of the Five Republics) features a tall white column holding a bust of Bolívar. When erected in 1842, this was the world's first monument dedicated to *El Libertador*. The park also has soil from each of the five countries Bolívar emancipated.

But of all Mérida's parks, perhaps the best-loved is **Los Chorros de Milla** with its beautiful cascades. Local legend says that an Indian princess whose

Angels and comics.

lover was murdered by the conquistadors cried so hard that her tears turned into the falls. There's a statue of the tragic princess at the park entrance.

In the heart of Mérida, the peaceful, green **Plaza Bolívar** is surrounded by stately government buildings, the main entrance to the university and of course, the **cathedral**. Construction on the cathedral was started in 1803, but damage from war and several earthquakes required continuous rebuildings, and the cathedral was completed in its present form only in 1958. The result is a rather gloomy architectural mish-mash, but to devout *Merideños* it is the most beautiful cathedral in the country. One of the paintings is supposedly of God.

Beside the cathedral is the **Palacio Arzobispal** (Archbishop's Palace) with its small museum of religious art treasures. There's also a **Museo de Arte Colonial** downtown that features religious paintings, precious metals, furniture and ceramics.

The entrance hall of the **Palacio de Gobierno** (Government Palace) has a monumental triptych by painter Ivan Belsky representing the three zones of Mérida state, from the steamy lowlands near Lake Maracaibo to the high plain to the Andes. In the formal reception room upstairs is a painting by Jorge Arteago of Bolívar's entrance into Mérida in the Admirable Campaign of 1813. The guards usually let you go in to have a look at the triptych, at least, if you present some kind of identification.

The **Universidad de Los Andes**, one of the largest and oldest in Venezuela, was founded in 1810 after first opening in 1785 as a seminary. A stained glass window over the entrance bears the Biblical quotation (in Latin): "You cannot hide a city on a mountain."

On the side streets near the plaza are a number of colonial houses that have been converted into shops and restaurants. Look for the National Monument plaques on their walls that give information about the history of the building.

The many small, typical restaurants downtown serve dishes like *truche andino* (trout caught fresh from moun- **Serious studies at Mérida university.**

222

tain streams) and usually accompanied by the small, sweet white potatoes grown in the area. *Carabinas* are the Mérida version of *hallacas*, which are *tamale*-like packets of cornmeal stuffed with meats and steamed in banana leaves. In the rest of Venezuela, *hallacas* are strictly a Christmas food, but in Mérida they are eaten throughout the year. Other local specialties are *pisca andina*, a soup with potatoes and eggs, and *mondongo* (tripe). Local drinks include *chica andina*, the Andean beverage made from corn, *mistela* and hot punches like *calentadito*.

Flavors of the Andes: Fruits and vegetables are the starring attractions at the city's main **market**, a block from the Plaza Bolívar. In season, look for baskets of sweet *fresas* (strawberries). There are always bags of *dulces abrillan-tados*, a chewy, taffy-like candy boiled into balls around an aniseed. You might find a few handicrafts such as cloth dolls and straw slippers.

If you have a sweet tooth or simply crave something offbeat during your stroll around Mérida, head straight for **Helados Coromoto** (Coromoto Ice Cream Parlor) in an orange stucco building just off **Plaza El Llano**. This is the home of 383 flavors – and counting. Owner Manuel Oliveira was searching for a new taste sensation when he dreamed up his first flavor – avocado. It took 50 kg (110 lb) of experimenting to get it right. From there, things sort of blossomed.

The flavor list takes up the entire back wall. There's pumpkin, whole wheat, soya, ginger, garlic, fried pork rind, tuna fish, fresh trout, shrimp, and wacky combos like grouper with guayaba. Among the most requested is *pabellón criollo*, a takeoff of the national Venezuelan dish of shredded beef, black beans, rice and plantains. Some flavors have fanciful names like *Te Amo* (I love you) and *Viajando con Polar Malta* (traveling with Polar malt beer).

Every day Helados Coromoto offers a short list of 88 flavors, and owner Oliviera whips up 15 fresh batches. He has applied to the *Guinness Book of*

A village coffee house.

Records for the title of "ice cream store with the most flavors."

High-wire adventure: Mérida's *teleférico* (cable car) is the highest and longest in the world, and it's a must for visitors to the state. The cars climb in four stages to the top of **Pico Espejo** at 4,763 meters (15,630 ft), where a large statue of the Virgen de las Nieves (Virgin of the Snows), patron saint of mountaineers, stands with open arms amid the swirling mists.

The *teleférico* station is located in the Barinitas section of town. Because the lines can be long, get there an hour before the first car departs (usually at 7.30 or 8am – check the sign at the entrance or with the tourist office at the airport). The *teleférico* operates daily except Mondays and Tuesdays, with the last car up leaving at noon, and the last car down from the top at 2pm, just as the thick mountain fog starts rolling in. Each stage of the ride takes 15 minutes or so, with short pauses at the stations.

No matter how warm it is in Mérida, there's always snow on Pico Espejo.

Take winter clothes. Most people carry sweaters, ski jackets and gloves, layering them on as they ascend.

The first part of the ride swoops up and over the **Río Chama** gorge, and soon the entire city of Mérida, surrounded by thick forest, is spread below. La Montana station, at 2,440 meters (8,000 ft), offers a view of nearly the entire Chama Valley. You may notice several white dots on the mountains at the other side of the valley; they are astronomical observatories. The station has a little restaurant/bar.

The second stop is **La Aguada**, at an elevation of 4,045 meters (13,272 ft). You'll notice guides hanging around at each station who might offer to take you on a hike or a mule ride. This is also the starting point for most organized treks, on foot, horseback or mountain bike – as well as a favorite start for hang gliders.

En route to the third station, **Loma Redonda**, at an altitude of 3,444 meters (11,300 ft), you'll be flying over treeless *páramo*. It's here that some people begin to feel a bit woozy or lightheaded

The view over Mérida.

or to experience a shortness of breath – all symptoms of *soroche* (altitude sickness). There's oxygen at each station, and a doctor at the top. If you start to feel uncomfortable, take it slow. Drinking or eating something may help. Don't hesitate to ask for oxygen if you're getting queasy.

Just a short walk from the Loma Redonda station, past the shrine to the Virgin, you can see the twin lagoons, **Los Anteojos** (The Eyeglasses), shimmering black in the valley. From this level, expeditions depart for **Los Nevados**, a 400-year-old Indian village that's about a six-hour hike or mule-ride away along a steep, narrow trail. Some 2,000 people live in this agricultural settlement, where potatoes, garlic, wheat and beans are farmed. Villagers haul their produce by mule to the *teleférico* station and whisk it down to Mérida in the cable cars. Visitors to Los Nevados can arrange to stay with local families, and the charge normally includes three hearty meals a day.

At the fourth station, the top, it's very cold. Fortunately, there's a shop selling comforting cups of hot chocolate, big slices of heavy cake, candy bars and other snacks. The rocky summit of Pico Espejo rises beside the platform, and if the weather isn't too gray or snowy, you can see the glacier on neighboring Pico Bolívar. A very fit hiker could reach Bolívar from here in three to five hours, but it's a tough journey.

Venezuelan tourism pamplets talk about skiing the glaciers, but this must be the fantasy of some sadistic copywriter. There are no lifts and at this high altitude the climb back up would be excruciating, if not downright impossible. One Venezuelan magazine suggested astronaut training for those considering skiing the Andes and pointed out that Pico Bolívar would be out of the range of European slopes; it soars over the Matterhorn and Jungfrau by more than 600 meters (almost 2,000 ft).

Excursions into the Andes: The Mérida environs offer a number of day trips for those interested in food, history and local culture. Just outside the capital, on

Atop Pico Espejo.

the El Valle highway en route to the Valle Grande hotel, is a fun little **jam factory** that seems bent on dreaming up as many flavors as Helados Coromoto. José and Rhoda Ramírez so far market more than 60 varieties of jams and marmalades. Among the more unusual flavors are angel hair (similar to cotton candy), tamarind (star fruit) and rhubarb. (Venezuelans believe the latter works as a laxative, so if you choose this flavor, be prepared for snickers from your fellow customers.)

The Ramírezes, agricultural engineers, launched El Valle jam factory in an effort to encourage young people from the area to start cottage industries instead of moving away.

There are several trout farms in the Mérida area that are open to visitors. A few decades ago the government introduced rainbow trout from North America. The industry has flourished.

Besides Truchicultura El Baho near **Santo Domingo**, you can visit El Paraíso at **Mucunutan**, where big Mucuchies dogs stand guard over the tanks fed by icy spring water piped in from the mountains. If you're lucky, you may get to feed the fish from a large bag of nutrient-rich pellets called "trout wheat." When you see how they gobble the stuff up, you'll understand how it takes only a matter of months for the fish to grow to market weight. They're mechanically scaled, gutted, individually packaged and shipped off by plane to restaurants around Venezuela and the US Eastern Seaboard.

Spanish outpost: One of the most popular day trips from Mérida is a visit to the restored colonial village of **Jají**. Buses leave from Mérida, and cab drivers will also negotiate a price to take you there. The 40-km (25-mile) ride southwest offers splendid views, following a winding mountain road washed by streams and waterfalls.

The government restoration of Jají was completed in 1971. Houses have traditional wooden gratings on the windows, and no commercial signs are allowed. Most everything worth seeing is clustered around the plaza with its white

Left, statue of the Liberator on Pico Bolívar. **Below**, handwoven rugs, an Andean specialty.

church trimmed in blue, shops and a 400-year-old inn called **La Posada de Jají**. The inn has rooms with balconies that face the plaza or overlook the central courtyard. Local folkloric groups play live music on Sundays. It's all very charming, but sometimes the place is almost overwhelmed by tourists, mostly Venezuelans.

La Azulita is a little village near Jají. The main attraction here is the mysterious Cueva del Pirata (Pirate's Cave). Although pirates raided towns along the southern shore of Lake Maracaibo during the 17th century, some miles north of La Azulita, it is not known if they came up into the mountains or if the cave's name is pure fancy.

Another touristic town is **Los Aleros** (The Eaves). It is modeled on a 1930s Andean village, right down to a few cars of that era parked along the narrow streets. There are exhibits with people performing traditional skills like spinning wool and dipping candles, as well as humorous little vignettes presented by costumed locals. Not far away and in stark contrast to the historic theme of Los Aleros is a rather weird amusement housed in the **Cave of the Weeping Woman**, a horror house in a tunnel with mechanical witches posed to scare the living daylights out of visitors.

Pueblo Nuevo del Sur is another historic town, about an hour's drive from Mérida. Although this one has not been restored, it was declared a national monument in 1960 which theoretically provides it some protection. Built on the site of an Indian village in 1700, it was once an important regional market. *Burros* remain the key form of transportation. There are no restaurants or hotels, so visitors will have to be content with a leisurely stroll around and a peek in at the colonial church of Santa Rita.

Farm holidays: If you're interested in staying at a working *hacienda* while in Mérida, there are several in the area that have opened their doors to guests. The old but beautifully restored **Hacienda Escaguey** near **Mucurubá** is the family estate of Rolando Araujo, a Caracas attorney. Guests sleep in rooms lining

The mists roll in on the mountain village of Jají.

the cobblestone courtyard – some might have been part of the stable in the days when animals and people shared the same roof. You can watch the farmhands at work and visit the dairy operation, where cows are milked by machine and cheese is made in big rounds.

If you drive southwest along the Transandina highway through Mérida state via Bailadores, you eventually arrive at Táchira state. You'll pass more little Andean villages like **La Punta**, where a high point of the year is El Baile de los Vasallos de la Candelaria (Dance of the Vassals), performed for the Virgin of La Candelaria in late January and early February. Fireworks and parades are among the festivities.

The road drops down to Lagunillas, the original location of Mérida, while the temperature climbs. The Festival of San Isidro in May harks back to the area's once-great Indian population. On May 15, vespers are said at the Chapel of Pueblo Viejo and Saint Isidro is carried in a procession by folks dressed like bears, monkeys and devils.

Estanques is the start of tropical Mérida. Sugar cane and bananas are the important crops here. The village boasts the **Capilla de la Santa Cruz** (Chapel of the Holy Cross), with its lavish gold baroque altarpiece. It was presented by King Carlos III to a local grande dame, Doña María Ramírez de Urbina, in 1726. Unfortunately, the chapel is in disrepair and seldom open to visitors.

The road starts to rise again, and at **Santa Cruz de Mora**, coffee is cultivated. **Tovar**, the second largest city in the state, is the heart of coffee and sugar-cane country. Oxen are still used to turn the machine to crush the cane.

The Transandina continues to climb to **Bailadores**, near the border with Táchira state. You're once again in the mountains, and the scenery is exceptional. Bailadores means "dancers," and it is said that the name originates from the quick movements made by the light-footed Indians during battle with Captain Rodríguez Suárez (illicit founder of Mérida) and his troops. The Indians fought fiercely but futilely.

Beside the Plaza Bolívar in town is a house that *El Libertador* made his headquarters in May 1813, at the launch of the Admirable Campaign. The building was in ruins when it was bought by the government and restored into a museum.

Province of dictators: Outside Bailadores, the highway rises steeply into the mountains and rolls on into Táchira state, the home of many Venezuelan dictators. It has produced at least five strongmen in the 19th century, including perhaps the most notorious of all, Juan Vicente Gómez.

The portraits of various native sons displayed in the bars and homes of Táchira show that some locals are still proud of the mark these *andinos* made on the country. But why would such an isolated region yield such a surprising number of dictatorial rulers? One historian claims *táchirenses* possess "deep and unbending patriotism stimulated by their condition of being a frontier people." Less fawning observers have noted how Andeans tend to appoint their cronies to influential positions, ensuring a more or less inherited line of power.

Left, Juan Félix Sanchez church. **Right**, look, no hand rails!

THE WEST COAST

Compared to the East Coast with its flashy resorts, Venezuela's West Coast seems a bit wild and undeveloped. That, of course, is precisely its attraction, especially for foreign visitors. The West's wilderness areas – from cloud forests to islands of mangroves or sand dunes – are incomparable, and colonial history lives on in fascinating cities like Puerto Cabello and Coro.

If you want to get to know the West Coast, set aside at least a week of exploring. Leave Caracas via the *autopista* to Route 1, a modern super-highway which winds south then west to the agro-industrial city of Maracay. From Maracay you can head north across the mountains, through the magnificent cloud forest of Henri Pittier National Park, to a string of little fishing villages with glorious, palm-fringed beaches.

Or you can skirt Lake Valencia to the important industrial center of Valencia City, where the decisive battle of Carabobo took place. North from Valencia you'll reach the thriving port city of Puerto Cabello, with its notorious colonial fort. To the west are the reef-formed islands of Morrocoy National Park, home to exotic birds and a paradise for snorkelers and divers.

From there, continue northwest to Coro, the first capital of the Province of Venezuela, with its interesting colonial mansions. Just outside of town – this is no mirage – are sand dunes and camels. The Paraguaná Peninsula, dry and dotted with cactus and scrub, offers remote, windswept beaches.

Departing the capital: After leaving Caracas and en route to Maracay, you will pass **San Mateo**. Nearby is the family *hacienda* of Simón Bolívar, a sugar and cacao plantation dating to 1593. Bolívar was born in Caracas in 1783, but spent much of his childhood here in the country, where he was educated by his free-thinking tutor, Simón Rodríguez. Later he brought his bride, María Teresa Rodríguez del Toro y Alayza, to the *hacienda* expecting to settle into the life of a country squire. His destiny changed when María Teresa died of a mysterious fever several months after the honeymoon. The 20-year-old Bolívar was devastated but shortly after became politically active. He never remarried, yet is said to have taken hundreds of lovers.

During the war for independence, the Bolívar estate became a military camp when José Tomás Boves ("the butcher") surrounded and attacked Bolívar and his troops. In a patriotic move, one of the republican soldiers ignited the armory, blasting himself and many of Boves' men off the face of the earth. The Bolívar family home is now a museum; there is also an exhibit on the production of sugar.

Maracay is the modern, thriving capital of Aragua state. Its name comes from an Indian chief who lived in the area with his Aragua tribe at the time of the conquest. The fortunes of the region have always been made in agriculture – coffee, cacao, indigo, cotton, tobacco and other crops.

Preceding pages: white sand and palms at Chichiriviche. **Left**, colonial grace at Choroní. **Right**, graceful reflection.

The brutal dictator Juan Vicente Gómez (1908–35) bought several houses in Maracay and governed here from 1912 until his death. It is said that, fearing assassins, he never slept in the same bed two nights in a row. Gómez is largely responsible for making Maracay what it is today. He cleared an escape route over the mountains to the sea that is now a well-traveled road, built a zoo, a bullring, opera house, parks and fountains. He started Venezuela's first air service, to Maracay, Maracaibo and Ciudad Bolívar. Maracay's **Museo Fuerza Aerea Venezolana** (Aeronautical Museum) displays a couple of dozen historical aircraft.

Natural wonderland: There are two routes from Maracay across the mountains to the enticing beaches at Cata/Cuayagua and Choroní. Both cross the Cordillera de la Costa through the magnificent Rancho Grande cloud forest. The 107,800-hectare (266,374-acre) site was set aside in 1937 as Venezuela's first national park. Initially called Rancho Grande Cloud Forest, it was

renamed **Parque Nacional Henri Pittier** in 1953 to honor the Swiss botanist who classified 30,000 Venezuelan plants and promoted the national park system.

Snakes, frogs, monkeys, ocelots, bats, opossums, armadillos, kinkajous, skunks and deer thrive in the humid environment of the cloud forest. The highest mountains in the park rise to about 1,280 meters (4,200 ft). Portachuelo Pass, a V-shaped dip in the terrain, serves as a migration route for insects and birds. William Beebe, the first naturalist to use the laboratory, claimed he had to wear glasses to protect his eyes from the migrating butterflies – as many as 200 brilliant species.

More than 500 species of birds make their home in the cloud forest. Mary Lou Goodwin, head of Venezuela's Audubon Society, calls Rancho Grande at dawn "without doubt, one of the rarest, most exquisite experiences a birdwatcher can have anywhere in the world." Endemic birds include the handsome fruiteater, blood-eared parakeet and helmeted

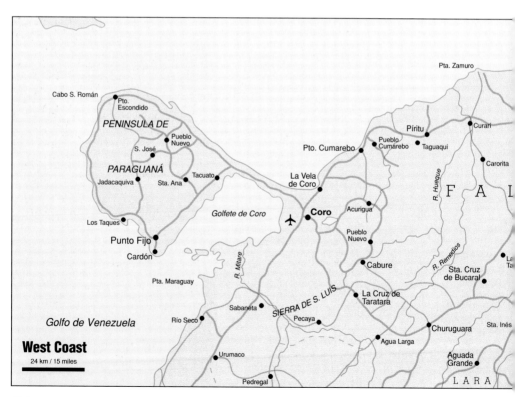

West Coast

24 km / 15 miles

curassow. You might also see harpy eagle, white-tipped quetzal and flocks of lilac-tailed parrotlets.

The road to Cata traces the path carved out as an escape route for the dictator Gómez. It passes Rancho Grande, a hotel Gómez was having constructed when he died. Upon hearing the news, the workers laid down their tools and walked away. The half-finished building was eventually converted into a biological research station. Beebe, who studied at Rancho Grande in the 1940s, wrote a book about his experiences called *High Jungle*.

After you cross the mountains and start to descend to the coast, you'll pass through **Ocumare de la Costa** with its twin plazas, each commemorating unsuccessful landings during the independence struggle – one by Francisco de Miranda in 1806 and the other by Bolívar in 1816.

Nearby **Cata** is a long crescent beach on a tranquil bay. Unfortunately, two tall apartment towers mar the view. But for the most part, Cata remains a rustic place where you can string your hammock under the palms, pitch a tent or hitch a ride with fishermen to the eastern point of the bay and **Catita Beach**. Five km (3 miles) inland from Cata is the old village of Cata, once part of a cacao plantation. **Cuayagua** lies 13 km (8 miles) east. Its beach is paradise, but the rough waters are usually braved only by surfers.

Hard road to paradise: The other road from Maracay through Henri Pittier Park is famous for its hairpin turns. It's only 48 km (30 miles) as the crow flies to **Choroní** on the coast, but the twisting, turning drive takes at least an hour and a half. Gaily colored buses loaded with beachgoers cross the mountains, grinding gears and sometimes meeting head-on coming around blind curves along the precipitous, one-lane road. Waterfalls wash across the pavement and you'll see cars pulled over with people bathing and picnicking. A splendid canopy of bamboo stretches overhead, obscuring the sky. The air is refreshing and grows cooler as you climb. On the

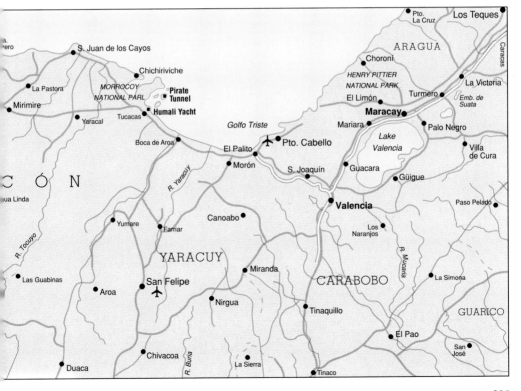

way down to the coast, you'll pass little roadside stands selling refreshments as chickens roam loose in the yard.

A few kilometers from the sea, you'll drive smack through the middle of Choroní, a charming village of one-story pastel houses built flush up to the road. Choroní was once at the heart of a rich cacao-growing region, with *haciendas* powered by back-breaking slave labor. In colonial times, Dutch and Spanish merchant ships plied the coast, spiriting cargoes of cacao, coffee and sugar across the Atlantic. The journey was fraught with danger – bloodthirsty English pirates stalked the entire coast and sometimes came ashore for raids.

That is why Choroní, like Cata and many other towns of the epoch, was built back from the sea – to afford some protection from the marauders. Tiny **Puerto Colombia**, the port for Choroní, is right on the water, with its fleet of brightly painted wooden boats moored in a little river flowing into the sea. A string of bars and seafood shacks lines the dusty main road that ends at the waterfront. Here, on the *malecón*, is where the sensual *tambores* are danced with wild abandon under the stars on weekend nights. *Tambores* are big hollow drums used to pound out a pulsating beat while one or two couples dance in the center of a rum-swilling crowd. Women from the ring take turns stepping in and trying to butt out the female of the couple, using quick steps and hip thrusting motions. The crowd claps along, egging on the dancers.

The area's principal beach, **Playa Grande**, is about 400 meters/yards east of Puerto Colombia. It's wrapped around a bay lined with coconut trees and a few open-air snack bars. This is where the crowds flock with their radios and paddle-tennis racquets.

In the opposite direction from town is isolated **Playa Escondida** (Hidden Beach), reached by wading through a stream, trekking along an unmarked jungle path, then climbing down a rocky cliff. It's remote and wild, with a frenzied surf and big crashing waves. Quite frequently the beach is totally deserted. **The beach, Choroní.**

Swimming here is strictly for the hardy.

Several local beaches are reached only from the sea, by fishing boat from Puerto Colombia. Go down to the waterfront in the morning and bargain for your transportation. **Chuao**, about 20 minutes away by boat, is a lovely little beach on a gentle bay. You can walk into the cool, enchanting forest. The small community of Chuao is set some kilometers back inland.

Club Cotoperíx, a hotel built in two restored colonial houses in Puerto Colombia, offers rooms with full board, including transportation and a picnic lunch or barbecue at local beaches, as well as walks through the forest to see the ruins of cacao *haciendas* and bathe in waterfalls. The club is an effort by Caracas businessman Polo Casanova to rejuvenate the local economy. Choroní carpenters made all the furniture for his hotel, local fishermen supply the fish, and farmers harvest the fresh fruits and produce that go into the club's bountiful meals. Book ahead in Caracas.

Back in Maracay, if you head west,

Hotel room in Choroní.

skirting **Lake Valencia**, you'll arrive at the flourishing capital of Carabobo state, Valencia. The lake area is believed to have been one of the earliest inhabited places in Venezuela. Archaeologists have unearthed ceramics and other evidence of early Indian cultures, along with fossils of mastedons, armadillos, tapirs and sloths. One of the most important sites in the country for petroglyphs is Valencia's extensive **Parque Nacional Piedras Pintadas** (Petroglyphs National Park).

Lake Valencia is shrinking. It was twice as large as its present size (30 km/20 miles long) when the city of Valencia was founded in 1553. Industrial waste is partly to blame, and a four-year cleanup costing hundreds of millions of bolívares has been launched.

Valencia has grown into one of Venezuela's largest cities despite a tumultuous past. Less than a decade after its founding, it was nearly destroyed by the invading forces of Lope de Aguirre, the mad conquistador on a quest to find El Dorado (*see Aguirre the Mad, page 34*).

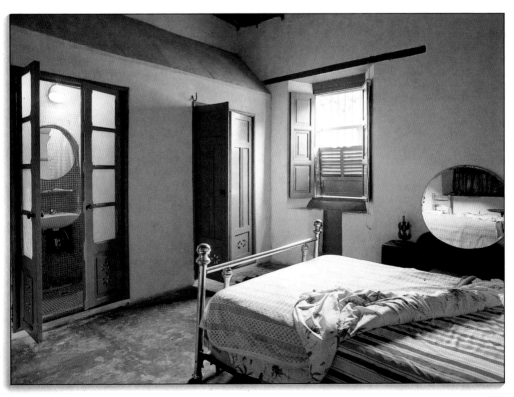

The city was later attacked by Caribe Indians, sacked by French pirates, and devastated in the earthquake of 1812.

While Valencia was the setting for the decisive battle of Carabobo in the war of independence, in 1826 it became the first city to resist Bolívar's union, Gran Colombia. It held an assembly declaring Venezuela a sovereign state and for a brief time stole the role of federal capital from Caracas.

Attractions include the **Teatro Municipal** (Municipal Theater), built in 1892 to emulate the Paris Opera House, and closed in 1971 to be renovated for the 150th anniversary of the battle of Carabobo. But instead of taking eight months as planned, the theater was not finished for eight *years*. The ceiling, painted by Herrera Toro, is a national monument.

Valencia's 200-year-old **cathedral** boasts a statue of the Virgen del Socorro (Virgin of Succor) in a bejeweled gown. In 1910 this became the first statue in Venezuela to be crowned – with the pope's permission – in recognition of the many favors granted by the Virgin. The priceless crown is hidden away in a bank vault and brought out only for special services.

The legendary General José Antonio Paez, who forged a formidable army of *llaneros* (plainsmen) and served as Venezuela's first acting president, then the first elected president of the republic, lived in Valencia for a time. The **Casa Paez** has a patio with murals depicting nine battles the general fought. Over some of the windows are inscriptions of his favorite sayings.

The **Plaza de Toros Monumental de Valencia**, the bullring, is the second largest in the Americas after Mexico City's. It holds 27,000 people.

Twenty-five km (15 miles) southwest of Valencia, on Route 5, the **Safari Carabobo Reserva Animal** (Auto Safari Carabobo) features tigers, giraffes, ostriches and other African creatures roaming on 150 hectares (370 acres). Visitors drive round a 14-km (9-mile) circuit. The baboons love to hitch rides.

Some 7 km (4 miles) further on from

Left, Choroní fisherman. **Below**, Henri Pittier National Park.

Valencia lies the **Carabobo** battlefield, scene of the June 24, 1821 victory that virtually secured Venezuela's independence from Spain. There's an impressive monument to the heroes who took part in the battle, with a large reflecting pool and an equestrian statue of Bolívar. At the entrance to the site is a diorama explaining the battle.

Gateway to the West: Leaving Valencia by Highway 1 north, you will arrive at the industrial behemoth of **El Palito**, a state-owned oil refinery, which marks the place where you bear right for **Puerto Cabello**. This large, natural port tucked into a bay at the eastern end of Golfo Triste often handles more cargo than La Guaira, its chief competitor. Puerto Cabello has been an important harbor since its founding in the middle of the 16th century. Almost from the start it was plagued by pirates who tried to intercept Spanish galleons loaded with gold, silver and other riches.

After a time, Dutch merchants gained a foothold. Cacao and coffee, indigo and cotton moved from Venezuela to the Dutch islands via Puerto Cabello. The Spanish government made a pact with powerful Basque merchants, promising them a virtual monopoly if they squelched the Dutch game. The group formed the Guipuzcoana Company in 1728 and erected a fort at the harbor entrance in 1732. The company also established offices and warehouses, stimulating the local economy, yet it was despised by the *porteños* (as people of the port were known). But with government support, the company flourished until 1785. After independence, the Guipuzcoana headquarters became the customs house. **Casa Guipuzcoana** now houses a library and city offices.

Fortín San Felipe, also known as **Castillo Libertador**, was the last Spanish stronghold on Venezuelan soil. Following their defeat at the battle of Carabobo, Spanish troops retreated here and managed to hold out for two years. In the 1900s, the fort was put to grim use by the dictator Gómez who had his political enemies chained in the dungeons. You can still see the messages

Fortress at Puerto Cabello.

the prisoners scratched on the walls. The fort is reached by a quick motorboat ferry; tour guides are available at the site explain the history.

Paseo Malecón is a long waterfront park with fountains and cannon. Brilliant red hibiscus bushes splash color against the blue Caribbean beyond the seawall. The *malecón* is especially popular with the locals at dusk, when everyone turns out to catch the cooling breezes. Vendors peddle coffee, *arepas* (fried cornmeal patties stuffed with a choice of fillings) and *empanadas de atún* (tuna turnovers). Seafood restaurants overlook the ocean at the far end of the marina – a perfect spot for watching the sun set. Even the cargo ships anchored offshore start to look romantic after a rum or two.

The pedestrian street, **Calle de los Lanceros**, is named for the patriots who ended the Spanish grip on Puerto Cabello by a surprise attack from the mangroves. They swam part of the way, carrying only their lances. Soon after the surrender of the fort, the Spanish left Venezuela. In November 1823, General Paez rode in a victory parade down the narrow cobblestone street with his lancers. Today the *calle* is a pleasant place to stroll and look at exhibits set up by local artists. Note the second-floor wooden walkway linking two buildings on opposite sides of the street. At the end of the passage is the unusual wooden bell tower of **Rosario Church**.

Plaza Monumento El Aguila (Eagle Monument Square) holds a statue dedicated to 10 North Americans who were executed by royalists in 1806, while fighting in Venezuela's independence war under Francisco de Miranda. The general had recruited about 200 Americans in New York to stage an ill-fated landing. The monument, located on Calle El Aguila across from the naval facility, is just one of many in this patriotic city where streets bear names like *Democracia* and *Independencia*.

Venezuela's great rail journey: It costs less than a dollar to take the country's last remaining passenger train from Puerto Cabello all the way to the end of

A *hacienda* near Maracay.

the line at **Barquisimeto**. The 173-km (108-mile) ride takes about four hours, with several stops. The train runs twice a day during the week and three times daily on weekends. The cars have red plastic seats and many of the windows are shattered from rocks lobbed by children along the route.

Puerto Cabello is hot year-round, which makes the seashore especially enticing. Beaches east of town include **Quizandal**, which offers restaurants and is jammed on weekends. More beautiful and less hectic is **Isla Larga**, a coral island reached by a 15-minute boat ride from Quizandal. There are two underwater wrecks for divers and snorkelers, and you can camp in the white sand. Kiosks and vendors sell snacks. Go prepared for the sun – there's no shade. **Patanemo Bay**, about 12 km (7½ miles) from Puerto Cabello, is a wide half-moon fringed by coconut palms.

West of Puerto Cabello is a large hill topped by the **Fort Solano**. Bankrolled by the Guipuzcoana Company and finished in 1770, it was the last colonial fort built in Venezuela. A long, winding road leads up to the ruins.

The community of **San Esteban** is a few kilometers southwest of Puerto Cabello. It was a popular retreat for wealthy merchants from the city. Only one colonial house survives; the other mansions date from the mid-19th century. Near the school are the ruins of the home of General Bartolomé Salom, a hero of the independence war and a loyal friend to Bolívar. The site is maintained as a monument, and there's an eerie, life-sized statue of the general sitting in a hammock.

Striking out west to Morrocoy National Park, you'll pass the ugly, state-owned petrochemical complex at **Morón**. Morón's other claim to fame is its absurd **Monument to the Mosquito**, a large dead mosquito lying at the base of an obelisk. It commemorates one of Venezuela's great medical triumphs: malaria was a major killer until a determined eradication campaign from the end of World War II until the 1960s loosened the disease's grip.

Exploring the mangrove swamps in Morrocoy National Park.

Nature reserve: In Falcón state, about a four-hour drive straight from Caracas, lies **Morrocoy National Park**, created in 1974 to protect the many mangroves, sea-bird rookeries and coral reefs. As you approach, you'll pass copra plantations and decrepit seaside shacks. Although Morrocoy is becoming a hot spot for weekending *Caraqueños* and overseas tour groups, there's still a lot to be done to beautify the area.

The park itself is a paradise for snorkelers, divers, waterskiers and bird-watchers. There are about 30 *cayos* (cays, or reef-formed islands), some quite large with palm trees and mangroves, others low-lying with pure white sand. The mangroves are nesting grounds for frigate birds. scarlet ibis, pink flamingos, crested herons, cormorants and ducks frequent the salt flats to feed.

The town of **Tucacas** guards the eastern edge of the park. Nowadays it's a muddy, rundown village that's showing signs of revival thanks to tourism – a major condominium resort with marina has opened, and smaller hotels are springing up. But it was once a thriving port of Dutch merchants who traded with the nearby islands.

Divers flock to Tucacas to visit the Submatur shop, owned by Mike Osborn. Eighteen years ago, this native of Guayana almost single-handedly introduced the sport of diving to Venezuela. Submatur rents equipment, conducts NAUI courses and operates tours with a small fleet of dive boats.

Morrocoy offers both beach and boat dives and is ideal for beginners, Osborn says. He describes the underwater experience as typical "Caribbean-type diving," relatively calm and shallow (20–25 meters/70–80 ft maximum), with visibility from 6 to 30 meters (20–100 ft), with all kinds of Caribbean fish and coral, as well as sponges and turtles (see *Beneath the Waves*).

At the Tucacas waterfront, you can hire a fishing boat to visit Smugglers' Channel (also called Lovers' Channel), a maze of mangroves where you'll spot dozens of bright orangey-red starfish, bigger than your hand, lying on the

Loading up bananas at Tucacas.

shallow bottom. **Isla de Pajaros** (Bird Island) is where magnificent frigate birds nest in December and January. Other common species include the brown pelican, brown booby, scarlet ibis and tropical cormorant. Boats can drive past to see the flocks crowded in the trees and circling overhead, but are not allowed to land – the island is off-limits for conservation reasons. It's a mystery why the birds favor this particular cay out of the many at Morrocoy, but a local pilot claims there is a heat blast that the birds like to float on.

There are about 400 caves in the park. You go by boat to a landing built in the mangroves then walk to **Cueva del Indio** (Cave of the Indian), actually a tranquil, vine-crossed clearing in the forest surrounded by rocks decorated with petroglyphs. **Cueva de la Virgen** (Cave of the Virgin), also reached by boat, is a shrine for local fishermen, who have placed little holy figures in niches of the cliff face. One bizarre effect is a pair of praying hands sticking out of the rock. It's 11 km (7 miles) north from here to

Chichiriviche, gateway to Morrocoy's northern cays. The route passes land that was formerly part of the Rockefeller dynasty's gigantic King Ranch. You'll see grazing cattle and all kinds of fruits, vegetables and spices thriving, including mangoes, pineapples, breadfruit, plantains, apples, oranges, cotoperix, bay, basil and coriander.

Growing popularity: Like Tucacas, Chichiriviche is a town undergoing a touristic transformation with hotels rising out of the muddy potholes. It was one of the earliest spots noted on the maps of the conquistadors and a launching point for their expeditions inland. When the explorers found the salt deposits on Cayo Sal and discovered the great fishing, many settled. Agriculture, fishing and trade were the mainstays until the 1920s when oil was discovered. Then Chichiriviche became a transhipment port for petroleum products until the deposits declined in the late 1930s. The locals returned to sowing the land. Chichiriviche was incorporated into the national highway sys-

The untouched cays near Chichiriviche.

tem in the 1940s and now has a major factory exporting cement. Tourism is developing by fits and starts.

On the long causeway into town from the main highway, birdwatchers can spot American flamingo, scarlet ibis, roseate spoonbill, herons and ducks feeding in the shallows. At dusk the birds come to roost in the mangrove swamp. The best months to see flocks of flamingos are November to early March.

There are seven main cays in the northern part of Morrocoy National Park. **Cayo Muerto**, just offshore, has an outpost for the Ministry of the Environment. Coral-ringed **Borracho** is known by scuba divers for its exquisite underwater views, while **Bahía de Cuare** boasts oyster beds and flamingos. The tiniest, aptly named **Pelón** (Bald), is a treeless strip of sand some 50 meters (55 yards) long – a genuine "desert island." Peaceful **Varadero** has a forest of palm trees and a 3-km sweep of beach. **Cayo Perasa** is another coral-ringed beauty, and **Cayo Pescadores**, as the name implies, is favored by fishermen.

One of the most distant – and the most popular hands-down for sun-worshippers – is **Cayo Sombrero**. Here Venezuela's "beautiful people" romp on the sand, quaff icy beers, doze in hammocks tied between palm trees, snorkel in pursuit of colorful parrot fish, or lounge in sleek, racy motorboats anchored near the shore (although there is talk of restricting the boats as their anchors damage the reef). The farther side of the island attracts a family crowd, with parents and kids splashing in the gentle surf and brightly-colored tents pitched among the palms.

A couple of small stands and vendors sell drinks and food on Sombrero, but you should take plenty of provisions – including mosquito repellant – when you visit any of the cays. Launches carry about 10 people and there's a set fare for the journey. If it's a slow day, you can usually bargain.

Adjacent to Morrocoy is the **Refugio de Fauna Silvestre de Caure** (Caure Wildlife Refuge), with its protected mangroves, birds and animals including deer, ant-eaters, peccaries and snakes.

Spanish elegance: The next stop on this West Coast route is the colonial city of **Coro**, the first capital of the Province of Venezuela. You can drive via **Barquisimeto** (called "The Music Capital" for its many folk bands) and through the **San Luis mountains**, which takes about six hours. For a quicker trip, follow the coast.

Coro, with its shady parks, colonial mansions and gracious ambience, was one of the earliest settlements in South America. The capital of Falcón, the country's driest state, it is located at the base of the arid Paraguaná Peninsula. Coro means "wind" in Arawak. It's a fitting name, for the gusting east winds have formed shifting *médanos* (dunes) that cover a 28-km (17-mile) strip of coast and part of the narrow isthmus to the peninsula. The dunes are protected as the **Parque Nacional Los Médanos de Coro**. Camels are available for hire from Los Médanos Hotel.

The city of Santa Ana de Coro was founded by Juan de Ampiés in 1527. In

A frigate bird in the Morrocoy mangroves.

a rare event for the conquest era, he was welcomed by the local chief, Manaure. Ampiés maintained peace with the Indians by dealing fairly with them and shielding them from the slave raids that were common on the coast at that time. Sadly, this unusual harmony was short-lived. In succeeding years, a series of German governors interested only in finding gold used Coro as a base for their expeditions. They ruled by exploitation, and the Indians fled.

After a period of decline in the 1600s, Coro began to flourish in the 18th century, becoming the supplier for Bonaire and Curaçao, some 104 km (65 miles away). Tobacco, hides, mules and all kinds of food were shipped from La Vela de Coro, east of the capital. Today the car ferry *Almirante Luis Brión*, operated by Ferrys del Caribe, leaves La Vela on Mondays and Fridays for Curaçao and Aruba.

The Venezuelan flag was planted for the first time on August 3, 1806, at La Vela, by Francisco de Miranda. The tricolor flew over Fort San Pedro, which has since been demolished, but a monument to the flag remains.

Modern-day Coro is a thriving agricultural center that uses irrigation to grow medlars, papayas, custard apples, mangos, oranges, lemons, bananas and cashews. The city is perhaps best noted for its beautifully-restored mansions, dating from the 1700s when trade with the Dutch islands flourished. Most are located along **Calle Zamora** near **Plaza San Clemente** with its old chapel and wooden cross. The cross was supposedly carved from the tree under which Ampiés met Chief Manaure.

The Coro **cathedral** was one of the first churches in Venezuela, started in 1531. Built like a fortress, its tall tower has gun slits. And indeed the cathedral improvised many times as a fort during the pirate attacks of the 16th century. The citizens prepared for these frequent onslaughts as best they could, the wealthiest building secret caches or tunnels to hide their riches. Even today there are tales of secret tunnels with hidden treasure.

The sand dunes of Coro.

The **Casa del Sol** (House of the Sun), located across from San Clemente chapel, boasts a sun design on its door. Built in the 17th century, the house has served as a private residence, a monastery and a college. Today it is the courthouse.

Colonial relics: Opposite is **El Balcón de los Arcaya** (Arcaya House), a national monument and one of the few two-story buildings in Coro. It was built by a Spanish nobleman in the late 17th century, and bought about 100 years later by Don Ignacio Luis Díaz de Arcaya, remaining in his family's possession to this day. The balcony runs on two sides of the house. There is a lush patio and, upstairs, the doors and ceilings are decorated with elaborate carvings. The house sheltered troops during the independence struggle, and you can see bullet-holes in the doors and windows. There are tales of secret tunnels and ghosts of ladies in long dresses with mantillas dancing to the music of a ball. An exhibit features colonial and pre-Columbian pottery and fossils.

Further down on Zamora is the **Casa de las Ventanas de Hierro** (House of the Iron Windows), with its beautiful baroque doorway. The wrought-iron grilles were imported from Seville at a time when the locals used only wood. They caused quite a sensation. Later iron grilles became typical all over the country. A painting of San Pedro in one bedroom disguises a door leading to a secret hiding-place in the ceiling.

Next door is the **Casa del Tesoro** (Treasure House). The house belonged to prominent Bishop Mariano Talavera y Garcés, a relative of the patriot Josefa Camejo. It was rumored to have a secret tunnel and years of digging finally produced one 8 meters (26 ft) underground – but no treasure was ever recovered. Also on Zamora is the **Museo de Lucas Guillermo Castillo** (Diocesan Museum), a former convent with colonial art, gold and silver, a large collection of wood carvings of saints – some in naïve style – and Indian relics.

Coro has long had a significant Jewish population. The Dutch islands were

An isolated farm on the Paraguaná Peninsula.

a haven for Jews fleeing the Inquisition in Spain, and when Venezuela's war for independence erupted, they offered support to the new republic and were among the first to trade with the rebels. There is a Jewish Cemetery, said to be the oldest still in use on the continent. The **Casa de los Seniors** (Senior House) was owned by the Senior family of Curaçao, who were well-known Jewish merchants. Bolívar slept here in 1828.

Barren landscape: The Paraguaná Peninsula, which was originally an island, became linked over time to the mainland by a long isthmus of sand. Pirates took refuge in this desolate landscape of cactus and brush to plan their numerous attacks.

Today there are said to be more goats than people. In the rural eastern part of the peninsula, goatherding is a common livelihood. The people sell goat's milk cheese and *dulce de leche coriano* (goat's milk fudge). *Chivo en coco* (goat in coconut sauce) is a specialty throughout the region. There are also cottage industries producing traditional leather work, pottery and furniture carved from cactus wood.

Just north of the narrow isthmus, the town of **Santa Ana** has a *cerro* (hill) that is a national monument. It rises 815 meters (2,673 ft), and from the summit you can see most of the peninsula on a clear day. The rare Tocuyo sparrow nests on the hill.

Adicora, to the east, is nestled in a protected bay. The smaller beach near town has fine sand and shady palms. Adicora's colorful houses show the early Dutch influence in architectural details like window grilles with pedestals and decorated caps, paneled doors, and shutters painted in contrasting colors. There are no hotels here, but the simple restaurants feature fresh fish and seafood including lobster.

The heroine of Venezuelan independence, Josefa Camejo, was born in 1791 at the family ranch of Aguaque, north of Pueblo Nuevo. Josefa's family, the Talaveras, were ardent republicans in the loyalist stronghold of Coro. Josefa married Juan Nepomuceno Briceño, second in command to General Rafael Urdaneta, and accompanied him on the Llanos campaign. In 1821 she invited everyone – including the Spanish troops – to her birthday ball. When suspicions were aroused, Josefa killed the royalist commander and her forces proceeded to Pueblo Nuevo, where the Spanish garrison gave up.

The northern tip of the Paraguaná Peninsula is a wilderness of cactus and salt beds. **Cabo San Ramón**, at the tip, is a cape where pelicans dive and fishermen cast their nets beneath the rocky cliffs. In contrast to the rest of the peninsula, the western side is modern and developed, thanks to the oil refineries that opened in 1947.

Today **Punto Fijo** has a population of 70,000 people, making it the largest city in Falcón state. Multi-lane highways lead to the beaches that – in contrast to the east – offer light breezes and calm waters. The beaches at **Villa Marina** and **Punta El Pico**, formerly contaminated, have been tidied up and offer great shelling prospects. But be warned: there is no shade.

Colonial facade in Coro.

THE LLANOS

The Savannah is beautiful and terrible at the same time; it easily accommodates both beautiful life and atrocious death. The Llanos are terrifying; but this fear does not chill one's heart; it is hot like the great wind of its sunburnt immensity, like the fever from its swamps.
– Romulo Gallegos, *Doña Barbara*

The vast, blisteringly hot plains known as the Llanos hold a special place in Venezuela's mythology, something akin to the Great Plains of the United States, pampas in Argentina and Outback of Australia. Opened up as cattle country in the 19th century, the area became a wild frontier of cowboys and ranchers that Venezuelans can still become dewy-eyed about – even though most modern Venezuelans, wedded to the metropolitan bustle of Caracas or hedonistic pleasures of the Caribbean, would never dream of actually going there.

For in many ways the Llanos have been left behind in Venezuela's mad scramble towards modernity. Taking up fully a third of the country's land mass, the region contains only a minuscule fraction of its population. There are few paved highways, its towns are dusty and apparently half-asleep, while hard-bitten *llaneros* (as this Venezuelan breed of cowboy is known) still chase herds on horseback across the plains (*see page 255*).

Along with this lingering "Wild West" feel, the Llanos comprise one of the great wildlife-watching areas of South America. More bird species can be seen here than in the United States and Great Britain combined, and in such abundance that binoculars are hardly necessary. Crocodiles inhabit the area's lagoons and can be seen wandering across its roadways. Jaguars prowl its fields, bats swoop through its skies, and, if you're lucky, fresh-water porpoises can be spotted in the Orinoco tributaries that are the region's veins.

A macho past: Eleven Spanish families were the first settlers to move into the Llanos, setting up the first cattle ranch near the modern town of Calabazo in 1548. Leather and salted meat were crucial in colonial Venezuela, and the march of hooves proved unstoppable: 200 years later, over 130,000 head of cattle roamed the enormous *hatos* or ranches of the Llanos while local Indian tribes had all but disappeared.

Despite the Llanos's economic importance and the contribution it made to the independence struggle (*llanero* troops made up the backbone of Bolívar's army), the area aroused mixed emotions in Venezuelans in the rest of the country. While its inhabitants were admired for their toughness, honesty and frontier spirit, they would at first be feared as barbaric, then later mocked for their backwoods slowness and lack of sophistication. Their homeland was viewed as a hot and primitive backwater best avoided by civilized folk.

Finally, when oil was discovered on the coast in the 1920s, the country began turning its back on the Llanos completely; after all, the government rea-

Preceding pages: a lineup of *llaneros*, Venezuelan cowboys. **Left**, the man with the golden grin. **Right**, *llaneros* rope a steer on Hato Doña Barbara.

soned, if Venezuela needed beef, it could be imported just as cheaply from abroad. The Llanos stagnated for decades, and only after the oil crisis of the early 1980s did Venezuelans again think of developing the vast resources to the south.

Even so, there is a lingering feeling that the Llanos somehow embody the "real Venezuela." Romantic photographs of the Llanos still hang in Venezuelan bars, Venezuelan dignitaries occasionally dress in the typical *llanero* collar of the *liqui-liqui*, and the Llanos provide the setting for the most famous Venezuelan novel: *Doña Barbara*.

Written by Romulo Gallegos in 1929, it is a melodramatic and bleakly sexist work about a woman, Barbara, who is gang-raped when young and learns to dominate and destroy men in revenge. By a mixture of seductiveness, malice and the threat of witchcraft, she becomes the virtual ruler of the otherwise male-dominated Llanos – that is, until an upright man from Caracas awakens her long-repressed feminine instincts and finally destroys her.

The novel nicely sums up Venezuelans' ambivalence towards the Llanos. The hero, Santos Luzardo, finally marries Doña Barbara's abandoned daughter – bringing the refined elements of the urban dweller together with the raw, natural spirit of the frontier.

Harsh backlands: Traveling through the roughly 300,000 sq. km (116,000 sq. miles) of the Llanos has never been easy. In the wet season (May to November), the area is flooded by rains so that it can look like an inland sea, and cattle have to be driven to outcrops of higher ground or they will drown. Then, in the dry season (December to April), the sun beats the Llanos into a virtual desert, and photographs show the bones of dead animals whitening on the cracked earth.

The dry season is often called *verano* or "summer" and the wet season *invierno* ("winter"), a custom begun by the first Spanish settlers who tried to relate their strange new climate to what they remembered in their homelands. Curiously, the dry season is the best time of year to see wildlife, since animals con-

The dry season.

gregate around a smaller number of lush lagoons that can more easily be reached. All year round the heat of the Llanos is intense – although "winter" is much more humid. In both seasons, the desolate plains are hauntingly beautiful.

Independent travelers with their own transport can drive south from Caracas across the Andes to the northernmost fringes of the Llanos – known as the **high Llanos** – where it is possible to find remote riverside areas for camping. The people of the Llanos are famous for their hospitality, and there is usually no problem staking out a hammock on private property or even, often, staying for a night on a farm. Unfortunately, because of the distances involved, driving deeper into the Llanos can involve several grueling days of travel across monotonous countryside, so it is recommended only for the most committed motorist.

Calabazo is the major urban center of the northern Llanos, and the first town with reasonably comfortable facilities. As the first permanent settlement in the region (it was a feared penal colony in colonial times), Calabazo has a number of colonial buildings still in use. The baroque 18th-century cathedral is probably the most imposing construction in the whole Llanos area.

But foreign travelers are more likely to want to skip Calabazo and fly directly into the heartland of the Llanos proper (the **low Llanos**), taking one of the daily flights from Caracas to **San Fernando de Apure**, the capital of Apure state. From there, journeys can be organized with local agencies to one of the several operating *hatos* or cattle ranches that accept paying visitors – giving a unique insight into a rural world that has survived in a virtual 19th-century cocoon.

Remote outpost: The city of San Fernando (population 40,000) itself has little to recommend it. The wide, dusty streets are mostly lined by undistinguished buildings, although one, the old **Palacio Barbarito**, is worth having a look at: this was where hunters at the turn of the century would bring egret feathers for export to Europe and the

Crocodile *motif* **in San Pedro de Atacama.**

United States. The trade in these feathers was so valuable that it was the cause of ambushes, gun fights and blood feuds. Locals say that one particularly large shipment of egret feathers actually led to seven deaths, changing hands several times before finally arriving in San Fernando for sale.

Nearby in **Plaza Camejo** is a bronze statue of Pedro Camejo, one of the most famous *llanero* lancers who fought in the independence struggle, heroically dying at General Paez's feet at the battle of Carabobo. Ringing the statue are glass containers with samples of earth from various battlefields around the country and an unusual concrete fountain based on a crocodile motif. Within sight of the plaza, leather craftsmen often set up informal stalls from the backs of their pick-up trucks, selling new saddles, stirrups, bullwhips and leather boots. Other stores sell small carvings made from *azabache*, a petrified wood that is like a smooth black stone. Meanwhile, at the Apure River docks, motorboats and *bongos* (big dug-out canoes) load goods for delivery as far away as Ciudad Bolívar.

Into the wilderness: The real attractions of the Llanos begin beyond the San Fernando town limits. There are almost no hotels in the whole area, so it is necessary to stay in one of the several ranches that accept tourists. They include **Hato Doña Barbara** (perhaps the most unusual of the options), **Hato El Cedral**, **Hato Pinero** and **Hato El Frío**. All have installed reasonable facilities for sleeping overnight and offer horse riding and four-wheel-drive tours in the Llanos.

Those with their own tents may want to visit the new National Park in southeastern Apure called **Cinaruco-Capanaparo** after the rivers bordering the park. This can only be attempted during the dry season, since in the wet the whole area is virtually underwater. A good base to visit this area might also be the **Adventure Camp Los Indios**, set up between the Cunaviche and Cunavichito Rivers.

All of these bases must be reached

Round-up time.

THE LLANEROS

The *llaneros* of Venezuela stand along-side the gauchos of Argentina as the finest horsemen in the history of South America. The true *llaneros* have now all but died out, and their descendants are rapidly losing any pride in the *llanero* traditions and dress. But even so, small groups of these tropical cowboys can still be seen on ranches in the Llanos, rounding up and branding cattle using traditional skills or listening to melancholy *llanero* ballads.

The *llaneros* come from a racial mix dating back some 400 years, combining the blood of Spanish frontiersmen, escaped black slaves and local Indians. It was during the lawless, chaotic colonial days that the *llaneros* developed the distinctive customs that can still, on occasion, be seen today: their own style of rodeos and rounding up cattle, and their own tropical variation on the classic cowboy dress – wooden stirrups, woollen ponchos (often worn in the rain, despite oppressive heat) and straw hats.

A haunting form of music began to accompany *llanero* ballads, usually about romance or knife fights, sexual conquests, hard drinking or skill in breaking horses. In this macho cult, leaders were given respect based on their skills in the field, and once proven, could demand complete loyalty.

The German scientist and explorer Alexander von Humboldt was impressed by the *llaneros'* toughness, especially their diet of pure salted meat, but also noted their laziness. "Being always in the saddle, they fancy they cannot make the slightest excursion on foot," he recorded. Despite their abundance, cows were never milked, and during summer, *llaneros* preferred to drink fetid yellow water rather than dig a well.

Even so, the hard-living *llaneros* became a truly terrifying fighting force during the wars of independence at the turn of the 19th century, first on the side of the Spaniards and only later with Bolívar. They made up the backbone of the Liberator's army, fighting without food or pay – instead taking both from the towns and villages they brutally pillaged. *Llaneros* did not even need to be supplied with arms, since they took a fresh supply of lance points from every outcrop of palm trees they came across.

In the end, the average *llanero* gained little from his contribution to Venezuela's independence. By law, every *llanero* down to the lowliest private was given some land as reward – but the small plots proved impossible to work profitably. Wealthy officers were easily able to buy up the smaller lots, and a new landowning class was born. Most families owning *hatos* today are descended from these purchasers.

The rest of the 19th century saw the increasing profitability of beef for export to Europe, along with the declining freedom of the *llanero*. But just as the Venezuelan cowboy began to disappear as part of an identifiable group (and threat to established order), writers and intellectuals began to romanticize him as embodying important traits of the "national character": independence, toughness, an egalitarian spirit born of living in the wild. It was a Kiplingesque mish-mash of values similiar to those being praised in diminishing frontiers as far away as Argentina, Australia and the US, with the *llanero* standing in contrast to the sickly, Europeanized city-dwellers, cut off from the primal forces of nature. ■

Llanero gaze.

from San Fernando, driving along a highway that parallels the Apure River for much of the way. Small towns like **Achaguas** and **El Saman** begin to appear, each with a "Wild West" atmosphere so strong that they feel like a Latino version of old Hollywood film sets. In **Mantecal**, the largest settlement en route, unshaven men stand on the unpaved street corners, thumbs hooked in their jeans and cowboy hats cocked at a Clint Eastwood angle. Occasionally a *llanero* will amble by on horseback, or tie up his mount at a roadside post. Even in the bars – where everyone is served standing up – the bargirls send beers sliding from one end of the counter to the other, like something out of *The Magnificent Seven*.

In these steaming rural outposts, people tend to work from 4am to around noon, leaving the afternoon for a long siesta. Even the truck drivers seem to stop work then, hitching up their hammocks in the shade beneath their rigs. Also noticeable in these towns is the reasonably sized Indian population:

there are some 120 indigenous communities spread throughout Apure state, with some groups maintaining a semi-nomadic movement.

The heart of the Llanos: Beyond Mantecal, the landscape changes from monotonous scrub to the classic Venezuelan savannah. The grassy plains now stretch off to the horizon in every direction, with the only trees on the occasional isolated hillock (called *metas*) lost in the distance.

Driving through here, it is easy to sympathize with the renowned German scientist Alexander von Humboldt, who was aghast at the landscape during a journey in the 18th century. "There is something awful... about the uniform aspect of these steppes," he wrote. "All around us the plains seem to ascend to the sky, and the vast and profound solitude appears like an ocean covered with seaweed. Through the dry mist... the trunks of palm trees are seen from afar, stripped of their foliage and... looking like the masts of ships descried upon the horizon."

The Llanos offer some of the world's best bird-watching.

The roadway here is elevated for the rainy months when the Llanos becomes a virtual inland sea, but in the early 70s the Venezuelan government started building dikes to help control the devastation and save water for the dry season. Now for most of the year the countryside is a collection of small muddy lakes teeming with wildlife.

These highways of the western Llanos are lucky to see an automobile every hour, so it is easy to pull over for some wildlife-watching without being disturbed. A great deal can be seen just from the road. Lone white egrets pick amongst the reeds. Screeching clouds of fluorescently-colored birds erupt from their lakes, making dazzling patterns against the horizon. And 2-meter (6-ft) long crocodiles – known as *bavos* – sun themselves in the mud by the lagoons' shores, although they will disappear in a flash at any noise.

Traditional ranch: The classic example of a working ranch that can be easily visited is Hato Doña Barbara, named after Romulo Gallegos' novel. It has had a new building added for paying guests, with simple but very comfortable rooms. Several days can easily be whiled away riding or taking short excursions into the peaceful countryside, while bird-watchers have been known to become obsessed for weeks.

The real name of the Hato Doña Barbara is Hato La Trinidad de Arauca. But the new title is not completely a tourist beat-up: part of the farm's lands were actually owned by the Señora Francisca Vazquez de Carrillo, the historical figure on whom Doña Barbara was based.

The current owner is Señor Hugo Estrada, a garrulous 50-year-old who usually sports a tropical shirt and baseball cap as his ranch gear. Estrada gave up his lucrative legal practice in Caracas to take over the remote property which has been in his family for five generations, and he comes out with the family scandals with disarming speed. It appears that Estrada's father had fancied himself as a poet more than a farmer, allowing the *hato* to decay almost to the

The capybara, a swimming rodent unique to the Llanos.

point of destruction: it went from 18,000 head of cattle to 3,000 in a few years. Finally the family started legal proceedings to take control away from him.

The heat and loneliness of the Llanos may have pushed the elder Estrada over to the battier side of senility, as a quick stroll around the ranch suggests. The family house, with its white and pink pastel color scheme, looks as though it belongs in the suburbs of Miami or Orlando. Embedded in the masonry are tiny, almost unnoticeable models of Mary and Jesus. An airplane propeller twisted in an accident into the form of a giant four-leafed flower has been set on a pillar like a sculpture. Exotic creatures like ant-eaters (that hug one another constantly) and chameleons are gathered in the property, as well as teams of local guinea pigs called capybaras on leashes.

But for the *pièce de résistance*, one must choose between the "Ship of Stones" – a 10-meter (30-ft) long enclosure, made of bricks in the shape of a ship's hull, sitting in the middle of the garden with dozens of Orinoco turtles inside – and a giant statue of Christ surrounded by little angels each representing a Venezuelan Indian, a black, a white and a mixed-race *mestizo*. This latter was inspired by a Venezuelan poem and hit-record called *Pintame Angelitos Negros* (Paint Me Little Black Angels). ("My father was a little out of control," the younger Estrada explains, and one pictures him as as a kind of watered-down Kurtz out here in the Llanos, exercising absolute power in his small domain.)

Exploring the ranch: A more recent addition to the *hato* is a replica of **Doña Barbara's house**, a typical 19th-century building of adobe and thatch. Inside are some antique odds-and-ends gathered from various parts of the farm. The house is set near the original Doña Barbara's tomb: because she was widely believed to be a witch, priests refused to have her buried in consecrated ground. She was rumored to have been buried with hidden treasure, but it was not until 1986 that thieves finally worked up the

A saddle sale in San Fernando.

courage to violate the grave. These days Venezuelan tourists make the pilgrimage here, and a small plaque has been laid by the Mexican actress who played Doña Barbara in a 1941 film.

But the real attraction of the *hato* is seeing its everyday workings. Early in the morning *llaneros* can be seen rounding up the longhorn cattle around the ranch, often chasing after them with lassoes. Demonstrations of their extraordinary riding skills are put on, along with swinging cattle to the ground by their tails.

Milking cows by hand is another nearly-disappeared tradition that is kept up at the *hato*. The ritual is fascinating: the milker sings to the cows to relax them as he leads them from the pen, usually something like "*P-u-u-u-u-t-a*" (whore in Spanish) rhythmically repeated or "*G-o-o-o-ld mine... you're so ugly today, looks like you woke up at three in the morning.*" All the while he caresses the cow's back and eases himself into position to begin the milking.

Wildlife excursions: From all of the *hatos* in the area, horseback trips can be made into untouched wilderness areas. (It is best to try this at around dawn, when the day is coolest). Birdlife is prominent, and it is not surprising to ride over a ridge in the farm and see a lagoon full of pink flamingos sieving with their beaks for food – and to be able to watch them unmolested for several minutes before they disappear in a graceful cloud. The colors of other birds are dazzling, from striking red to green and yellow.

All birds on the property are protected, ensuring their abundance. The same ecological instinct, however, has not been extended to the crocodiles. Their meat and skins can be sold for a total of US$60, so they have been hunted to virtual extinction on many of the *hatos*. The Llanos is also home to a unique creature called the capybara – a giant, river-going guinea pig. These cuddly little creatures are a staple food of the Llanos, and were once nearly hunted to extinction when the Catholic Church declared them to be a fish (because they swim!) and therefore fit to be eaten on Fridays.

Other water creatures are not so cute. The rivers of the Llanos are infested with piranhas and electric eels, which deliver a nasty shock (Alexander von Humboldt stood on one to see if it was alive and it gave him a jolt that would pain him for the rest of his life). So swimming is not recommended, despite the overwhelming heat.

Although they are extremely rare, it is not unheard of to spot a puma in the wild, but most visitors will be lucky to see one of their tracks in the mud.

Even without this pleasure, however, a stay in the Llanos turns out to be surprisingly affecting. Along with the heat and barrenness, the extremes of flooding and dryness, there is the serenity of being lulled to sleep by grasshoppers on a humid night, or watching the slow dawn over empty cattle pastures. Many find, much to their surprise, that the images from the Llanos linger on in the memory much more clearly than one more Caribbean beach or the glass skyscrapers of Caracas.

Local Arauco Indian.

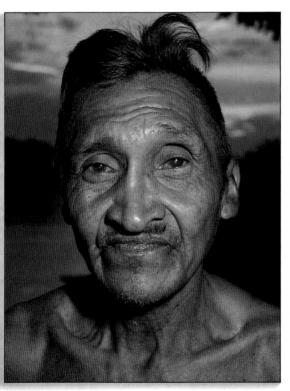

THE ORINOCO DELTA

The massive Guayana region – not to be confused with the neighboring country, (British) Guyana – sprawls over almost half the territory of Venezuela. Although the Spaniards never found the El Dorado they so feverishly sought here, Guayana in modern times is proving to be a treasure trove of gold (some 12 percent of the world's gold reserves are found here), diamonds, iron ore and bauxite, the raw material for aluminum.

Most industry – the mines, the smelters, the refineries – is centered around the Lower Orinoco River at Ciudad Guayana. Of historical interest is the colonial river port Ciudad Bolívar, which figured prominently in the wars of independence. And near the Atlantic coast is the vast Delta Amacuro, home to the Warao Indians, who live in platform houses over the water and skilfully manoeuver their dugout canoes through the delta's maze of channels.

Trade center: The capital of Bolívar state is a relaxed and charming colonial city, **Ciudad Bolívar**. Once the headquarters for the revolutionary Simón Bolívar, it was the scene of the country's first Congress and its first newspaper. Angostura bitters were invented in Ciudad Bolívar, and world-acclaimed kinetic artist Jesús Soto was born here.

Ciudad Bolívar was founded in 1764 with the name Santo Tomás de la Guayana de Angostura – *Angostura* (Narrows) for short – because it is situated where the mighty Orinoco River is less than a mile wide. During the independence struggle, Simón Bolívar used Angostura as a base to regroup after his early defeats.

On February 15, 1819, the Liberator installed the Congress of Angostura and gave his celebrated speech proposing the ideals of a free and united South American federation. Twenty-seven years later, Congress renamed the city in honor of Bolívar. For the next century, Ciudad Bolívar was the key transshipment point for goods from the interior to markets around the world.

Ciudad Bolívar developed in tandem with its sister city, **Soledad**, across the river, which could be reached by boat. It was only in 1967 that Soledad and Ciudad Bolívar were linked by the magnificent **Angostura suspension bridge** – the first bridge to span the Orinoco. It stretches 1,678 meters (5,505 ft), and is 57 meters (187 ft) above the river at its highest point.

Small motor launches still ferry passengers between the two banks from early morning to late at night. The boats depart as they're filled and the ride takes about 20 minutes.

Slow rhythm of life: Today, Ciudad Bolívar is a city of 100,000 people, but it retains the feel of a small town. With the average temperature 28° C (82° F), shade is cherished. The traditional homes face the Orinoco and have floor-to-ceiling windows and gardens of leafy trees. Commerce grinds to a halt in the heat of the day while people enjoy a siesta. In the evenings, families relax in the breeze of an open doorway or stroll along by the river.

Preceding pages: the banks of the Orinoco. **Left**, the Orinoco delta. **Right**, a room with a view, Ciudad Bolívar.

The waterfront remains a hive of activity, with many of the older shops located in the arcade on **Paseo Orinoco.** Here craftsmen work in precious gems and fashion gold into distinctive brooches shaped like orchids. Look for bargains in gold pieces, but gems are priced better elsewhere.

Across the street, overlooking the river and the Angostura bridge, is the **Mirador Angostura** (Angostura viewpoint) built on the base of the colonial **San Gabriel fort**. Keep an eye out for freshwater dolphins. There's a soda fountain with outdoor tables and the area is crowded with students and couples. You can also see the calibrated rock, **Piedra del Medio**, which shows the depth of the river. Normally the Orinoco is highest in August and lowest in March, the end of the dry season. At time of high waters, you might spot fishermen casting nets for *zapoara*, a local delicacy.

On Paseo Orinoco, not far from the Mirador, is the **Museo Correo del Orinoco** (Ciudad Bolívar Museum). In this building Bolívar established Vene-zuela's first newspaper as an official tool of the government, and had it published in English as well as Spanish to keep his British troops apprised of his policies. *Correo del Orinoco* (*The Orinoco Mail*) was printed on a press bartered in Trinidad for 25 mules. The press is housed in the well-preserved building, along with photos of the old city, paintings and ceramics.

Half a dozen blocks up from Paseo Orinoco is the **Plaza Bolívar**, with statues representing the five countries Bolívar liberated – Venezuela, Colombia, Ecuador, Peru and Bolivia. Bordering the plaza is the cathedral, dedicated to **Nuestra Señora de las Nieves** (Our Lady of the Snows) – a curious choice, since snow is unknown here. The building, painted a buttery yellow with white trim, was started in 1765, but little progress was made until Governor Don Manuel Centurión established a fund by taxing fighting cocks and *guarapo*, a sugar-cane liquor. The cathedral was eventually completed in 1840, and restored in 1979.

The colonial main plaza of Ciudad Bolívar.

South of Plaza Bolívar lies the **Casa de los Gobernadores de La Colonia** (Colonial Government House), built for the Spanish governors with money from the cathedral fund. The influential Don Manuel Centurión lived here from 1766 to 1777, while settling the fledgling district, founding new towns and opening the first secondary school.

In a room off the balcony of the house, an agonized Bolívar turned his back on the execution of the popular, mixed-blooded General Manuel Piar, who was shot by firing squad against the side wall of the cathedral on October 16, 1817. A leader in the independence struggle, Piar had refused to subordinate to Bolívar and was accused of encouraging Venezuela's *pardos* (mixed bloods) and slaves to begin their own rebellion. Before Piar's controversial end, he was held prisoner at No. 33 Calle Bolívar, just off the plaza.

Nearby is the elegant, salmon-colored **Casa del Congreso de Angostura** (Congress Building), built in 1766 by Governor Centurión to house the Colegio Nacional de Guayana (National College of Guayana). In Bolívar's time, it was the site of the Congress of Angostura.

From 1818 to 1819, Bolívar stayed at the **Quinta de San Isidro** (San Isidro House), owned by his friend, José Luis Cornieles, a member of the municipal council of Angostura. At that time the *quinta* was part of a coffee plantation out in the country, but today it has been swallowed by the city and is located on Avenida Táchira. The house, which is open to visitors, rests on a gigantic rock called the **Laja de San Isidro**.

Bolívar supposedly penned his address to the Congress of Angostura under a tamarind tree that is still thriving in a corner of the yard. Another story tells that the Liberator tied his horse to the tree. Perhaps he did both...

Historic mixer: Although Angostura is now known as Ciudad Bolívar, the old name lives on in the world-famous Angostura bitters. A key ingredient in the still-secret recipe is derived from the bark of a local tree. A mixture of this substance with honey is said to have saved the life of German naturalist Baron Alexander von Humboldt in 1800, stricken with a fever following an expedition to the Upper Orinoco.

Angostura bitters were invented by J.G.B. Siegert, a fugitive German chemist who came to Venezuela with volunteers for Bolívar's campaign. Many were sick with yellow fever and there was a crying need for doctors, so the German rose to a prominent position. He became chief physician at the provincial hospital and served as master surgeon to Bolívar's troops.

And of course, he whipped up the bitters – initially as a cure for stomach upset. The recipe was produced in Angostura from 1824 until 1875, when the federal wars caused the factory to be relocated to Port-of-Spain, Trinidad, where it's bottled even today.

On a more contemporary note, Ciudad Bolívar's **Museo de Arte Moderno Jesús Soto** (Jesús Soto Modern Arts Museum) features works by native son Jesús Soto, the world-famous kinetic artist. He was born here in 1923 and can

Spanish mansion where Bolívar read to the Congress of Angostura, Ciudad Bolívar.

occasionally be seen around town. You'll recognize him by his trademark droopy moustache.

Mineral center: If you plan to visit mining operations while in Guayana, you might want to stop in at the **Museo Geológico y Minero** (Geology and Mining Museum), near the main entrance to the university. The small display features models with explanations of Venezuela's principal mines, including Cerro Bolívar and El Callao.

Inquire at Ciudad Bolívar airport about arranging for a bush pilot to fly you to one of the mining sites. These days, the mines are controlled by the National Guard, so don't expect the wild and woolly atmosphere of the not-too-distant past. One thing is still true of mining sites – the high price of supplies. Take food and don't be surprised if accommodations are pretty basic.

You could also rent a car and drive to **Ciudad Piar**, built for the mining company workers. As you head south, you'll see Venezuela's largest iron mountain, the hulking **Cerro Bolívar**. Rediscovered in 1947 by United States Steel geologists, the mountain had looked promising to Sir Walter Raleigh back in 1595. But Spanish governors failed to act, and it wasn't until 1750 that Capuchin monks set up the first forges on the site.

Outdoor enthusiasts might enjoy an expedition to the spectacular **Pará Falls** on the Caura River, a tributary of the Orinoco. Dugout canoes leave from the small outpost of Maripa, a three-hour drive west of Ciudad Bolívar. It takes about a day by canoe, and about another day to climb the steep 7-km (4-mile) trail up the gorge to the top of the 200-meter (650-ft) falls.

Mining heartland: Guayana's key iron mines are located near the convergence of the Caroní and Orinoco rivers, 100 km (60 miles) downstream from Ciudad Bolívar. The Orinoco is a "white" river, while the Caroní is a "black" river. Their mingling has been described as "coffee and cream."

In the 1940s, Venezuela granted mining concessions to Bethlehem and US Steel. They invested a fortune in development programs which transformed the region into one of the world's most rapidly industrializing areas. Exploitation of all Guayana's resources was put into Venezuelan hands in 1961, when the government formed the powerful Venezuelan Guayana Corporation (CVG). CVG controls the mining of ore and other minerals, exploration for oil and natural gas, and the development of hydroelectric power.

Ciudad Guayana, Venezuela's boom town, was also born in 1961. The CVG fused Puerto Ordaz and San Félix with the industrial zone of Matanzas. The cities are linked by a double bridge over the Caroní. The population of this thriving metropolis is already nearing the 500,000 mark.

Ciudad Guayana boasts gargantuan steel, aluminum and iron ore plants. Aluminum is Venezuela's biggest foreign-exchange earner after oil, with production being expanded to 634,900 metric tons (700,000 tons) a year. The target is 1,814,000 metric tons (2 million tons), and Venezuela aims to be-

A break at the San Félix market.

266

come a world aluminum leader by the year 2000. Steel is also a key foreign-exchange earner. You can visit Sidor, the state-owned steel plant, at Matanzas.

Puerto Ordaz was built in 1952 by the Orinoco Mining Company as its administrative headquarters for shipping iron ore abroad. At the wharf, you can see ore whisked by train from Cerro Bolívar being loaded onto barges, and bauxite arriving from the motherlode discovered in 1977 upriver at **Los Pijiguaos**. Many industrial executives make their homes in this part of Ciudad Guayana, while the workers tend to live in **San Félix**.

Salto La Llovizna, the Caroní's most spectacular falls, are found in Parque Llovizna, reached by boat from the Hotel Inter-Continental Guayana or by the road south towards El Pao.

Nearby are the ruins of **Caroní Mission Church**. The Spanish Capuchin monks who founded their first mission in the area in 1724 became successful cattle and horse breeders, established towns, schools and even had their own

army. General Piar, who freed Guayana, seized control of the missions in 1817 and used their wealth to finance the patriot cause.

Downstream from Ciudad Guayana are the **Castillos de Guayana la Vieja**, two forts built to protect San Tomé, Guayana's first Spanish settlement, against English, French and Dutch pirates. They can be reached from San Félix by car; they're only 35 km (22 miles) away, but the dirt road is so poor it can take an hour and a half.

Founded in 1595, remote San Tomé played a crucial part in ending the career of the famed English explorer, Sir Walter Raleigh. In 1618, the city was burned by the English under orders from Raleigh, who was searching for gold to buoy his flagging fortunes. In the scuffle with the Spanish troops, Raleigh's elder son was killed, along with the Spanish governor. Spain retaliated by seizing English merchant ships and suspending trade. To restore relations, King James I had Raleigh beheaded.

The forts are positioned on rocks high

above the river. San Francisco was built from 1678 to 1681, on the site of the former monastery of San Francisco de Asís. The second fort, San Diego del Alcalá, is perched on a nearby hill. It was built in 1747 and was often called *El Padrastro* (The Obstacle). But even *El Padrastro* couldn't protect San Tomé from the pirate assaults, and eventually the settlement was moved upriver.

Giant dam: Another side trip from Ciudad Guayana follows the Ciudad Piar highway for about an hour and a half south along the Caroní River to **Guri Dam** (also known as Represa Raúl Leoni). Guayana's industrial development has relied on the hydroelectric power provided by this monolith, which currently supplies half the country's electricity and meets the needs of consumers as far away as Caracas. Ground was broken in 1965 for the phased construction. When complete, the complex will power the entire country with energy to spare. Tours are available.

The dam's gigantic reservoir, Guri Lake, will eventually be the fourth largest lake on the continent. It is becoming one of the world's hottest sport fishing venues, featuring two of Venezuela's best freshwater game fish, the feisty, saber-toothed *payara* – so ferocious it eats piranha for breakfast – and another notorious fighter, the *pavón* (peacock bass). Indians use piranha on headlines to catch *payara* weighing up to a whopping 14 kg (30 lb). *Pavón* get as large as 8 kg (18 lb). Organized fishing programs at Guri operate on the catch-and-release philosophy, with sportsmen keeping only what they can eat.

The archaeological site, **Cueva del Elefante** (Cave of the Elephant), is not far from Guri. From the highway, you'll see a big rock formation resembling an elephant. It conceals a cave with paintings over 2,000 years old. The designs and simple human and animal figures are on the back wall of the 20-meter (65-ft) deep cave and can be seen from its mouth. Visitors are warned not to enter because of dangerous fungi. The best time to get a good look is late afternoon, when the sun is at the right angle.

A dip in the Orinoco.

The Delta: As the Orinoco and a score of other rivers flow to the coast, they form one of the world's largest deltas. Curiously, the region is named for the Amacuro River, instead of the Orinoco. The Delta Amacuro territory became Venezuela's 21st state in 1991.

The Delta has a 370-km (229-mile) base on the Atlantic, and comprises 40,240 sq. km (15,533 sq. miles) of jungle and mangrove swamps sliced by countless estuaries and a maze of *caños* (channels). The river splits into 70 mouths flowing into the sea.

The Delta Amacuro is actually two distinct deltas – the high, and relatively dry Alto to the north, and the low, flood-plagued Bajo. The Bajo is home to about 15,000 Guaraunos (Warao) Indians. The name *War-aroas* means "canoe people," and, in fact, *Orinoco* is a Warao word meaning "father of our land." The Warao have adapted so completely to their watery domain that children may learn to paddle a dugout before they can walk. Warao dugouts range from about 6 ft (a couple of meters) long to more than 10 meters (30 ft). The big ones hold up to 50 people.

The typical Warao dwelling is the *palafito*, a pile house perched on the trunks of *moriche* palms sunk through the mud. A long roof slopes over the open sides of the *palafito*, reaching almost to the floor. Walkways on piles connect the various houses in each community.

Tucupita is a sweltering river port with a population of about 30,000, located 110 km (68 miles) from the Atlantic. It was founded by Catholic missionaries, supposedly on the spot where an Indian chief named Tucu, who strayed in the jungle, blew his *pitó* (conch horn) for help. The *paseo* along Calle Mánamo is the place to watch the river traffic. It's also where you can hire motorized *bongos* (dugout canoes) to explore the delta. This is done informally, and the price is negotiated. You'll have to get a savvy guide to show you the remote channels where you might see freshwater dolphins, exotic birds, howler monkeys and *babas* (small alligators).

An easy catch in Lake Guri, one of South America's great fishing spots.

THE LOWLANDS OF MARACAIBO

Oil and heat. *Goajira* and *gaita*. Contraband runners and Indian ranchers. Maracaibo, the sweltering city beside one of the world's biggest oil reserves, brings in the money that the rest of Venezuela spends.

Oppressive heat: For visitors, the most obvious aspect of the country's second city is its temperature, one of the highest in Latin America: it rarely drops below 29.9°C (85°F) and soars well above that at midday. In case the mercury level alone is insufficient, add in a humidity level of at least 80 percent and you can see why the mere mention of Maracaibo can make a *Caraqueño* wither. Tourists have been known to fly into the city, walk out into the blast-furnace temperatures and immediately return to the air conditioned airport for the next flight out. Even Maracaibo's position on the banks of South America's largest lake is not enough to assure cool breezes or respite from the relentless sun.

Maracuchos, as local residents are known, have their own method for beating the heat. At midday, activity grinds to a halt as those who can escape to the shade and fans of their homes. Everyone else heads for the shadow of a tree, cold drink in hand, to wait out the oven effect. Don't expect, then, to find stores open from noon to 2pm in this city. Some stay shut until 4pm. Once evening arrives and the temperatures drop from broil to simply bake, *Maracuchos* haul chairs out into the sidewalks in front of their homes and do the local equivalent of stoop-sitting until they fall asleep.

That's not to say the *Maracuchos* are inactive. Their traditional music, the *gaita*, does not let them be. *Gaita* literally means bagpipe but this folk music has nothing to do with the Scottish musical instrument. Venezuelan *gaita* is played by large bands using *maracas*, four-string guitars called *cuatros* and twanging *furrucos*. While musicians belt out fast-paced folk rhythms, singers improvise verses, often satirical.

Although the origin of *gaita* is un-known, there are theories it has Persian roots or that it came to the Americas with Spanish priests. Then, as now, lyrics were political. Religious *gaitas* dedicated to the saints surface only in December, the month dedicated to this type of music.

During *gaita* season, the best-loved local bands head to Caracas for appearances in restaurants, in theaters and on television. The competition is fierce to come up with a song that, for its harmony, ingenious lyrics, or both, catches the fancy of Caracas audiences. The *gaita* that tops the music charts at year end guarantees its band an extended stay in the limelight.

Oil capital: Although heat is the most obvious characteristic of Venezuela's second largest city and *gaita* its most entertaining, to most of the world Maracaibo means just one thing: oil. It is impossible to separate the city from the petroleum wealth that has filled it with whitewashed highrises and, outside the city, the luxury homes of European and North American petroleum

Preceding pages: fish heads for dinner. **Left,** Maracaibo steaks are famed around Venezuela. **Right,** a Goajira Indian woman.

engineers. Maracaibo's economic importance gives it an inflated notion of its touristic value. Undoubtedly, the city has intriguing offerings but it falls low on the list of "must" stops for visitors.

Until they were levelled in the 1970s, charming colonial buildings brought travelers to Macaraibo. They dated from the time when the Spanish, giving up their futile search for gold, recognized that Maracaibo had other value. The city became, like Puerto La Cruz, Puerto Cabello and Colombia's Barranquilla and Cartagena, a transit point for voyages across the Atlantic Ocean. Galleons bound for Spain were loaded at Maracaibo with the gold, silver and other riches collected from across the continent. British pirates anxious to nab the booty frequently raided the city.

In later years, a different kind of European came to the port. Maracaibo became the starting point for missionaries bent on converting local Indians to Christianity – a task that continues to this day. In the 1800s, brisk trade between Venezuela and the nearby Dutch islands boosted Maracaibo's commerce. But it was the 1922 discovery of a vast pool of oil that brought the city fame and fortune. The crude that gushed from the well known as Barroso No. 2 left no doubt that Venezuela was blessed. The influx of foreign petroleum companies and engineers began.

The oil boom shaped the city and its people. Maybe it's the heat or maybe it's the hard labor required to sweat out a living in the oil fields or on the region's cattle ranches, but something toughens the short and stocky *Maracuchos*. Easily identifiable by his accent, a *Maracucho* would think nothing of walking into a Caracas bar garbed in a hand-lettered T-shirt bearing a politically sensitive message.

Nobody is likely to bother him, either; *Maracucho* machismo is legendary in Venezuela. (And everyone knows *Maracuchos* have a penchant for carrying handguns – which they'll use to defend their honor.) Unlike Andean dwellers, who are often the butt of jokes in Caracas, *Maracuchos* are well-liked

The colors of Maracaibo's Santa Lucía district, one of the last parts of the city not to be redeveloped.

by *Caraqueños*, who are impressed by their feistiness and fierce patriotism.

Reshaped city: Government coffers loaded with oil money bankrolled urban development based on the Venezuelan notion that "modern is best." Maracaibo's oldest neighborhood, **El Saladillo**, was razed. The few multi-colored adobe homes that escaped the wrecking ball can be found along the edges of **Plaza Bolívar**, the focal point of the city. Peek inside their open doors and you'll see lace-covered tables with plastic flowers, a clutter of holy images and, inevitably, a color TV tuned to local soap operas.

El Saladillo occupied the seven blocks running between the Cathedral and the Basilica of Chiquinquirá. When it was razed, the empty lot that remained was turned into a pedestrian walkway bordered by trees and flowering bushes, dotted with fountains and decorated at intervals by outdoor sculptures commissioned by Venezuelan artists. While modern and clean, the walkway known as **Paseo de Las Ciencias** suggests nothing of the colonial charm of the antiquated neighborhood that once stood there, the heart of the city and the area where legend has it that *gaita* music originated.

The *paseo* begins at Plaza Bolívar, where the Cathedral, Casa de Gobierno and Casa Morales are located. The century-old **Cathedral**, remodeled in recent years, is home to the Cristo Negro, or Black Christ. Local residents say the crucifix and church where it hung were burned in an Indian raid in 1600 but the Christ statue nailed to the cross survived, although permanently blackened by the smoke and flames. The devout claim the statue has miraculous powers and special petitions are made to the religious figure.

Flirting police and traffic tie-ups: To one side of the white-domed church is the **Casa de Gobierno**, the state capital building also known as the Palace of the Eagles. Police officers stationed outside flirt (with varying degrees of success) with women passing by, politicians drive up and park in the no-park-

Religious icons outside the cathedral.

ing spots and there always seems to be a traffic jam outside.

Next door is **Casa Morales**, a restored two-story home built in the 18th century to serve as the official residence of the royal governor of Maracaibo province. As the only colonial mansion still standing in Maracaibo, it is now used as museum and headquarters for the Venezuelan Bolivarian Society. Although some of its architectural details, including its wooden balcony, make it a noteworthy structure, its true value is historic: this is where the Spanish Armada signed its capitulation to the independence forces following a naval battle on Lake Maracaibo in 1823.

A flogging before surrender: When Spanish naval commanders shut themselves into the mansion to decide what to do following their naval defeat, locals outside taunted them to surrender. Ana María Campos, a servant, yelled across the plaza for General Francisco Tomás Morales to capitulate and angered the Spanish officer so much that he ordered her stripped and publicly beaten. The

spunky *Maracucha* was dragged across the plaza and down two blocks to the **Convento de San Francisco**, now located next to the restored **Mercado Central**, a colorful outdoor market.

The Casa de Morales sits beside the **Teatro Baralt**, a luxurious theater for live performances during its heyday and, for several years now, under restoration. The theater was built in 1883 to celebrate the centennial of Simón Bolívar's birth, then replaced in 1929 with an 800-seat art deco building. In the country's first oil boom of the 1930s and 1940s, Carlos Gardel sang tangos there under what are claimed to be the continent's largest ceiling murals.

The Baralt was neglected and eventually turned into a movie theater before it was closed in the 1970s and a campaign began to restore it.

The walkway ends at the **Basilica of Our Lady of Chiquinquirá**, which appears from a distance to have an elaborate Romanesque facade. Look again. It is painted, not sculpted there. The basilica is the focal point each November 18 for the start of a weeklong festival, the Fería de la Chinita. The festival dates from 1749 when a young girl found a floating board in the lake and took it home where, as legend claims, the image of the Virgin Mary appeared on the wood. Now kept in the basilica, the image is known as the Virgin of Chiquinquirá or affectionately as *La Chinita*. It is carried through the streets during the festival, which is marked by a beauty contest, circus, bullfights, baseball games and plenty of music.

From jail to gallery: A few blocks southeast of the basilica is the new **Anthropology Museum**. The yellow building is unmistakable with its Egyptian-style facade and high trapezoidal windows. Once a prison, it has been converted into a series of galleries dedicated to the region's Indian culture, photography exhibits on Maracaibo and rooms of paintings and sculptures by local artists.

Much of the city is designed to accommodate the foreign petroleum engineers hired to guide operations at the oil derricks sticking up from Lake Maracaibo. Luxury hotels, fine restau-

Sunday service in Maracaibo cathedral.

rants (including the **Restaurante Paseo**, billing itself as Venezuela's only revolving dining room), and upscale shops serve these families. There are so many North Americans in the city that the US operates a consulate; an English library is found at the **Centro Venezolano-Americano**. Many of the expatriates came years ago when Venezuela was pioneering offshore drilling; locally born engineers now make up the younger ranks of the executive ladder.

In this city of engineers, a construction marvel is the 10-km (6-mile) long **Rafael Urdaneta Bridge**, one of the world's longest prestressed concrete spans and a symbol of the city. The bridge links both sides of the strait separating Lake Maracaibo from the Caribbean, around which are perched small towns like **Santa Rosa de Aguas**, a picturesque extension of Maracaibo where houses are built on piles and the fishing and swimming are good.

Colonial relic: Back in the 17th century when English, French and Dutch pirates, including the notorious Henry Morgan, began raiding Maracaibo, a defense was needed. So a fort was built on **San Carlos Island** at the mouth of the gulf. On July 24, 1823 it became the scene of the great naval battle that broke the Spanish authority in Venezuela for good. In 1902, that same fort was shelled by a German battleship after Germany, Italy and Great Britain banded together to blockade the coastline when Venezuela failed to pay its foreign debt.

Later the fort was used by Venezuela's dictators as a prison; the messages those political prisoners scratched on the walls of their cells still remain. Today, the old cannons from San Carlos are used as sea breaks.

Near San Carlos is **Toas Island** with excellent fishing, undeveloped beaches and lovely scenery. To get there, rent a boat at the pier in the fishing town of **San Rafael El Moján**. If you venture as far as the side of the lake in the evening, you might be able to see the Catatumbo Lightning, also known as *San Antonio Faro* (Saint Anthony's Beacon). This climatic phenomenon is similar to heat

The Guajira market.

lightning – lots of flash but no thunder.

Maracaibo's famous **oil derricks** are on the east coast of the lake, some distance from the city. Massive quantities of crude petroleum are still sucked from beneath the lake but the derricks closest to the shore are no longer operating and boat trips to see them have become increasingly difficult to arrange.

The jumping-off point for oil operations begins at **Cabimas**, where the hundreds of towers that have come to symbolize the city can be seen from landside. Hire a taxi; the drivers know exactly where the best vantage point is. Technically, because of fears of sabotage, it is illegal to photograph the derricks. Many people do anyway, although some degree of caution may be recommended since the derricks are still checked sporadically by the National Guardsmen, who are not known for being cooperative with tourists.

Venice, Caribbean-style: Just 45 km (27 miles) north of Maracaibo lies **Sinamaico Lagoon** where residents live in houses perched on stilts above the Limón River. The lagoon, a paradise of mangroves and coconut trees, is home to Paraujano *mestizos*, mixed-blood Venezuelans who identify with their Paraujano Indian roots. The Paraujanos make mats, *esteras*, from a papyrus-like reed that grows in the shallows, and they live from fishing. This is the "Little Venice" with the raised houses called *palafitos* that inspired the country's name; the houses connect to each other by a series of boardwalks.

For excursions on the lagoon, head to **Puerto Cuervito**, where motorboat owners take visitors on tours.

But the predominant Indians here are the Goajira, Venezuela's single largest indigenous group and the only Indians ever seen in the cities dressed in traditional clothing. The trademarks of the Goajiras are the multicolored caftans, or *mantas*, worn by the women, and the sandals with huge pompons. Goajiras have their own laws, their own language and their own customs. Many Goajira chiefs in Maracaibo and Zulia State have accumulated massive wealth from

The *palafitos* (houses on stilts) on Sinamaico Lagoon.

cattle ranching and some still remember the days when women were a symbol of power and prestige, traded for cattle. The region produces half the milk consumed in the country and more than a third of its meat.

Like the Goajira Indians across the border in Colombia, this tribe wants little to do with non-Indian affairs and it has successfully blocked the Venezuelan government from infringing upon many of its customs and native rights. Goajiras are not required to carry *cédulas*, the government-issued identification cards that everyone else – even children – must keep in their possession in Venezuela. Since the Goajiras do not recognize political borders, an arrangement has been made by which they may move between Venezuela and Colombia without the need for passports or government permissions.

While police and military officers meticulously scrutinize cars traveling between the Colombian border and Maracaibo, this search for drugs, guns and other contraband usually does not inconvenience the Goajiras who travel unimpeded in buses designated for them. This immunity from modern governments is probably what drew the infamous Papillon to hide out with these nomadic Indians during his first unsuccessful escape from the prison on Devil's Island. Older Goajira women wander through Maracaibo in their traditional, brightly colored *mantas*, but many younger Goajiras are abandoning Indian garb for Western clothes.

Every Monday, Goajiras leave their ranches and load their psychedelically painted trucks for a trip to **Paraguaipoa**, a town heavily populated by Indians. By dawn, hundreds of Goajiras have congregated in **Los Filuos** market to sell neon-colored tapestries, cotton *mantas* and finely woven hammocks. You may see women dressed in black; under local tradition, if an Indian leader – or *cacique* – dies, all the women of the tribe dress in mourning. By noon in Los Filuos, when the heat becomes unbearable, the Goajiras' commerce has been completed and they are gone.

The eye of the chameleon.

TRAVEL TIPS

GETTING THERE

BY AIR

From Europe, direct flights to Caracas are available on Venezuela's national airline Viasa, and with Iberia, British Airways, Air France, KLM, Lufthansa, Alitalia, Swiss Air and Portugal's TAP. Viasa, American Airlines, Avensa, Aeropostal, and Canadian have direct flights from the United States and Canada. (Viasa also flies weekly from New York direct to Margarita Island.)

Caracas is accessible by air from nearly all Latin American countries and several Caribbean islands, including Aruba, Cuba, Curaçao, Puerto Rico and Trinidad. Aerotuy has regular flights between Venezuela and Grenada.

A popular route from Australia or New Zealand is the once-weekly Aerolineas Argentinas flight to Buenos Aires with a connecting flight to Caracas; alternatively, travelers can take a Qantas flight to Los Angeles with Viasa connections to Venezuela.

Recently, foreign carriers – particularly US and other South American airlines – have been examining route changes that would result in more frequent and convenient air services between North America and Venezuela, as well as Europe and Venezuela. Existing direct services from New York, Los Angeles and London to Margarita Island, in addition to direct services from Houston to Maracaibo, are expected to be increased in frequency.

Tourists on international flights from Venezuela pay a US$18 departure tax (in *bolívares* or US dollars). Viasa allows international travelers to check their bags the evening before a flight, thus avoiding delays associated with airport security and luggage weighing.

BY SEA

Venezuela's port of La Guaira has long been a regular stop for luxury cruise liners plying the Caribbean. Efforts are under way to bring more cruise traffic to Puerto La Cruz, where Carnival Cruises has opened a resort hotel. Cruise ships also stop at Porlamar, on the island of Margarita, and at Ciudad Bolívar on the Orinoco River.

The *Almirante Brion* car ferry runs between the Muaco Pier near Coro and the islands of Aruba and Curaçao. It is best to book a week ahead at Ferrys del Caribe in Coro at (068) 519 676 or in Caracas at (02) 562 0409. From Venezuela's east coast, daily ferries take passengers and cars between Margarita island and Puerto La Cruz as well as Margarita and Cumaná. Book at Conferry in Caracas (02) 782 8544, in Porlamar at (95) 616 397, Puerto La Cruz (81) 668 767 and Cumaná (93) 661 462.

BY ROAD

Venezuela shares borders with Colombia, Brazil and Guyana. There is regular bus and taxi service at the border with Colombia at Cúcuta, but travelers from most countries are required to have visas if they enter Venezuela by land at this point. (The requirement is different if you arrive by air. See Travel Essentials below.) Visas can be obtained at the Venezuelan consulate in Cúcuta although the process is a chaotic one and may take a couple of days to complete. You will be asked to provide two passport-sized photos (color or black and white).

TRAVEL ESSENTIALS

VISAS & PASSPORTS

Visas are not required for Colombians and Venezuelans traveling between the two countries. However, other South and Central Americans must be in possession of a visa. Citizens of Canada, the United States, Australia and all European countries except France and Portugal do not need visas. They may enter the country by air with a valid passport; tourist cards are issued aboard the plane. All visitors may be required to show an airline ticket out of the country.

Tourist cards are valid for up to 60 days (the immigration officer stamping your passport will ask how long you want to stay) and must be surrendered to tourism officials on departure. Visas are normally good for 30 to 60 days. Visits may be extended at the discretion of the Foreign Ministry's Directory of Foreigners (Dirección de Extranjeros), commonly known as the DIEX, on Avenida Baralt in El Silencio, Caracas, although officials are frequently uncooperative. An alternative is to take an inexpensive flight to a nearby Caribbean island and return with a new tourist card.

Carry your passport and tourist card with you at all times. Some travelers recommend making copies of your passport and other valuable documents and depositing these in the hotel safe. If the originals are lost or stolen, the copies facilitate arranging replacements from your local embassy.

MONEY MATTERS

Petroleum wealth has given Venezuela a fairly stable monetary system. Although the unit of currency, the *bolívar*, is no longer at the 4.3-per-dollar level that it enjoyed for years before the so-called "Black Friday" devaluation in the early 1980s, it fluctuates little. (US$1 was worth about 60 *bolívares* in early 1992). *Bolívar* notes come in denominations of 1, 2, 10, 20, 50, 100, 500 and 1,000. Coins are available worth .25 (*medio céntimo*) .50 (*céntimo real*), 1, 2 and 5 (*fuerte*) *bolívar* denominations, as well as small tin slugs worth .05 (*puyas*), which are normally received only as change in grocery stores. Coins are often in short supply, worsened by the increased popularity of the subway, or Metro. It would be wise to hang onto any coins coming your way in order to avoid long ticket lines at the Metro and to make phone calls.

Money can be changed at competitive rates at both banks and *casas de cambio* (exchange houses). The best-known such house is Italcambio. It and other *casas de cambio* in Caracas are found in Sabana Grande and downtown on Avenida Urdaneta. Hotels and even some shops will also change US dollars. There are 24-hour currency exchange offices at the airport; the exchange counters within the waiting areas of the international airport do not open until 9am and they close at 5pm so leftover *bolívares* should be changed before checking in for flights and passing through to the waiting areas.

Venezuela is highly computerized, especially in banking, and credit card purchases and cash advances are common and easy. Cash advances are also available at the hundreds of automatic tellers scattered around the capital. Before traveling, check with your credit card company to obtain the addresses of participating banks.

Tips are given to porters, room service, hair dressers and service station employees. Restaurants add a 10 percent service charge to meal tabs but diners in fine restaurants generally add up to another 10 percent for the service staff if merited. Cabbies are not tipped, although when they use a meter to determine fares the total is usually rounded up.

HEALTH

Although malaria has been reported in some jungle regions, Venezuela has few persistent health problems. No shots are required to enter the country; travelers visiting remote jungle regions should consult their physicians regarding the need for innoculation against yellow fever and courses of anti-malarial tablets. These should be taken two weeks before entering a malarial zone and for several weeks afterwards.

Compared to other Latin America capitals, Caracas has few streetside food vendors; most common are licensed hot dog carts run by white uniformed employees wearing caps which help to give the appearance of a hygienic operation. However, it is best not to purchase food that is prepared on the street.

Most importantly, drinking water should be avoided unless it is bottled. When asking for fruit juices or *batidos* (whipped fruit drinks), request that they be made with bottled water.

However, don't let fear of tap water make you avoid liquids altogether, because dehydration is not unusual under the Caribbean sun. Make sure you come well prepared with a hat, sunglasses and strong sun screen. (It is difficult to find high-strength sun blocks in Venezuela.) Mosquitos can be a problem in some beach areas and in the Llanos; take insect repellent (also best brought from overseas).

If you visit the Llanos, do NOT swim in the rivers since many are infested with sting rays, electric eels and crocodiles. Watch for chiggers (blood-sucking parasites) on clothing if you wander through tall grasses or pasture areas. Swimming in the Amazon or "Lost World" areas is, however, usually safe.

In the Andean state of Mérida, be alert for signs of altitude sickness, including headache, fatigue and nausea. Rest is the best remedy until your body becomes adjusted to the thin air.

Motion sickness sufferers should bring their own medicine or buy *dramamina* (Dramamine) at local drugstores.

WHAT TO WEAR

Except for the Andean region near Mérida, Venezuela is hot all year round, even scorching in some places, and lightweight clothing is obligatory. That's not to say a suitcase full of shorts will suffice. Caracas is a formal city where you'll rarely see anyone in shorts, although jeans are becoming more common. In the evenings, some restaurants and nightclubs require jackets and ties for men. In general, though, casual clothing and comfortable shoes will be just fine.

Bring an umbrella if you are in Venezuela during the rainy season, which runs from May through November; torrential rains begin without warning and drench you before you have time to find shelter. At the beach, bathing suits, footwear (as a protection against the hot sand) and a towel are all you'll need. Venezuelans are known for their skimpy beach wear, including *tangas*, but nude and topless sunbathing are illegal.

The evenings cool down in Caracas so you might want a light sweater or windbreaker. Temperatures in the Andes vary according to elevation and time of year. The best time to visit Mérida is November to May when skies are clear and the mercury hovers in the low 20°s Celsius (70°s Fahrenheit) during the day and goes as low as 5 degrees Celsius (41 degrees Farenheit) at night. (In the cooler months from June to October, night temperatures hit freezing.) A warm jacket or heavy sweater is recommended for the evening and a poncho or waterproof windbreaker is a good idea if you are hiking. In the Llanos, cotton trousers and shirts will protect you from the effects of the sun and bugs.

Although December through March is considered the "high season" for foreign visitors to Venezuela (mostly by travelers who view this as a Caribbean country and want to escape their own country's winter), Venezuela can be visited all year round. The beaches have sun and warm water 12 months of the year, Mérida can be visited even in the winter and the jungle has no defined high or low tourist season.

WHAT TO BRING

Caracas is one of South America's best stocked cities, although some types of contraceptives are unavailable and travelers should bring their own personal medical supplies. A money belt is recommended since thefts are on the rise. Film is available in Venezuela and developing fees are reasonable. Take a plastic bag to store your camera away from sand and sea at the beach. English language books are sold in Caracas and Maracaibo bookstores and airport newsstands; expect them to be expensive. US and European magazines are sold at newspaper kiosks throughout the capital.

GETTING ACQUAINTED

CLIMATE

Venezuela has tropical and subtropical weather. Caracas is temperate year round, with warm days in the 80's Fahrenheit and cooler evenings. During the rainy season, it rains daily – and torrentially – for short periods of time. At the beaches, it is hot all year. Temperatures in the Andes vary according to elevation, ranging from 70–85° F (21–30° C) during the day and dropping to freezing at night.

TIME ZONES

Venezuela's time corresponds with Atlantic Standard Time in the United States, making it an hour behind New York; when the US is on Daylight Savings Time, clocks in Caracas and New York coincide. Venezuela is 5 hours behind UK time and 6 hours behind mainland Europe.

WEIGHTS AND MEASURES

Venezuela uses the metric system.

ELECTRICITY

Venezuela has 110 volt, 60-cycle outlets throughout the country.

BUSINESS HOURS

Commercial outlets in Caracas give their employees a midday break so shops are open from 9am–noon and 2–6pm Monday to Friday, 9am–noon on Saturday. Offices generally operate from 8am–noon and 1.30–5pm weekdays. Bank hours are from 8.30am–11.30am and 2–4.30pm from Monday to Friday, but note: bank holidays are frequent. Outside the capital, the tradition of the siesta also survives and it is common for stores and businesses to close from noon–2pm or, in some cases, until 3 or even 4pm. Shops are closed on Sundays.

FESTIVALS & PUBLIC HOLIDAYS

January 1: The first day of *Año Nuevo* is a public holiday. It is nearly impossible to find a restaurant open on New Year's Day.

Carnaval: The week encompassing Ash Wednesday is not celebrated as raucously in Venezuela as in other countries. Monday and Tuesday of the week before Lent are holidays.

Semana Santa: Holy Week, ending with Easter Sunday, is one of the biggest holidays of the year. Most employees work only until the Wednesday of this week (some only until noon) then they head to the beaches for four days of celebrations.

May 1: International Workers Day is a holiday.

June 24: The anniversary of the Battle of Carabobo, a turning point in the Independence War, is a public holiday.

July 5: This is the Venezuelan Independence Day, marked by parades and public ceremonies.

July 24: Liberator Simón Bolívar's birthday is a public holiday.

October 12: Día de la Raza, or Columbus Day, is a holiday.

December 25: In this Roman Catholic country, Christmas is a family holiday. Streets become clogged with vendors and shoppers in the two weeks before Christmas. No shops, restaurants or businesses are open on Christmas Day.

COMMUNICATIONS

NEWSPAPERS

Boasting that it is South America's best English language newspaper, the *Daily Journal* is found on newsstands around the country every day, including Sunday. Geared toward expatriate business executives, it concentrates on financial and political news with pages devoted to the arts and cultural events.

The country's leading morning dailies are *El Diario*, a slick but serious tabloid, and more staid *El Universal* and *El Nacional*. Afternoon papers are more sensational; they include *Ultimas Noticias*, *El Mundo* and *2001*.

BOOKS

A number of good bookstores are scattered around Caracas, with a handful lining the Sabana Grande pedestrian boulevard. There you can pick up Spanish language novels by authors from around the country, as well as history books on Venezuela.

If you're in the market for English-language books, however, your options are narrower. Lectura, at Locale No. 129 downstairs in the Centro Comercial Chacaíto beside the Chacaíto Metro station, has some English language novels, as does Steele's bookstore on Calle Baruta, off the Sabana Grande pedestrian mall. The Hotel Tamanaco has a limited selection of English-language novels, usually by US authors, and the Centro Americano-Venezolana has a reading library at its office on Avenida Principal Las Mercedes, just three blocks south of where the pedestrian boulevard ends at the Chacaíto Metro station. Undoubtedly one of the better bookstores for its English-language selection is the *librería* located on the sub-ground floor of the Centro Plaza commercial complex on Avenida Francisco de Miranda, midway between the Parque del Este and the Los Palos Grandes stations. Other English-language reading material can be found at the English Bookshop at the Concresa shopping center in Prados del Este, the upscale neighborhood on the east side of the city.

Nature enthusiasts can also visit the Audubon Society Bookstore, downstairs in the Centro Commercial Paseo Las Mercedes (near the door to the parking lot).

POSTAL SERVICE

The main post office in Caracas is at Plaza la Candelaria, on Avenida Urdaneta. Hotels also handle mail. However, mail service is hit and miss; postcards to and from Venezuela have been known to take up to a year to arrive while others show up in just a week and packages have no guarantee of reaching their destination unless mailed *certificado* (certified). Be careful with packages, too, because the Venezuelan postal service is very strict about wrapping requirements. First of all, you must be able to show officials the contents of the package if required (leave one end open until they give you the green light) and the parcel must be covered in a white cotton cloth and sewn shut. It's not as difficult as it might sound because outside the post office you'll find vendors willing to stitch the parcel for you or rent the necessary supplies for you to do it yourself. For important or rush items, you might want to try any of the multitude of carrier services in the country, including Federal Express and DHL.

TELEPHONE

Don't expect too much from the phones, although with persistence you can usually get a call through. Venezuela's low tech phone service is the country's shame, although the government is attempting to sell it to foreign investors. To operate public phones, you'll need 1 *bolívar* coins; some phones also accept 2 *bolívar* coins.

Another way to tackle local calls on the street is to visit any of the phone company (CANTV: pronounced Can-Tay-Vay) offices scattered around the city and buy phone cards, disposable credit-card-sized slips you insert in public phones. A portion of the card's value is discounted with every call. The CANTV's main office is located on Avenida Libertador just where it runs into Avenida Andres Bello, east of downtown.

For long distance, national or international, there is direct dialing at most hotels and booths (*cabinas*) at the CANTV offices. For directory assistance dial 103.

EMERGENCIES

SECURITY & CRIME

Caracas has always had a problem with street crime, and it's not getting any better. Be on the lookout for the multitude of *motorizados* (messengers on motorcycles who wind their way through city traffic): some of these bikers will ride right up onto the sidewalk, snatch a purse or necklace and roar away. It's best to leave good jewelry, especially gold chains, at home. Other *motorizados*, though unintentionally, have been known to knock down and seriously injure pedestrians crossing the street. (*Motorizados* generally ignore traffic lights and stop signs.) Purse snatchers and pickpockets on foot are also a problem. Avoid deserted streets in the evenings and keep identification on you at all times. The police can ask for ID at any time.

For emergencies in Caracas, call the Radio Patrulla (similar to a police emergency radio system) at 811 1222. Victims of sexual assault receive assistance and counseling from AVESA at 575 4165. For fires, call the Omberos Caracas (Fire Department) emergency number 166. Private ambulance services are Ambulancias Plan Caracas (Tel: 545 4545) and Ambulancias del Este (Tel: 320 750). Medical clinics where English is spoken include the Policlínica Americana (Tel: 951 6836 and 951 5322) and Clínica Instituto Médico La Floresta (Tel: 285 2111).

Tow truck services are available from Grúas La Trinidad (Tel: 935 913), Grúas Las Minas (Tel: 930 506), Grúas Satelite (Tel: 239 4364) and Grúas Ibarra (Tel: 310 191 and 338 045).

Taxis should have a registration sticker in their front windows. If the cab looks like a private vehicle that someone has simply stuck a TAXI sign on, avoid it. Most of these unregulated *piratas* are okay but occasionally their drivers are actually thieves – and tourists are ideal targets. If you have any trouble with a cabbie, you can report the taxi registration number to the police or the tourist office, Corpoturismo.

GETTING AROUND

ORIENTATION

Caracas is the main jumping off point for visits to Venezuela, although many travelers go straight on to Puerto La Cruz or Margarita when they enter the country.

Caracas, located about midway along the country's northern coast, is not hard to manage, particularly if you obtain a good map with the Metro system indicated. The city lies in a long narrow east-west valley, bordered to the north by Mount Avila – a good landmark for orienting yourself during walking tours.

The most complicated part of Caracas is its unorthodox method of indicating addresses. Street numbers are rarely used and street names are only somewhat valuable since many of them extend for considerable distances. Instead, street corners are named and intersection are given as reference points.

High rise buildings have names (as do private residences) so a typical address might be: Residencia Las Palmas (the name of an apartment building) on Avenida Las Palmas near Avenida Andres Bello (the intersection) in La Florida (the name of the neighborhood). If unfamiliar with the city, make sure you get as many landmarks as possible when given an address. Most taxi drivers and bus drivers know their way around, but it helps when you can refer to nearby parks, corporate buildings or shopping centers.

From Caracas, there is convenient and regular bus, *por puesto* (shared taxis) and airline service all over the country. The best highways also leave from this hub, heading to the beaches just over the mountains from the capital, to the highlands, along the eastern coast on what is called the Gold Coast circuit and along the western Caribbean coastline. Caracas is the business, political and social capital of the country, although other cities such as Maracaibo and Puerto La Cruz have well developed hotel, restaurant, bank and shopping services.

When Venezuelans talk about *la playa*, the beach, or *la costa*, the coast, they mean El Litoral, which is the central area coast closest to Caracas. Otherwise they specify beaches to the east, such as Puerto La Cruz, Cumaná and Carúpano, or beaches to the west, including Puerto Cabello and Morrocoy. Mérida refers to both the city and the state with that name and is synonymous with the Andes mountains.

Scorching hot Maracaibo, on the shores of the continent's largest lake, is the focus of the oil industry which pumps heavy crude from deposits below the lake. And San Fernando de Apure is the principal starting point for visits to the Llanos, or grasslands where cattle graze under the gaze of rough and ready cowboys.

Reference to the Lost World means the Gran Sabana, Venezuela's prehistoric landscape where flat-topped mountains set the background for an eerie, relatively unexplored plateau north of the country's steamy jungle region, which for most visitors begins with a flight to Puerto Ayacucho.

Offshore, Margarita is the most popular island destination, a dry spot of land floating on the Caribbean and offering beaches to please every taste.

Visitors with a short time in the country might try to arrange a trip in which they spend a couple of days in Caracas then take a day trip to Los Roques, the spectacular Caribbean archipelago accessible by flights aboard Aerotuy propeller planes.

With a taste of what the Venezuelan beaches have to offer, Ciudad Bolívar, on the banks of the Orinoco, might be a good second option. From this historic city, travelers can head off in Aerotuy planes to the Kavak Camp – reached by flying over Angel Falls – or by Avensa jet to the airline-owned camp right beside the world's highest waterfalls. (Note: the Avensa camp has more demand than it can meet and you must have a reservation to get on these flights. Book as far in advance as possible.)

From there, it is possible to fly to Mérida (via Caracas) for a taste of the Venezuelan highlands then onto San Fernando de Apure for a look at the Llanos – still one of the least visited tourist destinations. The trip can be concluded at one of the mainland beaches near Puerto La Cruz or sunning and shopping on the resort island of Margarita.

MAPS

Bookstores and kiosks in Caracas sell city maps. Gas stations have highway maps. The national tourism office Corpoturismo on floors 36 and 37 of Torre Oeste in Parque Central has folders and brochures of touristic sites. It has a 24-hour bilingual tourist phone line set up to answer questions at (02) 507 8829 and 573 8983.

TO AND FROM THE AIRPORT

An airport shuttle bus leaves from under the Avenida Universidad bridge at the north end of Parque Central every half hour starting at 4am and is the least expensive way to get to and from the Maiquetía airport; the fare is about $1.25 and travelers are dropped off at the airport terminal door. At night, take a cab to the airport bus stop as the area is unpleasant to walk to after dark. Buses from the international terminal stop running about 8pm but next door at the domestic terminal they continue

until the last flight has arrived, usually about midnight. It is just a short walk between the two terminals.

Probably easier for first time visitors is to take a taxi. A cab ride between downtown and either airport terminal runs to about $15; there is a cab information booth where you buy a ticket (located next to the money exchange booth directly ahead as you leave the baggage collection area) and a list of prices (calculated according to city zones) at the airport. Although a multitude of independent *taxistas* offer lifts from the airport, paying directly at the taxi booth ensures getting an officially registered driver.

For any flight leaving from the Simón Bolívar International Airport in Maiquetía outside Caracas, allow at least two hours travel time to the airport. Traffic can be horrendous on the mountain highway; when roads are clear the trip takes less than 45 minutes but seasoned travelers talk about being stuck for hours in traffic jams, especially during peak travel periods such as Christmas, Easter, weekends and summer holidays.

In Puerto La Cruz, Maracaibo, Porlamar and other cities, city buses pass the main roadway outside the airports. Ask at the airport tourism information offices for details. There is cab service at all airports.

DOMESTIC TRAVEL

BY AIR

Venezuela's domestic flights are comfortable, generally run on time and are among the world's cheapest, thanks to the oil-rich country's policy of subsidizing jet fuel prices. The only hitch is that you must be at the airport at the time the airline requires or your seat will not be held. Air transportation is a fabulous bargain for the price and is highly recommended except for trips in which you want to see the countryside en route.

The two major domestic airlines, Aeropostal and Avensa, serve most major cities. The smaller Aerotuy, with regularly scheduled tourist flights and charter service, specializes in propeller plane flights to Los Roques islands, Canaima, Angel Falls and the Amazon region. It has daily scheduled services to Gran Roque in the Los Roques archipelago from Maiquetía, Barcelona (near Puerto La Cruz) and Porlamar on the island of Margarita.

Aerotuy packages range from day trips to overnight stays in guest houses with beach and/or fishing excursions to cruise and diving programs on a 76-foot (23-meter) motor cruiser. It is also possible to get to Los Roques on the small airline CAVE, by hitching a lift or chartering a plane from the Aeroclub at La Carlota, the military airport in Caracas, or chartering a helicopter from Helicópteros del Caribe at Maiquetía.

Be sure to confirm all airline reservations at least 72 hours in advance (and reconfirm 24 hours in advance). The airlines will give you a reconfirmation number on a slip of paper to avoid problems when you check in for the flight, which you should do at least an hour in advance to assure your seat.

BY RAIL

There is passenger service on only one rail line, the four-hour ride between Puerto Cabello and Barquisimeto. Tickets can be purchased at either train station no sooner than two hours before the train departs; passengers should be wary of pickpockets and purse snatchers aboard trains. In towns along the route, stone throwing has become popular and the train has both Plexiglas windows and metal grilles that must be raised (the conductor will let you know when). Snacks and cold drinks are sold aboard.

This train is about the least expensive form of travel in the country – less than a dollar for the entire route, but the scenery is dull and the journey is longer than on a bus.

BY BUS

Long-distance ground transportation is in buses (*autobuses*) or shared cabs called *por puestos* or *colectivos*. Every city has a bus station (*terminal terrestre*) where bus companies offer their services. Fares are regulated so the main consideration should be the condition of the vehicle. (Ask what *anden* or platform the bus loads at so you can take a look.) Tickets may be sold in advance but more often you line up on a first-come, first served basis and pay on board. The buses stop frequently at rest areas.

For travel from Caracas, head to the Nuevo Circo bus terminal – a pair of fume-filled lots of idling buses and *por puestos*. (The terminal is located beside the Metro's La Hoyada station.) One lot is dedicated to east-bound travel and the other to west-bound. Here you can also get short distance mini-buses to El Litoral beaches or Colonia Tovar. There are ticket offices inside the buildings at Nuevo Circo although most passengers simply follow the hawker calling out the name of their destination; they are inevitably led to the next bus heading in the direction they want.

To get to your destination quicker, the best option is a *por puesto*. In Caracas, these are small mini-buses that travel both in and outside the city. However, they may also take the form of full-sized cars that take up to five passengers. They leave as soon as they are full and stop only for gas. Whether the *por puestos* are more comfortable than the buses is somewhat subjective. Riding five or six passengers to a car on a long trip may not be more comfortable than a bus, although it will always be faster.

For short trips to the beach area outside Caracas (or for inter-urban travel in other parts of the country), the mini-buses used are often cramped. Travel light and look for a mini-bus that is not full in order to get your choice of seat.

BY SEA

Fishing boats can be hired at any beach town; the arrangements are informal and you should agree on a price in advance. If the plan is a round trip affair where you're dropped off at a beach and then collected later, don't pay the bill until you have been safely returned to your starting point. Most of these boats are simple wooden affairs; some carry no life jackets. (Ask in advance.)

Long term yacht rental, with skippers, is available at the Caraballeda Marina near the Macuto Sheraton hotel at El Litoral or by checking the classifieds in *The Daily Journal*. Yachts destined for Los Roques can be chartered by booking in the US through Lost World Adventures (phone toll-free: (800) 999 0558 or (404) 971 8586).

A ferry service is available from Cumaná and Puerto La Cruz to Margarita Island. Make sure you locate the nearest open emergency exit as soon as you board the ferry. All are required by law to carry life vests and safety equipment but some have blocked a few of their emergency exits.

BY CAR

Car rentals are easy in Venezuela. Travelers must present a valid driver's license from their country of residency (or an international license), passport and credit card. The minimum driving age is 18. Rental agencies have a number of offices, including at the airports, and reservations for across the country can be made in Caracas. Car rental agencies include Hertz (reservations in Caracas at 952 5511 and 952 8611), National (Tel: 344 611 to 15 in Caracas), Budget (in Caracas at 283 4333).

Venezuela's highways are among South America's best, although landslides can occur on mountain roads during the rainy season. Gas stations are found at regular intervals along major highways. The biggest danger, unfortunately, is other drivers. Although traffic generally does not travel at the rapid speeds found in the United States and many European countries, accidents are frequent. Drivers here are aggressive and drinking and driving is not an uncommon combination, especially at the end of a beach weekend. Be defensive and steer clear of erratic motorists. There is no law requiring seat belt use in Venezuela.

PUBLIC TRANSPORT

Caracas has just about every type of public transportation available, including South America's newest subway, or Metro. The Metro stations are clean and orderly; maps on the walls show routes and there is an information booth for commuters with questions. Tickets can be purchased with coins from self-serve machines or from attended windows. The subway operates from 6am to 11pm. East-west routes run from Los Palos Grandes to Propatria, while the short north-south spur goes from the El Capitolio station to Las Adjuntas or, alternatively, the Caricuao Zoo. The Metro is still under construction and above ground Metro buses carry passengers along future subway routes. To take a Metro bus, ask for a ticket that is *integrado*.

Above ground, city buses run a number of routes. They look like repainted Bluebird school buses and are the least expensive – and slowest – way to travel. A quicker option are the urban *por puestos* or minibuses that stop wherever you request. Destinations are posted in the windows of buses and *por puestos* (although the system may be confusing for those who don't speak Spanish or don't know the city well). Buses have designated stops; flag down a *por puesto* by waving your arm as one goes by.

With the exception of the parks, Plaza Bolívar and the Sabana Grande boulevard, Caracas is not made for walking. Sidewalks are poorly maintained and frequently are cut off by highways. *Caraqueños* are used to the quick and easy public transportation, and when giving directions they will frequently describe a place as *demasiado lejos* or too far to reach on foot.

Caracas and Mérida have yet another type of public transportation: cable cars, or *teleféricos*. The Caracas *teleférico* from the city up the Avila mountain to the park at its peak had been out of service for several years at press time. The Mérida *teleférico* offers the only public transportation route to Venezuela's snow-capped Andes.

Taxis are in abundance in nearly every Venezuelan town and city. Cab drivers tend to overcharge tourists, although even at the inflated rate, taxi fares are usually under US$5. If the cabbie has no taxi meter (and even those who do usually claim it's out of commission), agree in advance on a fare. The price of a ride can differ dramatically at different times of the day (after 10pm on Friday and Saturday nights, for example, prices can double or even triple). During rain or rush hour, a ride that normally takes 15 minutes can take an hour – and the drivers know it. Be suspicious, too, of fictitious holidays that cab drivers cite in adding surcharges to the fares. They are legally allowed to hike prices after midnight and on national holidays. Venezuelans do not normally tip cabbies but, if the ride is metered, they round up the fare. If the cabbie has carried luggage, a tip is in order.

WHERE TO STAY

CARACAS

Hotel Avila, Avenida Washington, San Bernardino. Tel: (02) 515 128, 515 155, 515 119 and 529 690. Fax: 523 612. If Caracas had to identify its traditional hotel, it would be the now somewhat faded Avila, built by Nelson Rockefeller and tucked against the base of the Avila mountain, away from the noise and traffic of the downtown areas. Its outdoor swimming pool is one of the city's most inviting and the exuberant flora springing up around the hotel add to the Caribbean *ambiente*. $$$

Anauco Hilton, Parque Central, Edificio Anauco, El Conde. Tel: (02) 573 4111 and 573 5702; US reservations (800) HILTONS. Telex: 21886. Fax: (02) 573 7724. This is the best of the Hilton chain's two Caracas properties. The Anauco Hilton has modern balconied suites overlooking the city's fine arts neighborhood. $$$

Caracas Hilton, Avenida Sur 25, Urbanización El Conde. Tel: (02) 574 2322; US reservations 800 HILTONS. Telex: 21171. Fax: (02) 575 0024. $$$

Hotel Eurobuilding, Calle La Guairita, Chuao. Tel: (02) 959 1133, 922 740; in the US toll free at 800 325 EURO. Fax: (02) 922 069. This luxury hotel is where Cuban leader Fidel Castro stayed when he was in Caracas. $$$

Hotel Tamanaco Inter-Continental, Avenida Principal de Las Mercedes, Las Mercedes. Tel: (02) 924 522, 208 7000, 208 7030, 208 7040. Telex: 23575 HIGLV. Fax: (02) 208 7951. The Tamanaco is synonymous with luxury and fine service. Perched on a hill overlooking the upscale Las Mercedes residential area, its view is lovely. However, visitors who want to explore the downtown area may find the location inconvenient as it is not near any Metro routes. $$$

Hotel Lincoln Suites, Avenida Francisco Solano near Jerónimo. Tel: (02) 728 576 through 728 579. Fax: (02) 725 503. This new hotel is right in the heart of the action. Situated along the Sabana Grande Boulevard, the Hotel Lincoln Suites offers one of the best locations for lodging in the city, although its service is uneven. It is walking distance from two Metro stations and several bus lines. $$

Plaza Palace, Avenida Los Mangos, Las Delicias. Tel: (02) 724 821 through 4829. Telex: 24129 HOPLA VC. Fax: (02) 726 375. The Plaza Palace may be Caracas' best bargain. Recently renovated, one block from the Sabana boulevard and with an English-speaking staff, this hotel has air conditioning, televisions and easy prices. $

BARQUISIMETO

Barquisimeto Hilton, Carrera 5, entre calles 5 y 6, Urbanización Nueva Segovia. Tel: (051) 536 022, 542 945 and 543 201; in US (800) HILTONS. Telex (395) 51464. Fax: (051) 539 601. In a residential area overlooking the Valle de Turbio National Park, this hotel has swimming pool, tennis courts and access to a golf course. $$$

CHORONÍ

Hotel Club Cotoperix, Puerto Colombia. In Caracas, tel: (02) 573 5241. Space must be reserved ahead for rooms in this restored colonial home. Rates include meals and drinks, boat rides to isolated beaches, excursions into Henri Pittier National Park and tours of former *cacao haciendas*. $$
Hotel Alemania, Puerto Colombia. Reservations can be made by calling in Caracas (02) 986 2698. This used to be the standard hotel for English-speaking expatriates in Caracas. As Choroní's popularity has gone up, so have the prices at the rustic Alemania. Food here is still good, though. Book well in advance for Friday and Saturday nights. $

CHICHIRIVICHE

La Garza, Avenida Principal de Chichiriviche. Tel: (042) 86 126 and 86 048. $
Hotel Mario, Calle 7 con Calle G. Tel: (042) 86 114 and 86 115. $

CIUDAD BOLÍVAR

Hotel Río Orinoco, Distribuidor San Rafael (off Ciudad Bolívar El Tigre highway), near Angostura Bridge. Tel: (085) 42 011; reservations in Caracas, tel: (02) 782 8433; in the US (800) 275 3123. Fax: (085) 42 844. This is the best hotel in town with a swimming pool, discotheque-bar and good restaurant that specializes in delicious fish dishes.
Hotel Laja Real, opposite the airport. Tel: (085) 27 911. A simple but comfortable hotel with a pool and good restaurant, close to the center of town. $

CIUDAD GUAYANA

Hotel Inter-Continental Guayana, Parque Punta Vista. Tel: (086) 22 2244. Telex: 23575 HIGLV. Fax in Caracas: (02) 208 7951. Good views here perched on a lovely lagoon. Restaurant, bar, tennis courts, gym and a pool. $$$

COLONIA TOVAR

Selva Negra. Tel: (043) 51 415. $
Alta Baviera. Tel: (043) 51 333 and 51 483. $
Two hotels easily found on the main road.

CORO

Hotel Miranda, Avenida Coro. Tel: (068) 516 645 and 516 732; reservations in Caracas, tel: (02) 507 8815 and 507 8816. This three-story hotel has pool, tennis court, garden and restaurant and is situated right beside the airport. $$
Hotel Los Médanos, Avenida Esteban Smith. Tel: (068) 599 449. Just east of Coro, this moderately-priced hotel has 40 rooms spread among several buildings and cabins, as well as a pool and discotheque. Inquire here about renting camels to ride across the dunes. $$

CUMANÁ

Hotel Cumanagota, Avenida Universidad. Tel: (093) 653 115. This hotel has a fabulous outdoor swimming pool and an ocean view. $$

GRAN SABANA ("Lost World")

In Canaima, the **Avensa Camp** and **Jungle Rudy's** are both very expensive and often booked out weeks in advance. Reservations can only be made through travel agents. Rustic hammock accommodation in private houses is on a first come, first served basis.

In **Kawaik**, the lodge is slightly less expensive ($$) and can be booked through Aerotuy airlines or Lost World Adventures in either Caracas or the US.
In Caracas:
Edificio 3-H, Officina 62, Boulevar de Gran Sabana. Tel: (02) 718 644. Fax: (02) 717 859.
In the US:
189 Autumn Ridge Drive, Marietta, Georgia. Tel: (800) 999 0558 and (404) 971 8586.

Lost World Adventures is also the contact for the Kawaik lodge near the Brazilian border.

EL LITORAL

Macuto Sheraton, Caraballeda. Tel: (031) 944 300, 944 318; reservations in Caracas, tel: (02) 782 9408. Telex: 31165 SHEMA VC. Fax: (031) 944 318. On the beach with a freshwater pool, marina and luxury accommodations. $$$
Meliá Caribe, Caraballeda. Tel: (031) 945 555; reservations in Caracas, tel: (02) 729 314. Lovely resort hotel run by the Spanish Meliá chain. $$$

THE LLANOS

San Fernando de Apure: There are several rough-and-ready hotels in town, but none you can book in advance or offering any degree of comfort.

Most visitors pre-arrange accommodation at a number of private *hatos*, or cattle ranches. **Hato El Cedral** northwest of El Frío and **Hato Piñero** near the town of El Baúl are booked through the Audubon Society in Caracas (Tel: 02 3813). **Adventure Camp Los Indios**, a cattle ranch/lodge between the Cunaviche and Cunavichito Rivers about four hours from San Fernando de Apure, is also open to overnight visitors. Contact the Audubon Society.

Hato Doña Barbara is a huge working cattle ranch owned and operated by the Estrada family but open to guests who stay in basic but comfortable rooms with private baths. All hearty, buffet-style meals included.

Birdwatching, visits to the forest to see howler monkeys, horseback riding to the sand dunes on the property and watching *llaneros* at their work are among the things to do here. Located at La Trinidad de Arauca, on the shore of the Arauca River southwest of San Fernando de Apure. Contact Lost World Adventures in the US at (800) 999 0558 or in Caracas at Edificio 3-H (entre Banco Metropolitano y Pasaje Concordia), Piso 6, Oficina 62, Boulevar de Sabana Grande. Tel: (02) 718 644.

You can make arrangements to overnight at the biological station at **Hato El Frío**, between Mantecal and El Samán de Apure; contact the La Salle Society in Caracas at (02) 782 8711, extension 232.

MARACAIBO

Hotel del Lago Inter-Continental, Avenida El Milagro. Tel: (061) 912 022 and 911 657. Telex: 23575 HIGLV. Fax in Caracas: (02) 287 951. This luxury hotel in the Intercontinental chain is Maracaibo's best and caters to oil industry executives and engineers. $$$
Kristoff, Avenida 8, No. 68–48 entre calles 68 y 69. Tel: (061) 72911, 72912, 72913, 72917 and 72919. $$
Maruma, Circunvalación No. 2, frente a la Zona Industrial. Tel: (061) 349 011 and 349 176. $$$
Cabimas International, Avenida Andres Bello, Sector Ambrosio, Cabimas (suburban Maracaibo). Tel: (064) 45 692, 45 694 and 45 703. This luxury hotel caters to oil industry executives and engineers, situated on the banks of Lake Maracaibo. $$$

MARGARITA

Margarita Hilton, Calle Los Uveros, Urb. Costa Azul Playa Moreno, Porlamar. Tel: (095) 615 044, 615 822 and 616 280; in US 800 HILTONS. Telex: 95353 HIMAR VC. Fax: (095) 614 801. $$$
Bella Vista, Avenida Santiago Mariño, Porlamar. Tel: (095) 618 264 and 614 831; reservations in Caracas, tel: (02) 507 8815 and 507 8816. This government-run hotel with two swimming pools is situated right on the beach. Its entrance is flanked by a landmark sculpture by Narvaéz. $$ to $$$

Margarita Concorde, Avenida Raúl Leoni, Porlamar. Tel: (095) 613 333. The hotel that boasts the most complete watersports offerings and a range of rental equipment. $$$

MÉRIDA

Prado Río, Avenida Hoyada de Milla. Tel: (074) 520 700. Sixty rooms in a lovely mountain setting with formal gardens, pool and restaurant. $$
Park, Calle 37 on Parque Glorias Pátrias. Tel: (074) 632 400; reservations in Caracas, tel: (02) 979 3246. Fax in Caracas: (02) 978 1497. A large and expensive multi-story hotel with good mountain views, restaurant, coffee shop and discotheque. $$
Valle Grande, Off Valle Grande Highway east of Mérida. Tel: (074) 443 011. Set in a grove of trees, this lodge has bungalows with kitchens, miniature golf and horse riding. $$
La Posada de Jají, Plaza Principal, Jají. Tel: (074) 35 182. Traditional and small, this has rooms with balconies and a good restaurant serving local foods. Live folk music on Sundays. $$
Los Frailes, Just off main highway to Mérida, Santo Domingo. Tel: (074) 88 144; reservations in Caracas, tel: (02) 562 3022; in the US through Avensa or Viasa airline offices. Perhaps the most charming of the Mérida area lodgings and certainly the best known, this neo-colonial structure was built on the site of a 17th-century monastery. It has comfortable rooms with wooden beams set around a cobblestone courtyard with a fountain. Ask ahead if you want to rent horses for riding. Advance reservations strongly recommended. $$

PUERTO LA CRUZ

Hotel Doral Beach, Avenida Américo Vespucio, El Morro. Tel: (081) 81 911 and 87 921; reservations in Caracas, tel: (02) 781 1833; in the US (Miami) at (305) 759 8071 and 751 3550. TELEX: 81307. This is a massive resort complex with 1,312 rooms and suites, a huge irregularly shaped swimming pool and a hotel right on the beach. Rental shop has bicycles, boats, surf boards, water skis and diving classes. $$$
Meliá Puerto La Cruz, Paseo Colón. Tel: (081) 691 311; reservations in Caracas, tel: (02) 729 314 and 729 317. Ocean view rooms. $$$
Maremares, Complejo Turístico El Morro. Tel: (081) 813 022; reservations in US 800 3 GOLDEN. This Golden Rainbow Resorts chain hotel is the newest addition to the Puerto La Cruz hotel roster and it offers a lagoon-style swimming pool, golf course and a long list of watersports activities. $$$

FOOD DIGEST

WHAT TO EAT

Venezuela has a good variety of food, from beef raised in the Llanos, to seafood, harvested from Caribbean waters, to mouth watering fruits and exotic juices. If you've never had passion fruit before, try it in juice form. Ask for *jugo de parchita*. The national bread is *arepa*, discs of fried or baked corn meal. *Arepas* are sliced open in the center and the heavy dough inside is scooped out before fillings ranging from shredded meat to cheese are spooned inside. Scrumptious deepfried fingers of crust-covered cheese, known as *tequeños*, are good snacks. The national dish is *pabellón criollo*, shredded beef, white rice, black beans and fried plantains. At Christmas time, the local version of *tamales*, known as *hallacas*, are available and are considered quite a delicacy. (For more information on local cooking styles and specialities, see the chapter on Cuisine.)

Venezuela has been a melting pot for immigrants and its roster of restaurants, especially in Caracas, clearly shows that. Along with typically Venezuelan dishes, it has every other kind of food imaginable, from Middle Eastern falafels, Mexican burritos and Japanese sushi to Brazilian *feijoada*, French cuisine and Szechvan Chinese dishes.

WHERE TO EAT

CARACAS

In this flashy capital, atmosphere is every bit as important as cuisine. *Caraqueños* thrive on novelty and they expect to be entertained, which is why top restaurants emphasize decor and food preparation. Caracas has one of the continent's most diverse selection of fine restaurants, with excellent seafood and ethnic restaurants.

Casa Juancho, Avenida San Juan Bosco, Altamira. Tel: (02) 334 614. Located up the hill towards the Avila from Los Palos Grande Metro stop, this restaurant's attractions are a garden setting and Spanish menu. The house specialty is roast suckling pig. Strolling minstrels perform at night.

Dama Antañona, Jesuitas 14 at Maturín. Tel: (02) 837 287. This lovely, restored colonial home in an old section of downtown (on a cross street up the hill toward the Avila from the Citibank building along Avenida Urdaneta) offers a selection of Venezuelan

dishes, including wonderful *sopa de jojoto* (corn soup). Excellent salad bar. Open for lunch.

Los Pilones, Avenida Venezuela, Esquina con Avenida Pichincha, El Rosal. Tel: (02) 718 376. This is the best place for *criollo* offerings like the national dish, *pabellon criollo*: shredded beef, black beans, rice and fried plantains.

Altamar, 3a. Transversal Altamira, between Luis Roche and San Juan Bosco. Tel: (02) 262 1813. This seafood restaurant presents a dazzling flamenco show along with its highly touted paella. Like Casa Juancho, it is in the restaurant district north of the Metro's Los Palos Grandes station.

Gazebo, Avenida Rio de Janeiro, Las Mercedes. Tel: (02) 926 812. You'll probably need to take a cab here because it is difficult to reach with public transportation. This internationally acclaimed restaurant sets the standard for *nouvelle cuisine* in Caracas, with its renowned gastronomic festivals and guest chefs like the Frenchman Paul Bocuse.

Lasserre, Avenida 3 near 3ra Transversal, Los Palos Grandes. Tel: (02) 283 4558. The menu is French and the atmosphere is elegant, helped by the rich antique furnishings and excellent wine cellar. This is northeast of the Los Palos Grandes Metro stop, behind the Centro Plaza commercial high rise.

Aventino, Avenida San Felipe at José Angel Llamas, La Castellana. Tel: (02) 322 640. Tucked in an elegant mansion and boasting the city's best wine cellar, this restaurant upholds a classical French reputation. The house specialty is pressed duck.

Cafe L'Attico, Avenida Luis Roche, Qta. Palic, Altamira. Tel: 261 2819. Very popular amongst young *Caraqueños* and homesick US expatriates, L'Attico could be transplanted directly from Miami. Still, the food is good and atmosphere wild, especially on weekends.

La Estancia, Avenida Principal, La Castellana. Tel: (02) 331 937. A colonial home converted into an Argentine-style steak house.

Much less formal and easier on the pocketbook are the Spanish *tascas* of La Candelaria, a neighborhood best not visited on foot at night. Here you can make a meal of the *tapas* – snack plates of fresh squid, wedges of *tortilla español*, garlic mushrooms and fresh-baked bread.

MARACAIBO

Mi Vaquita, Avenida 3H at Calle 76. There's nothing more appropriate than eating beef here in cattle country and Mi Vaquita may be the city's best steak house.

El Delfín, Calle 75 at Avenida 3H. Good seafood.

MARGARITA (Porlamar)

El Chipi, Avenida Santiago Mariño at Cedeño. Tel: (095) 32 648. This restaurant claims to have the best seafood on Margarita. The menu includes the local shellfish soup, *chipi chipi*.

D. Gaspar, Avenida 4 de Mayo. No telephone. Homemade pastas are the treat at this moderately-priced Italian restaurant.

PUERTO CABELLO

Sol y Mar, End of Malecón, off beach. No telephone. This open air seafood restaurant right beside the water serves up a good plate of freshly caught fish, shellfish or shrimp and is a lovely place to be at sunset.

THINGS TO DO

CARACAS

Caracas is an eclectic and electric city with something for everyone. Although much of its colonial roots have been destroyed, razed to make way for glittering high rises, tourists can still wander through the history-filled La Pastora neighborhood or visit Plaza Bolívar. The city's art museums are top-notch and its parks are lovely and well-kept. Although *Caraqueños* don't party late on week nights, this is definitely a night owl's city on weekends when discotheques, jazz bars and the city's theatrical district are in full swing. Movie theaters are plentiful and inexpensive by US and European standards and dining out – day or night – is a memorable experience at the city's finer restaurants.

City tours are available through a number of local travel agencies but Caracas is an easy city to get around in, so travelers may be inclined to just wander on their own. Recommended tour operators include:

Lost World Adventures, Edificio 3-H (entre Banco Metropolitano y Pasaje Concordia), Piso 6, Oficina 62, Boulevar de Sabana Grande, Caracas. Tel: (02) 718 644. Fax: (02) 717 859. In the US: 189 Autumn Ridge Drive, Marietta, Georgia. Tel: (800) 999 0558 and (404) 971 8586.

Morgan Tours, Edificio Roraima, Piso 9, Avenida Francisco de Miranda, Caracas. Tel: (02) 271 9265. Telex: 23516.

PUERTO LA CRUZ

The lure of this city is summed up in one word: beach. Local travel agencies offer inclusive day packages that include boats, lunch, jaunts to isolated beaches and tropical cocktails. However, travelers who speak some Spanish can use public transportation or rental cars and just as easily make their way to excellent beaches such as Playa Dorada and Playa Arapita. Most *por puestos* leave at regular intervals from stops along the waterfront boulevard, Paseo Colón. In addition, many hotels in Puerto La Cruz arrange day beach trips for their guests. At night, do what the residents of Puerto La Cruz do: stroll along the sea wall and people-watch.

From Caracas, Puerto La Cruz is served by Avensa and Aeropostal. It is also possible to travel by land in a bus or *por puesto* from the capital. Although a lengthy bus trip, the scenery along this route, also known as the Gold Coast, is spectacular. A third alternative is renting a car. The highway between Puerto La Cruz and Caracas is paved and well-marked.

MARACAIBO

Oil is what lures most visitors here: petroleum engineers come to work at what is one of the world's largest heavy crude deposits and tourists try to catch a glimpse of the derricks rising up from South America's largest lake. Although much of Maracaibo has been razed to make way for new highrises, there is still an intriguing colonial section of the city worth visiting. And this is the only urban area of the nation where you can see indigenous people still following their traditions. Goajiro men and women – mostly cattle ranchers – shop and socialize in Maracaibo in their Indian clothing.

Maracaibo is accessible on regularly scheduled buses from Caracas; there are also several flights daily between Caracas and Maracaibo on Aeropostal and Avensa.

MARGARITA

Venezuelans come to this island for its duty-free shopping. Most tourists come for the beaches, but it is possible to combine the two, adding in some seafood dining and a trip through the enchanting La Restinga mangrove lagoon. History buffs can take time out to explore the forts built in the Spanish era to hold back Caribbean pirates.

By land, you can travel by bus, *por puesto* or car to Cumaná, Puerto La Cruz or Carúpano, continuing onto Margarita by ferry. There are at least two ferry services to the island, each with more than one daily departure most times of the year. Margarita is accessible by air from Caracas and Puerto La Cruz.

MÉRIDA

Although best known as a Caribbean country, Venezuela has an Andean region with charming highland towns centered around Mérida. Here visitors ride the *teleférico* up to a snow covered peak, drink the local *chicha* or eat river trout and photograph the bright yellow *frailejones* flowers that bloom on the hillsides.

Buses and *por puestos* have regularly scheduled services between Mérida and Caracas, although the trip is a long and windy one. Easier are the Avensa and Aeropostal flights to this Andean city. There are several flights a day from the capital.

CIUDAD BOLÍVAR

Ciudad Bolívar is most often used as the jumping off point for visits to Angel Falls and Canaima, but it has a touristic value of its own. Perched on the banks of the Orinoco River, this is one of Venezuela's most historically important cities. City tours give a glimpse of the colonial architecture and balconies on houses while the local museums trace the beginnings of this city. Here, too, is the home, studio and museum of one of Venezuela's most famous artists, kinetic sculptor Jesús Soto.

Ciudad Bolívar is a port stop for cruise vessels plying the Orinoco. There is also daily air service on Aeropostal and Avensa from Caracas.

CULTURE PLUS

MUSEUMS

Museums and art galleries are usually open daily except Mondays.

CARACAS

Museo de Arte Contemporáneo, Parque Central (near Hilton Hotel and the Bellas Artes Metro stop). Tel: (02) 573 0075 and 573 0209. Open 10am–6pm every day but Monday; no admission charge. An excellent collection of Venezuela's top contemporary artists and others, including Botero, Picasso, Léger, Chagall and Matisse.
Museo de los Niños, Parque Central (Beside the Anauco Hilton hotel). Tel: (02) 573 3434. Open 9am–noon and 2–5pm; closed Mondays and Tuesdays. Small admission charge. Hands-on museum with exhibits geared toward children.
Museo de Bellas Artes and Galería Nacional, Adjoining Parque Los Caobos (Across from Natural Science Museum). Tel: (02) 571 0169. Easily accessible by the Metro; just exit at the Bellas Artes station. Open 9–noon and 3–5.30pm weekdays except Monday; 10 a.m–3pm on weekends. No

admission charge. Fine works by Venezuelan artists and a good sampling of Oriental and European art.
Quinta Anauco, Avenida Panteón, San Bernardino. Tel: (02) 518 517. Open Tuesdays–Saturdays from 9am–noon and 3pm–5pm; Sundays from 10am–5pm. Small admission charge. A lovely colonial house with period art and furniture.

CIUDAD BOLÍVAR

Museo de Arte Moderno Jesús Soto, Avenida Mario Briceno Iragorry and Avenida Germania. Open Tuesday–Saturday 9 am–noon and 3–7pm; Sunday 10am–5 pm. Located in Soto's hometown, this is a fine collection of the kinetic sculptor's art as well as works by other Venezuelan artists.
Casa de Correo de Orinoco, Paseo Orinoco at Carabobo. Open Tuesday–Saturday 9–noon and 3–6pm; Sunday mornings only. Exhibits on the history of the city and the printing press used for the country's first newspaper – the one that announced Venezuela's independence from Spain.

PUERTO AYACUCHO

Ethnological Museum of the Federal Amazon Territories, Plaza Bolívar.
Its presentation is not slick, but this is a good museum to find out about the indigenous cultures in Venezuela's Amazon region. At Puerto Ayacucho's Apostolic Vicarage (Vicaría Apostólica). Open irregular hours.

MARGARITA

Museo de Arte Contemporáneo, Francisco Narváez, corner of Igualdad and Fraternidad, Porlamar. Open daily except Monday, 10am–4pm. Although this highlights the work of the Margarita-born sculptor for whom the museum is named, contemporary paintings and sculptures by several other Venezuelan artists are featured.

THEATERS & MUSIC

CARACAS

Teatro Teresa Carreño and Ateneo de Caracas, Avenida 25 Sur (Across from Caracas Hilton, near the Bellas Artes Metro station). Tel: (02) 571 0521.
Teatro Municipal, Avenida Bolívar at Esquina Teatro Municipal, one block east of the Santa Teresa church. Tel: (02) 415 384.

CONCERTS

Caracas Symphony Orchestra performs at the Teatro Municipal, located about a block east of the Santa Teresa church downtown. Classical concerts are held at the Aula Magna of the Universidad Central, just south of Plaza Venezuela. Tel: (02) 619 811.

Regularly scheduled concerts featuring everything from Latin jazz to folk music can be heard at the Ateneo de Caracas across the street from the Caracas Hilton (near the Bellas Artes Metro stop). For Ateneo box office information, call 571 0521.

SPORTS

PARTICIPANT

Watersports: Most beach resort hotels rent watersports equipment, as does the Marina Mar beside the Macuto Sheraton at El Litoral. Snorkeling and diving equipment is also available through some of the tour operators and watersports equipment stores in Puerto La Cruz and on Margarita Island. The Margarita Concorde hotel rents windsurfing equipment.

Scuba Diving: A number of companies specialize in providing diving and snorkeling equipment and tank filling services in Venezuela. Some also rent equipment. They include:

Alcar, Campo Alegre. Tel: 33579 (Caracas).

Marina Divers, La Castellana. Tel: 261 5229 (Caracas).

Oceanside, Chacao (Caracas).

Sesto Continente, La Florida. Tel: 743 873 (Caracas).

Subma Tur, Tucacas, Morrocoy. Tel: (042) 84082 or 84679.

Tecnosub, La Trinidad, (Caracas). Tel: 933 369. In Puerto La Cruz, (081) 669 081.

Subma Tur, Marina Divers, Sesto Continente and Tecnosub also offer diver's certification courses.

Golf: It is difficult – and costly – to play golf in Venezuela if you don't belong to a local club, but some hotels have arrangements for their guests. At El Litoral, the Meli Caribe and Macuto Sheraton hotels have a standing arrangement with the nine-hole Caraballeda Golf Course. In addition, Arelys Tours, Tel: (02) 782 4680, can arrange facilities at a handful of courses in and around Caracas.

Tennis: The Caracas Hilton and Tamanaco hotels in Caracas have facilities, as do the Macuto Sheraton and Meliá Caribe hotels at El Litoral. In Puerto La Cruz, the resort hotels have courts or make arrangements for guests to use courts at private clubs.

Bungee Jumping: This fad has reached Venezuela. For information, telephone or fax Jessica Manca Graziadei of Extrem Caraibes at (02) 781 9750 in Caracas.

SPECTATOR SPORTS

Bullfights: Sunday afternoon bullfights are held at Caracas' Nuevo Circo bullring not far from the bus terminal area with the same name (near the La Hoyada Metro station). There are also Plazas de Toros in Maracaibo, San Cristóbal, Maracay and Valencia. In Caracas, tickets to the bullfights are sold at the ring and at Los Cuchilleros restaurant on Avenida Urdaneta just east of Plaza La Candelaria; the bar/restaurant is the hangout of local *toreros*. You only have to buy tickets far in advance if you want to guarantee yourself a spot in the shade.

Horse racing: La Rinconada, on the Panamerican highway just outside the city, is a fine track with horse races on Saturday and Sunday afternoons.

Basketball: Venezuela's professional teams play Fridays, Saturdays, Sundays and Mondays on the courts at Parque Miranda and Parque Naciones Unidas, at Avenida Páez, near the Universidad Santa María in the neighborhood known as El Paraíso. There is usually no need to buy advance tickets.

Bolas criollas is a form of lawn bowling. Many companies and public offices have their own teams and compete in tournaments.

Chess: Although you can join in, this is really a spectator sport in Caracas, where public chess boards draw fans on the Sabana Grande Boulevard half a block east of the Gran Café restaurant and under the bridge where Avenida Urdaneta and Avenida Fuerzas Armadas meet.

Baseball: While soccer is the rage in most South American countries, baseball is clearly the No. 1 sport here. Venezuela has turned out a number of players recruited by North American leagues, among them sluggers Tony Armas and David Concepción. US pros sometimes come to play in Venezuelan leagues during off season; games in Caracas run from October through February and are played at the Universidad Central stadium (south of Plaza Venezuela and the Plaza Venezuela Metro stop) at night and, sometimes, on Sunday and Monday afternoons.

NIGHTLIFE

LIVE MUSIC

Juan Sebastián Bar, Avenida Venezuela, El Rosal. Tel: (02) 951 5575. This comfortable jazz club has live music and a dance floor; order a plate of *tequeños* to accompany your drinks or try the Caesar salad.

Nueva Esparta, Avenida Los Marquitos, Sabana Grande. This spot draws locals to its dance floor, which features *gaita* bands at Christmas time. It's just north of the Sabana Grande pedestrian boulevard.

BARS

Dog and Fox, Avenida Rio de Janeiro, Las Mercedes. Tel: (02) 917 319. British pub atmosphere and a hangout for English-speaking expatriates.

La Bolera, Avenida Fuerzas Armadas, north of Urdaneta. This is the favorite haunt of the North American and British reporters who work at the *Daily Journal* newspaper across the street. La Bolera's fabulous snacks include Spanish *tortilla*.

Cafe L'Attico, Avenida Luis Roche, Qta. Palic, Altamira. Tel: 261 2819. The *in* place for young, well to do *Caraqueños*. (Also a restaurant.)

DISCOS

New York, New York, Centro Comercial Concresa. Tel: (02) 979 7745 or 1900.

My Way, Centro Comercial Ciudad Tamanaco, Nivel C-2. Tel: (02) 959 0441.

SHOPPING

WHAT TO BUY

In Venezuela you can pick up the latest in Caribbean fashion, good and reasonably priced leather shoes and some lovely handicrafts. The latter includes baskets from the jungle regions of the country, hand-woven hammocks, *naif* paintings and clay ceramics. As the unofficial headquarters for South America's music industry, this is also a good spot to buy music tapes, records and CDs. You can listen to the music before you buy and the range is wide, including *salsa*, *merengue*, Latin jazz, rock'n'roll and pop music. Perfumes and liquors are inexpensive in duty free Margarita and no one should leave the country without buying a bottle of the aged local rum or a can of rich Venezuelan coffee.

SHOPPING AREAS

Shopping malls are found all over Caracas and in most major cities. One of the favorite shopping spots in the capital is Sabana Grande, the pedestrian boulevard where shopping competes with people-watching. The largest collection of stores comes at the Chacaíto end of the boulevard. At the Plaza Venezuela end of the boulevard is Artesanía Venezolana, one of the city's best collections of handicrafts from around the country.

Caracas' Central Comercial Ciudad Tamanaco, better known as CCCT (pronounced Say-Say-Say-Tay), is Latin America's largest shopping mall, a glittering collection of stores including upscale and designer boutiques. It is located in the Chuao section of Caracas, beside La Carlota airport.

Paseo Las Mercedes is tucked into Caracas' ritzy Las Mercedes neighborhood not far from the Hotel Tamanaco. Among the shops at this shopping mall is a bookstore run by South America's oldest Audubon Society, which has its headquarters and store in the Sección La Cuadra area of the indoor complex; the bookstore has a good collection of picture books and guide books on Venezuela, as well as more academic volumes on local flora, fauna, folklore and culture. Open Monday–Friday 9am–noon and 2.30pm–6pm. Tel: (02) 913 813.

Just off Plaza Bolívar, in the heart of downtown, is a jewelry lover's paradise. Edificio La Francia is a single building divided into a multitude of tiny shops that sell only jewelry and watches. Venezuela's 18-carat gold is the highlight here and most of the jewelry is sold by weight, regardless of the amount of workmanship involved. Look for designs in the shape of orchids, the national flower. Edificio La Francia is open weekdays and Saturdays from 9am–5pm. Outside the building is a reasonably priced market for hammocks, baskets and other handicrafts.

In the Hotel Tamanaco, H. Stern has one of its well-known South American jewelry stores, selling exquisite gems, including custom-made settings.

FURTHER READING

GENERAL

Naim, Moisés and Piñango, Ramon (eds.). *El Caso Venezuela*. Caracas 1984. This collection of analytical essays looks at the country's modern-day political and economic system. (In Spanish.)

Lernoux, Penny. *Cry of the People*. Although it gives an overall view of the role of the Catholic Church and US foreign policy as it relates to social struggles in the whole of Latin America, there are specific references to Venezuela – where the late author once lived and wrote.

JUNGLE

Beebe, William. *High Forest*. A scientist's account of his research in the Rancho Grande Cloud Forest at Henri Pittier National Park.

Caufield, Catherine. *In the Rainforest*. A definitive report on the Amazon jungle, including a look at the Indians in Venezuela's rainforest and the New Tribes Missions trying to convert them.

LITERATURE

Gallegos, Rómulo. *Doña Barbara*. New York, 1948. The tale of a legendary, lusty and evil-hearted plainswoman who could outride even the best *llanero*. She cultivated the widely-held notion that she was a witch, probably to gain respect in a male-dominated society. Based on a real person and one of this renowned Venezuelan novelist's finest works, along with *Mene* and *Canaima* (also translated into English).

García Márquez, Gabriel. *Autumn of the Patriarch*. This Nobel Prize-winning author takes a look at a composite dictator. The character is based more than a little on Venezuelan dictator Juan Vicente Gómez.

Allende, Isabel. *Eva Luna*. A fictional tale about a storyteller, set in a town modeled on Colonia Tovar, and including many factual events. Allende, niece of former Chilean president Salvador Allende, was a columnist for the Caracas newspaper *El Nacional* before becoming a novelist. A book of short stories, *Stories of Eva Luna*, is the sequel.

HISTORY

Herrera Luque, Francisco. *Boves, El Urogallo*. Caracas 1987. This is a novelized version of one of the bloodiest periods in Venezuela's history, when renegade Tomás Boves and his army of disillusioned Indians and blacks began a wholesale slaughter of the country's Spanish and *mestizo* (mixed race) population. Herrera Luque, now deceased, was ousted from the Bolivarian Society because of this novel, which portrayed Liberator Simón Bolívar in less than glowing terms. (In Spanish.)

García Márquez, Gabriel. *The General in His Labyrinth*. This historical novel raised quite a controversy when it was published. Tracing the final days of Liberator Simón Bolívar, it shows the hero is a less than flattering light.

Lemaítre, Louis Antoine. *Between Flight and Longing*. New York, 1986. A biography of Teresa de la Parra, Venezuela's foremost woman of letters during the 1920s. This volume details how the feminist Parra paid dearly for refusing to accept a more traditional role as a wife and mother, instead dedicating her short life to writing.

INDIANS

Chagnon, Napoleon. *The Fierce People*. A fascinating and controversial scientific tome written by a French anthropologist who lived for years with the Yanomami Indians in the Amazon and concluded they are the most violent people on the planet.

O'Hanlon, Redmond. *In Trouble Again*. New York, 1988. Rip-roaring account of a wild Englishman's semi-scientific Orinoco river expedition deep into the Amazonas in search of the fierce Yanomami Indians.

LOST WORLD

Robertson, Ruth. *Cherún Merú*. The autobiographical story of a New York journalist who moved to Venezuela in the 1940s and became an oil company pilot and photographer. She led the first overland expedition to the base of Angel Falls (Cherún Merú).

Nott, David. *Angels Four*. A hair-raising account of how four men scaled Angel Falls in 1971 – the first successful attempt.

Conan Doyle, Arthur. *Lost World*. This 1912 work with amazing description of the Gran Sabana is even more impressive once you know that Conan Doyle never visited Venezuela. His writing was based solely on what he was told by those who had.

USEFUL ADDRESSES

EMBASSIES & CONSULATES

Argentina, Centro Capriles, Plaza Venezuela, Caracas. Tel: (02) 793 1103 and 781 8479.

Canada, Torre Europa, Avenida Francisco de Miranda, Caracas. Tel: (02) 951 6166.

Chile, Edificio Venezuela, Avenida Venezuela, El Rosal, Caracas. Tel: (02) 261 4941 and 261 5014.

Denmark, Edificio Easo, Avenida Francisco de Miranda, Caracas. Tel: (02) 951 6618 and 951 4618.

France, Edificio Los Frailes, C. La Guairita, Chuao. Tel: (02) 910 333 and 910 324.

Germany, Edificio Panaven, Avenida San Juan Bosco, Altamira. Tel: (02) 261 0181 and 261 1205.

Italy, Quinta Las Imeldas, Avenida Luis Roche, Altamira. Tel: (02) 261 0755 and 261 1779.

The Netherlands, Edificio San Juan, Avenida San Juan Bosco, Altamira. Tel: (02) 263 3622 and 263 3076.

Japan, Quinta Sacura, Avenida San Juan Bosco, Altamira. Tel: (02) 261 8333.

Russia, Quinta Soyuz, Calle Las Lomas, Las Mercedes. Tel: (02) 751 6037 and 752 5312.

Spain, Edificio Banco Unión, Camino Real, Sabana Grande. Tel: (02) 712 432 and 731 5444.

Switzerland, Torre Europa, Avenida Francisco de Miranda. Tel: (02) 951 4064.

United Kingdom, Torre Las Mercedes, 3rd Floor, Avenida Estancia, Chuao. Tel: (02) 751 1022 and 751 1232.

United States, Avenida Francisco de Miranda, La Floresta. Tel: (02) 285 2222 and 285 3111.

CULTURAL & COMMERCIAL ASSOCIATIONS

Centro Americano-Venezolano, Avenida Principal de Las Mercedes, Las Mercedes. Tel: (02) 752 7511 and 752 5511.

Venezuelan-American Chamber of Commerce (VenAmCham), Torre Credival, Piso 10, Oficina A, 2da. Avenida Campo Alegre. Tel: (02) 263 0833.

Dutch Association. Tel: (02) 263 3622 and 284 6819.

British Council, Edificio Torre La Noria, 6th Floor, Las Mercedes. Tel: (02) 915 222 and 915 443.

Cavenal (German-Venezuelan Association). Tel: (02) 241 2502.

Asociación Cultural Humboldt (German), Avenida Juan Germ an Bosco, San Bernardino. Tel: (02) 527 634.

AIRLINE OFFICES

Aerolineas Argentinas, Edificio La Previsora, Calle Real de Sabana Grande. Tel: (02) 781 8044 and 782 3311.

AeroPeru, 1ra. Avenida, Los Palos Grandes. Tel: (02) 261 9241, 216 8147 and 284 2510.

Aeropostal, Plaza Venezuela. Tel: (02) 575 2511 and 573 6511.

Air Canada, Simón Bolívar International Airport, Maiquetía. Tel: (02) 823 318.

Aerotuy, Boulevard de Sabana Grande, Edificio Grand Sabana, No. 174, Piso 2. Tel: (02) 726 195 and 717 375.

Air France, Avenida Francisco de Miranda, Parque Cristal. Tel: (02) 285 2311 and 283 2044.

Air Panama, Torre Diamen, Chuao. Tel: (02) 923 222 and 923 476.

Air Portugal, Avenida Francisco de Miranda, Edificio Canaima. Tel: (02) 951 0511 and 951 0381.

American Airlines, Centro Plaza, Torre B, Penthouse. Tel: (02) 914 222 and 283 8333.

Avensa, Avenida Universidad, Esquina El Chorro, Edificio El Chorro, Piso 12–13. Tel: (02) 561 3366 and 562 3022.

Avianca, Avenida Francisco de Miranda, Edificio Roraima. Tel: (02) 263 1322 and 337 311.

BWIA, Centro Plaza, Torre D, Piso 16, Los Palos Grandes. Tel: (02) 284 9111.

British Airways, Torre Británica, Altamira Sur. Tel: 261 8006.

NEW YORK
HOUSTON
MIAMI
GULF OF MEXICO
ARUBA
MARGARITA
CARACAS
SOUTH AMERICA

VIASA:
Venezuela's Official Airline
Flies From:
- New York
- Miami
- Houston

To:
- Caracas
- Margarita Island
- Aruba

From: CARACAS
To:
- Bogotá
- Quito
- Rio de Janeiro
- Sao Paulo
- Lima
- Santiago de Chile
- Buenos Aires
And Major European Cities.

Dominicana de Aviación, Avenida Casanova, Chacaíto. Tel: (02) 716 056 and 716 272.

LanChile, Avenida Rómulo Gallegos, Torre KLM, Piso 5, Santa Eduvigis. Tel: (02) 284 7155, 284 7511 and 283 8277.

Lloyd Aereo Boliviano, Avenida Tamanaco, El Rosal. Tel: (02) 951 5775 and 951 2745.

Varig, Avenida Principal, Los Ruices. Tel: (02) 239 4577.

Viasa, Torre Viasa, Avenida Universidad. Tel: (02) 572 1611.

TOURIST INFORMATION OFFICES

Caracas, Parque Central, Torre Oeste, Piso 36. Tel: (02) 507 8611. The office, not far from the Anauco Hilton hotel (and easy to reach via the Bellas Artes Metro stop) is open from 8am–5pm; questions can be answered in several languages including English 24 hours a day, seven days a week via a tourist telephone line: 507 8829 and 573 8983.

Maracaibo, Palacio de las Aguilas, Calle 95 (in front of Plaza Bolívar). Tel: (061) 225 109. Open Monday–Friday, 9–noon and 4–6pm. There is also a Tourism Information Office at the airport but it keeps erratic hours.

Cumaná, Palacio del Gobierno, Calle Bolívar (in front of Plaza Bolívar). Tel: (093) 23 799 and 26 616 and 24 449. An excellent Tourism Information Office is located at the airport, Aeropuerto Antonio José de Sucre; it is open from 6am–5pm.

Puerto La Cruz. Tel: (081) 762 827 and 763 140. A tourism information booth at the airport keeps irregular hours.

Mérida. A Tourist Information Office with city maps and, occasionally, brochures, is open sporadically at the airport.

ART/PHOTO CREDITS

INDEX

U – V

W – Z

A
B
C

E
F
G
H
I
J
a
b
c
d
e
f

h
i
j
k
l

INSIGHT GUIDES

COLORSET NUMBERS

You'll find the colorset number on the spine of each Insight Guide.

INSIGHT *pocket* GUIDES

EXISTING & FORTHCOMING TITLES:

● ●

United States: **Houghton Mifflin Company, Boston MA 02108**
Tel: (800) 2253362 Fax: (800) 4589501

Canada: **Thomas Allen & Son, 390 Steelcase Road East**
Markham, Ontario L3R 1G2
Tel: (416) 4759126 Fax: (416) 4756747

Great Britain: **GeoCenter UK, Hampshire RG22 4BJ**
Tel: (256) 817987 Fax: (256) 817988

Worldwide: **Höfer Communications Singapore 2262**
Tel: (65) 8612755 Fax: (65) 8616438

66 I was first drawn to the Insight Guides by the excellent "Nepal" volume. I can think of no book which so effectively captures the essence of a country. Out of these pages leaped the Nepal I know – the captivating charm of a people and their culture. I've since discovered and enjoyed the entire Insight Guide Series. Each volume deals with a country or city in the same sensitive depth, which is nowhere more evident than in the superb photography. **99**

Sir Edmund Hillary